Wordsworth's Counterrevolutionary Turn

Wordsworth's Counterrevolutionary Turn

Community, Virtue, and Vision in the 1790s

John Rieder

DELAWARE

Newark: University of Delaware Press
London: Associated University Presses

Associated University Presses
440 Forsgate Drive
Cranbury, NJ 08512

Associated University Presses
16 Barter Street
London WC1A 2AH, England

Associated University Presses
P.O. Box 338, Port Credit
Mississauga, Ontario
Canada L5G 4L8

The paper used in this publication meets the requirements
of the American National Standard for Permanence of Paper
for Printed Library Materials Z39.48–1984.

Library of Congress Cataloging-in-Publication Data

Rieder, John, 1952–
  Wordsworth's counterrevolutionary turn : community, virtue, and vision in the 1790s / John Rieder.
     p.   cm.
  Includes bibliographical references and index.
  ISBN 0-87413-610-5 (alk. paper)
  1. Wordsworth, William, 1770–1850—Political and social views.
  2. Literature and society—England—History—18th century.
  3. Counterrevolutionaries—England—History—18th century.
  4. Social ethics in literature.   5. Community in literature.
  I. Title.
  PR5692.S58R54   1997
  821'.7—dc21   96-52719
                                                                CIP

PRINTED IN THE UNITED STATES OF AMERICA

Contents

Abbreviations

Author is William Wordsworth unless otherwise indicated.

13BP	*The 13-Book Prelude.* Ed. Mark L. Reed. 2 vols. Ithaca, NY: Cornell University Press, 1991.
B	*The Borderers.* Ed. Robert Osborn. Ithaca, NY: Cornell University Press, 1982.
Burke	Burke, Edmund. *Works.* 12 vols. Boston: Little, Brown, 1865–67.
CEY	Reed, Mark L. *Wordsworth: The Chronology of the Early Years 1770–1799.* Cambridge, Mass.: Harvard University Press, 1967.
Cowley	Cowley, Abraham. *The Essays and Other Prose Writings.* Ed. Alfred B. Gough. Oxford: Clarendon Press, 1915.
GJ	Wordsworth, Dorothy. *The Grasmere Journals.* Ed. Pamela Woof. Oxford: Clarendon Press, 1991.
HAG	*Home at Grasmere: Part First, Book First, of The Recluse.* Ed. Beth Darlington. Ithaca, NY: Cornell University Press, 1977.
JTP	Thelwall, John. *Poems Written Chiefly in Retirement.* 1801; rpt. Oxford: Woodstock, 1989.
LB	*Lyrical Ballads and Other Poems, 1797–1800.* Ed. James Butler and Karen Green. Ithaca, NY: Cornell University Press, 1992.
LEY	*The Letters of William and Dorothy Wordsworth.* 2d edition. Ed. Ernest De Selincourt, rev. Chester L. Shaver. Volume 1: *The Early Years 1787–1805.* Oxford: Clarendon Press, 1967.
P2V	*Poems, in Two Volumes, and Other Poems, 1800–1807.* Ed. Jared Curtis. Ithaca, NY: Cornell University Press, 1983.

P1799 *The Prelude, 1798–1799*. Ed. Stephen Parrish. Ithaca, NY: Cornell University Press, 1977.

Paine Paine, Thomas. *Complete Writings*. Ed. Philip S. Foner. 2 vols. NY: Citadel, 1945.

PrW *The Prose Works of William Wordsworth*. Ed. W. J. B. Owen and J. W. Smyser. 3 vols. Oxford: Clarendon Press, 1974.

RC&P *The Ruined Cottage and The Pedlar*. Ed. James Butler. Ithaca, NY: Cornell University Press, 1979.

STCL Coleridge, Samuel Taylor. *Collected Letters*. Ed. Earl Leslie Griggs. 6 vols. Oxford: Clarendon Press, 1956–71.

STCPW ———. *Poetical Works*. Ed. E. H. Coleridge. Oxford: Oxford University Press, 1912.

SPP *The Salisbury Plain Poems*. Ed. Stephen C. Gill. Ithaca, NY: Cornell University Press, 1975.

Watson Watson, Richard, Bishop of Llandaff. *Miscellaneous Tracts on Religious, Political, and Agricultural Subjects*. 2 vols. London: T. Cadell and W. Davies, 1815.

Acknowledgments

I OWE MY LARGEST DEBT OF GRATITUDE TO MY FRIEND AND COL-
league Craig Howes, who read and commented extensively on
drafts of every chapter, and whose conversation and editorial advice helped shape this project at every stage of its progress.

Earlier drafts of portions of this book were presented at the
American Society for Eighteenth Century Studies Conference in
New Orleans, 1989; the Wordsworth Summer conference in Grasmere, 1989; and the Interdisciplinary Nineteenth Century Studies
Conference in New Haven, 1991. I extend sincere appreciation to
all of those who responded to my work on these occasions, particularly to Michael Ferber, Jonathan Wordsworth, and William Galperin, for their helpful suggestions. Special thanks are due to Ken
Johnston for his encouragement, advice, and generosity.

Much of the material in this book has been generated by my
teaching. I thank my students and my colleagues in the English
Department of the University of Hawaii for the way they have
sustained and challenged my work over the last fifteen years. I also
want to thank my own undergraduate and graduate school teach-
ers, starting with Leslie Chard, who introduced me to Romantic
poetry, and above all Geoffrey Hartman, who taught me how to
linger over and learn from Wordsworth's poetry.

Grants from the American Council of Learned Societies and the
University of Hawaii allowed me to spend a semester working on
this project at the Huntington Library in San Marino, California,
and the staff at the Huntington helped make that stay remarkably
profitable and enjoyable.

A part of chapter 3 appeared in an earlier version as "Wordsworth's Indolence: Providential Economy and Poetic Vocation" in
Pacific Coast Philology 23 (1988). Chapter 4, "Social Class and
Civic Virtue at the Scene of Execution: The Salisbury Plain
Poems," is a slightly revised version of the essay by the same title
that appeared in *Studies in Romanticism* 30 (1991). Thanks to the
editors of *Pacific Coast Philology* and to the Trustees of Boston
University for permission to reuse this material. Permission for
extended quotation from the newly edited texts in *The Ruined*

Cottage and The Pedlar, edited by James A. Butler, and *The Borderers,* edited by Robert Osborn, has been granted by Cornell University Press.

My strongest ally during the writing of this book has been Cristina Bacchilega. I can only hope that my writing has deserved the gift of her support.

This book is dedicated to the memory of Louise Rieder.

1

Wordsworth's Community of Recognition

WHY AT THE END OF THE TWENTIETH CENTURY DO WE CONTINUE to read William Wordsworth's poetry, write books and essays about it, and teach students to interpret it? Recent literary criticism has usually responded to such questions by asking how literature exercises power rather than how it gives pleasure. But this study argues that whatever power literature generates must be grounded in, and mediated by, pleasure. Therefore, where the most influential recent critics of Wordsworth's poetry have associated its considerable influence and durability with the way it promulgates a meliorist view of British society and thereby sustains and refigures a severely distorted field of vision, *Wordsworth's Counterrevolutionary Turn* will focus on the way the poetry constructs a fantasy of community and draws its readers into it. Instead of stressing repression as the keystone of the poetry's ideological effects, this book maintains that our culture reproduces the reading practices that keep poetry alive more by seduction and fantasy than by sheer overbearing insistence. The argument proceeds, then, by showing that the various fantasies of community in Wordsworth's poetry answer to widespread anxieties about social cohesion in late-eighteenth-century British writing; by describing in detail the way Wordsworth's versions of community shift and supplant one another as his subject matter becomes less explicitly political in the later 1790s, and by proposing that Wordsworth's poetry derives its most effective and influential sense of community from the play of participation and detachment in the literary experience itself rather than from reference to the idealized rural and familial communities that pervade his work. It begins, though, by noticing a curious but powerful abstraction in one of Wordsworth's most famous sentences about poetry, community, and recognition.

A MAN SPEAKING TO MEN

When Wordsworth wrote his famous definition of the poet as "a man speaking to men" (PrW1 138), he meant to reduce the relation between poets and their audiences to the essential proposition that poetry's cardinal virtue is its ability to re-create the face-to-face presence of a speaker to one or more listeners. Surely one needs to proclaim such immediacy as a goal only when its absence has become burdensome; for instance, when the mediations of print and poetic convention seem to obstruct poetic voice, or when "men" have lost the opportunity or the will to face one another. This weighty absence flattens the immediacy Wordsworth celebrates into an abstraction, so that the "men" of his slogan face one another not as concrete individuals but as "man." To put it another way, Wordsworth's formula turns "speaking" into a generic activity rather than the communication of a particular message. Whatever exchange of knowledge or ideas the poem transacts between the poet and the audience is liable to be overpowered by a mutual recognition of their shared humanity. The fundamental content of poetry, its transcendental signified, would then become this community of recognition. The centrality to Wordsworth's poetics of this peculiar community, a thing stranger and more revealing than it is usually taken to be, occasions the present inquiry into the various and complex communities of recognition envisioned and produced in Wordsworth's poetry during the decade following his return from France in 1792.

Like most visions of authenticity, Wordsworth's requires a present state of debasement as its foil. When Wordsworth asserts that poetry's highest calling is to bring "man" face to face with "men," he sets poetry the task of purifying various corrupt communities where men are not their proper selves and speaking has lost its immediacy. In Wordsworth's attack upon poetic diction, for instance, the merely fashionable poets' loss of their sense of themselves as common men or women corrupts their ability to speak genuinely. "Ambitious of the fame of Poets," he charges, the false poets mechanically adopted earlier poets' figures of speech, but "applied them to feelings and thoughts with which they had no natural connection whatsoever" (PrW1 160). Such mechanical and vainglorious repetition also contaminates its listeners. Intoxicated by pretty words that only play at being poetry, the audience loses touch with the "genuine language of passion" (PrW1 160) and so with their proper selves.

A similar debasement of language characterizes the highly charged opposition between rural and urban life in the "Preface to *Lyrical Ballads.*" In the city a "degrading thirst after outrageous stimulation" seems to be increased rather than satiated by the "rapid communication of intelligence [that] hourly gratifies [it]."

As a result, "frantic novels, sickly and stupid German Tragedies, and deluges of idle and extravagant stories in verse" threaten to drive England's noble literary tradition into eclipse. The sources of corruption are political ("great national events"), social ("the encreasing accumulation of men in cities"), and economic ("the uniformity of their occupations"). Each mode of corruption has a purified counterpart in rural life. There "the passions of men are incorporated with the beautiful and permanent forms of nature" instead of political turmoil. Rather than being cramped by "the sameness and narrow circle of their intercourse," rural inhabitants profit from it by falling "less under the action of social vanity." In the agrarian economy, the "necessary character of [rural] occupations" fosters simplicity, comprehensibility, and durability. Thus the "repeated experience and regular feelings" of rural life provide a "better soil" not only for the "essential passions of the heart," but also for the "more permanent and far more philosophical language" that Wordsworth advocates.[1]

Wordsworth lays the stakes in clearer view in the important letter he wrote to Coleridge from Goslar in late February 1799, comparing the "transitory manners reflecting the wearisome unintelligible obliquities of city-life" with "manners connected with the permanent objects of nature and partaking of the simplicity of those objects":

> Read Theocritus in Ayrshire or Marionetshire and you will find perpetual occasions to recollect what you see daily in Ayrshire or Marionetshire read Congreve Vanbrugh and Farqhar in London and though not a century is elapsed since they were alive and merry, you will meet with whole pages that are uninteresting and incomprehensible. (LEY 255)

Wordsworth links the peculiar type of unintelligibility associated with the dramatists just as closely to the city's commercial economy as he makes the durability of Theocritus's pastoral poetry depend upon an agrarian one. Theatrical spectacle models for Wordsworth the way representation can overpower substance; but, despite his disdain for most contemporary drama, the target of Wordsworth's antitheatricality is not the theater itself. His point, rather, is that urban alienation results from the treacherous basis afforded by representation or exchange as such for a healthy human community. Because London is a nexus of exchange, uprooted people and imported objects—"the quick dance / Of colours, lights, and forms; the Babel din; / The endless stream of men, and moving things" (7.156–58)[2]—flow by one so quickly and in such profusion there that, unable to grasp them in their substantial reality, the city-dweller is seduced into a rage for novelty or for consumption in itself, for its own sake.[3] Conversely, one of the main advantages the lower density of population affords to the inhabitants of rural areas would seem to be that natural objects, unlike human beings, cannot consciously pretend to be something else.

The "man speaking to men" must be nothing if not sincere, and in this respect especially his palpable identity is more important than anything he could possibly say. The paradox by which "speaking" might overpower the contents of speech here resembles the one whereby, at its most drastic, Wordsworth's antitheatrical tendency leads him to glorify solitude itself as an experience of true community compared to that of being a member of the urban crowd:

> Say boldly then that solitude is not
> Where these things are: he truly is alone,
> He of the multitude, whose eyes are doomed
> To hold a vacant commerce day by day
> With objects wanting life, repelling love;
> He by the vast Metropolis immured,
> Where pity shrinks from unremitting calls,
> Where numbers overwhelm humanity,
> And neighborhood serves rather to divide
> Than to unite. (HAG 89)

Wordsworth's paradoxical conflation of solitude and community raises his insistence on personal integrity to an intensity sufficient for it to counterbalance the threats posed by theatricality and urban experience. However, such a poetic solution seems to exact a rather heavy price in terms of social engagement.

The same hyperbolic insistence on integrity has an unsettling economic dimension, for instance. Just as Wordsworth's idealized agrarian economy provides a metaphorical base, so to speak, for his community of recognition, his distaste for the "rapid communication of intelligence" in the city points to a parallel discomfort with the more material basis for whatever community his poetry might hope to create or enrich, that is, with the commercial production and distribution of books. The same discomfort underlies his emphasis on "speaking" rather than writing in the "man speaking to men" formula, for Wordsworth well knew that the fate of his poetry was bound to the circuit of writing, publishing, and reading rather than simply speaking and listening. The "Essay Supplementary to the Preface" of 1815 is in large part an extended and somewhat embittered meditation upon this necessity, and the strange lines in *The Prelude* book 5 mourning the transience of books speak to the same anxiety. In fact, when Wordsworth collapses the distinction between speaking and writing he also erases another transaction that sometimes mediated the production of his poetry: that between the man, William Wordsworth, speaking, and the woman, Dorothy Wordsworth, writing. Although Wordsworth's subsumption of women into the universal "men" is significant in its own right, perhaps the more significant elision in this case involves confounding the production of Wordsworthian manuscripts and the role of women in Wordsworth's cottage industry with the speaking "man." Both a domestic and a commercial economy support the face-to-face meeting of men in Wordsworth's ideal poetic moment, but in the community of recognition the material production and dissemination of poetry are swept aside into the inessential.[4]

Wordsworth's idealization of his roots in the Lake District, then, could be interpreted as a way of redirecting anxieties about the production and distribution of his poetry into a quest for metaphysical origins. The community of "a man speaking to men" has actually been pulled free of its historical and social roots, as the universalistic conception of poetry Wordsworth defends in the 1802 "Preface to *Lyrical Ballads*" implies: "In spite of difference of soil and climate, of language and manners, of laws and customs: in spite of things silently gone out of mind, and things violently destroyed; the Poet binds together by passion and knowledge the vast empire of human society, as it is spread over the whole earth, and over all time" (PrW1 141). This is not to say, however, that Wordsworth's formula represses history or evades politics. On the contrary, it convenes poet and audience in a radically democratic scene. The oratorical situation of the "man speaking to men" no doubt models itself partly on the *polis* of classical Athens or the Roman republic's forum; and the humanity shared there, although Wordsworth names passion, knowledge, pleasure, and sympathy as its substance, derives its form from republican, civic virtue.[5] Wordsworth's ideal community of recognition emerges from the poet's transformation, from 1793 to 1802, of a version of the political animal into the humanity that discovers itself in poetry's "empire."

That is why the community that plays the crucial role in Wordsworth's autobiographical epic of alienation and return, the most extended instance in Wordsworth's poetry of a degraded community acting as a foil for a vision of genuine humanity and community, is constituted by the French Revolution, and especially by Wordsworth's exalted identification of a political community with a community of recognition in the Revolution's earlier phases. This combination promises, for instance, to transmute the urban crowd in all its theatricality and transience into an authentic civic body:

> Even files of strangers merely, seen but once,
> And for a moment, men from far with sound
> Of music, martial tunes, and banners spread
> Entering the City, here and there a face
> Or person singled out among the rest,
> Yet still a stranger and beloved as such,
> Even by these passing spectacles my heart
> Was oftentimes uplifted, and they seemed
> Like arguments from Heaven.
>
> (9.281–89)[6]

Wordsworth's enthusiasm for the Revolution and his later disillusionment with it obviously comprise a major episode in *The Prelude;* but the poem also constructs a significant parallelism between Wordsworth and the Revolution. The course of the French Revolution follows a plot of maturation in *The Prelude,* from its blissful dawn of hope to the "Herculean Commonwealth" strangling "the snakes about her cradle" (10.362–64), to the "young Republic" (10.582) struggling to moderate its course after the death of Robespierre. The Revolution, like Wordsworth, having suffered through a tragedy of betrayal, hopes to recapture the visionary promise of its youth.

Here Wordsworth and the Revolution part ways. The young poet survives his own crisis of depair "no further changed / Than as a clouded, not a waning moon" (10.916–17). France, however, eventually descends into Napoleonic imperialism:

>   when the sun
> That rose in splendour, was alive, and moved
> In exultation among living clouds,
> Hath put his function and his glory off,
> And, turn'd into a gewgaw, a machine,
> Sets like an opera phantom.
>
> (10.935–40)

Not only is the artificial revolutionary sun the imagistic counterpart of Wordsworth's true and constant moon, but also the debased and theatricalized demise of revolutionary hope completes the

French Revolution's role as counterplot to Wordsworth's maturation. The poet's epic ambition can nowhere be better measured than in his attempt to balance his private salvation against the Revolution's decline.[7]

The Prelude turns, in precisely this sense, in a "counterrevolutionary" direction. Wordsworth's turn away from the grand stage of historical events enables him to resolve his moral crisis in the supportive structure of a community of recognition provided by Dorothy Wordsworth and Samuel Taylor Coleridge (10.904–15). However, this turn only brings to a climax the poem's oscillation between epic ambitions and lyrical self-construction on the one hand, and between progressively wider, more threatening social contexts and recuperative, private meditations on the other. In Wordsworth's account the community of recognition merges with the healing influences of "Nature" and presents itself as a kind of gift, albeit one that presents a peculiar challenge or demand upon Wordsworth's faculties and his sense of duty. The question driving this book is to what extent such an account coincides with the evidence provided by Wordsworth's writings during the 1790s. Is the counterrevolutionary turn a self-serving myth or a heroic homecoming, a political abnegation or the poet's accession to a more profound awareness of social conflict, a defensive reconstruction or a substantial, confessional self-understanding? The key to answering such questions lies in understanding how much more complex and equivocal a construction Wordsworth's community of recognition is than he makes it appear to be.

Clearly Wordsworth's turn—or, as he would have it, his return—to poetry as the locus of authentic community and utopian desire takes part in a widespread mid-1790s movement away from political activism, and it involves the problematic, but classically sanctioned, ethical status of rural retirement as opposed to civic participation. This political context overdetermines and exacerbates both the dichotomy between agrarian and urban economies and the paradoxical value of solitude as a mode of experiencing genuine community. The odd results of this set of tensions pervade Wordsworth's poetry in the form of his persistent doubts about the rationality of the poetic vocation (the *locus classicus* would be the question "Was it for this" that opens Ms. JJ of *The Prelude* and that later versions associate with the parable of the false steward) and his recurrent association of poetic labor with passivity, parasitism, and "indolence" (for instance in "Expostulation and Reply," "Stanzas Written in My Pocket-copy of Thomson's *Castle of Indolence,*" "Resolution and Independence," and, perhaps most complexly, *The Ruined Cottage*). Not just the immediacy but, just as urgently, the comradeliness or fraternity of the "man speaking to men" formula reveals it to be a defensive gesture. Jon Klancher acutely observes that "the language of men" is one that Wordsworth's poetry represents rather than breathes,[8] and the life of the "common man" is even more vicariously projected into his poetic program. Wordsworthian sympathy is not just undercut or ironized by the distance that keeps the poet apart from those he watches so closely; rather, this separation is a constitutive element of much of his best work. I will argue here that this constitutive element, by which the Wordsworthian common man is always in some sense "still a stranger and beloved as such," articulates Wordsworth's historical situation in terms clearly limited by a certain class perspective.

Another way of putting this is that Wordsworth's community of recognition is one that unites the poet with his readers rather than with his characters. His poetry often tells stories of man's love for nature, man's love for man, of brotherly and familial bonds; but the poet's vision tends to be a kind of reading, an essentially distanced and spectatorial participation that more resembles the interpretation of a text than a mutual encounter. The materiality of Wordsworth's community has far less to do with the places and the people he points toward than with those who share his sympathy and his solitude; and his writing has exercised its enormous influence far less by virtue of the ideal agrarian community it fantasizes than by virtue of the literary form of community it modelled and virtually substituted for the rural one. If Wordsworth's vision follows the perspective opened to it by his class position, this may be ultimately of less importance than the way his writing invents and enacts the class practice we now recognize as, simply, literature.[9]

THE STATE OF THE QUESTION

Wordsworth scholars usually agree that the poet's thought underwent a profound change between the radical writings of 1793–94—the *Letter to the Bishop of Llandaff* and the earliest version of *Salisbury Plain*—and his composition of the major poetry of 1797 and after. Wordsworth's turn from the radical politics associated with abstract reason in the early 1790s to a less forthright politics that was matched, for whatever reason, with a more complex psychology of emotional life at the end of the decade has been variously interpreted: most often as positive growth or maturation, sometimes as disaffection, a retreat from or repression of his personal, political, or ideological commitments. The most important change in Wordsworth's writing from the *Letter to Llandaff* to "Tintern Abbey," however, is not that the politics formerly in Wordsworth's poetry are later left out, but rather that Wordsworth's way of representing a sense of community and his authority within it radically alters the articulation of politics and morality with one another. In the course of this development both Wordsworth's ideal and real communities of recognition take shape.

It has often been said that the literary values Wordsworth advocates in the "Preface to *Lyrical Ballads*"—simplicity of diction, spontaneity disciplined by habits of meditation, an emphasis on feeling rather than incident, and the sense of an immediate, private encounter between the poet and the audience—translate, as it were, the values of his earlier political beliefs into a different idiom. In fact, this particular argument is as old as Francis Jeffrey's attack on the "Lake School" in his 1802 review of Southey's *Thalaba,* and perhaps its most famous version remains the one made by William Hazlitt in *The Spirit of the Age.* Nonetheless the relation between Wordsworth's political commitments and his emergence as a major poet has seldom, if ever, been scrutinized more intensely than during the last decade. When one surveys the history and the current state of Wordsworth criticism from the point of view of this question, four interpretive themes stand out: the status of Wordsworth's self-representation; the content and meaning of the historical record, that is, of the political and social context of Wordsworth's writing; the contemporaneity and originality of Wordsworth's poetry; and the significance of his achievement in literary history. A brief survey of these four themes will illustrate the pertinence of focussing a lengthier discussion on Wordsworth's community of recognition.

Wordsworth himself established the dominant interpretation of his early career in *The Prelude*'s narrative of his crisis of moral despair, but the authority of his account has always been problematic. First of all there is the problem of his having suppressed entirely any mention of his affair with Annette Vallon, and along with it the related problems of how to read the "Julia and Vaudracour" story and how to interpret its removal from the autobiographical context in 1820.[10] Beyond the difficulties presented by what Wordsworth leaves out of *The Prelude,* however, lies the whole problem of what place we grant to the memories he includes. Are the childhood memories and the later moments of private vi-

sionary glory to be taken as accurate accounts or, as some Freudian readers would argue, as screen memories that obscure as much
as they reveal?[11] Whatever one's attitude toward psychoanalysis,
surely the conscious determination of literary form separates *The
Prelude's* goals from those of a faithful, accurate rendering of the
incidents of Wordsworth's life. Thus Wordsworth's most recent
biographer, Stephen Gill, differentiates his own use of *The Prelude*
from the more trusting approach of Mary Moorman by pointing
out the way Wordsworth's autobiography forces events into con-
formity with a heroic plot.[12] As Gill points out, one cannot hope to
understand and assess the importance of the literary construction,
William Wordsworth, unless he can be told apart from the actual
person of that name who wrote the poems. The poet at the center
of Wordsworth's community of recognition is clearly the former
of these two, the Wordsworthian self-portrait that Wordsworth's
writing ever more elaborately constructs and reconstructs, so that
he becomes more like an institution—for instance, the Gothic ca-
thedral Wordsworth proposed as the metaphor for his collected
poetry—than a person.[13]

The historical record regarding the young Wordsworth's stay in
France and his political activity, or lack of it, upon his return to
England has often provided a healthy corrective to the pieties and
downright obfuscations in Wordsworth's self-portrait.[14] Yet the
problem of deciphering that record and of understanding the political context of Wordsworth's writing remains an area of vigorous
debate. Although there is no doubt that Wordsworth eventually
became a political conservative, there remains considerable disagreement concerning how early and how thoroughly Wordsworth
abandoned his youthful radicalism.[15] Such disagreement is made
inevitable and irresolvable by virtue of the relation between poetry
and politics. For it is never simply a question of poetry either
including or excluding or even reflecting politics. On the contrary,
poems emerge into a complex interplay of discourses suited to
different purposes and circulating to different audiences, or to the
same audiences but within different institutional contexts of reception and response. Wordsworth's poetry, for instance, seems to be
quite closely allied to the public venue of the political pamphleteers
at some points, and to the conventions of magazine poetry at
others, while in his most serious work he often appears to disdain
publication and to look for recognition from only a small circle of
readers. There are profound differences among these alternatives,
not just in the content of what is represented, but in the social
action undertaken when Wordsworth represents himself to his vari-

ous audiences in the medium of his writing. If the act of representation itself can be pictured as a spectrum of possibilities with fully committed political advocacy at one end and pure literary mimesis at the other, then where in that spectrum one places a given utterance remains very much a question of tact or, as Volosinov puts it (and which amounts to much the same thing), of attending to the "social *multiaccentuality* of the ideological sign."[16]

Thus the debate over the politics of Wordsworth's poetry turns upon the critical decision of how one articulates the poems with other discourses. For instance, Wordsworth writes of his crisis of despair that "Nature's self, by human love / Assisted" led him through it; and the notoriously polyvalent associations of Nature pose a kind of "weary labyrinth" of choices for the interpreter as well (*Prelude* 10.921–22). No one can seriously doubt the powerful political charge that "Nature" carries in the age of natural rights or in a tradition where Hobbes, Locke, and Rousseau figure prominently. But does one gloss "Nature's self" by reference to French Revolutionary ideology, to the English republican tradition, or to classical political and ethical thought?[17] Or should one prefer a more obvious, intentional referent for Nature here, the Lake District landscape? This choice opens another branching path of possibilities leading on the one hand to the more or less politicized categories of aesthetic experience, and on the other to the social practices that took hold of and transformed the prospect of nature in Wordsworth's day.[18] And what about the alliance between "Nature's self" and "human love"? It often seems as if Wordsworthian Nature is a radically social concept that finds one of its strongest paradigms in the bond of the nursing mother and her child. The topic of domestic affection is as powerfully and pervasively political as that of natural rights, however. Emerging nationalist and commercial ideologies, the struggle between agrarian improvement and manorial paternalism, and a host of practical and theoretical questions that hinge upon the more or less benevolent and universal character of sympathy all converge here.[19] One's choices in this maze of readings no doubt depend on one's own political and philosophical commitments as well as on sensitivity to Wordsworth's art, and I am willing to ascribe my emphasis on problems of social class as much to my own agenda as to Wordsworth's.

The question of locating Wordsworth's artistic originality and assessing its thematic or ideological ramifications remains the central focus of most studies of Wordsworth's career. In the last decade that question has been dominated by the thesis, first announced by Jerome McGann, that Wordsworth was the first and chief spokesman of what McGann calls the Romantic ideology. The genealogy of this thesis would include, on the one hand, all those factors that have given rise to the New Historicism in literary studies, of which I will single out only one for mention here: a spreading agreement that academic literary critics needed to learn to think politically, memorably articulated for the 1970s by Richard Ohmann in *English in America*.[20] On the other hand, it is certainly important that the same decade's most striking thesis about poetic originality was Harold Bloom's theory of poetic influence. The common ground between Bloom's argument and McGann's is that the power of Wordsworth's originality in both cases draws its strength from the dynamics of repression. But where Bloom's Wordsworth struggles to repress Milton, the New Historicist Wordsworth of McGann, Marjorie Levinson, and Alan Liu represses social and political reality or, as Liu calls it, history.[21]

Take, for instance, Marjorie Levinson's reading of "Tintern Abbey".[22] Levinson charges that Wordsworth actively represses social, historical, and ideological themes: "'Tintern Abbey' achieves its fiercely private vision by directing a continuous energy toward the nonrepresentation of objects and points of view expressive of a public—we would say, ideological—dimension" (37–38). Levinson's primary example of a nonrepresented object is the abbey itself. She argues that, for Wordsworth, the juxtaposition of the monastic abbey and its squalid surroundings sets a sacralized but lost form of poverty against the "debased and destructive pauperism" of the present day (35). Thus the abbey "would have figured to Wordsworth the loss of a meaningful collectivity" (35); but in Wordsworth's sense of loss, nostalgia for the medieval institution coalesced with a flight from history, and especially from recent political history, to poetry (36). Levinson's abbey finally seems to be a metaphor both for Wordsworth's mature self and for the process of composition: "Having passed through Nature's refining fires, the abbey was reborn as a meditative spot, stimulus to and guardian of free—that is, nonpurposive, nonpartisan, ideologically innocent—thought" (29).

However correct it may be that Wordsworth's poem is powerfully inventive of what have subsequently become pervasive ideological gestures, Levinson's specific conclusion that the poem's originality, its "primary poetic action," lies in its "suppression of the social" (37) is deeply flawed. This has to do, first of all, with the poem's contemporaneity. Robert Mayo pointed out some years ago how entirely familiar the elaborate and specific title of "Lines Written a Few Miles above Tintern Abbey, on Revisiting the Banks of the Wye during a Tour, July 13, 1798" would have sounded to readers of the verse published in contemporary periodicals. There they encountered, for instance, titles like "Lines (Written at Old Sarum, in Wiltshire, in 1790)," "Verses Written on Visiting the Ruins of Dunkeswell-Abbey, in Devonshire," "Lines, Occasioned by the Recollection of Once Seeing Avondale, in the County of Wicklow," and so on (Mayo 492–93).[23] What anyone who takes the trouble to read these poems will quickly discover is how superficial a resemblance they bear to "Tintern Abbey." Wordsworth's resonant periods have little to do with such versification. Nonetheless these poems do establish something useful about the conventions of touristic meditation: that nonrepresentation of the social in this context requires no extraordinary energy. None of these magazine writers seems any more constrained than Wordsworth to mention unpleasant details like beggars or charcoal manufacture in the locales they describe. (There is, of course, another whole group of poems surveyed by Mayo that are obsessed with beggars.) In fact, despite the details included in the titles, there is rarely anything in a poem on, for instance, Tintern Abbey that distinguishes the scene from any other ruin. The monotony of the conventional images (for example, ruined abbeys and castles, river banks, sea shores, cliffs, suns setting, twilight gathering, moons rising) and attitudes (joy in solitude, rejection of the world and its cares, inspiration to think of spiritual matters, sympathy for simpler creatures) is simply overpowering. These conventions constituted a static register of signs alongside which real lives and real social conditions slid with very little effect. Absence of reference to an unpleasant social context is one of "Tintern Abbey's" most banal characteristics.

The point here is not merely to dismiss Levinson's scholarship or to call her reading of "Tintern Abbey" inept. On the contrary, her considerable learning and her eloquent, impassioned interpretation misconstrue the poem's power because of a theoretical error. That is, Levinson's analysis boxes the poem into a prematurely imposed opposition between referentiality and repression, whereas the detour along which the poem leads Wordsworth's social and political aims seems to me not to derive its power from suppressing the social but rather from actively constructing a particular kind of social body. To quote Slavoj Zizek's apt articulation of the strikingly different notions of ideology in current criticism, Levinson (like McGann and Liu[24]) constructs Wordsworthian ideology as a denial of political and historical realities, that is, as "a *partial* gaze overlooking the *totality* of social relations"; I want to stress, instead, that Wordsworth's communities of recognition embody "*a totality set on effacing the traces of its own impossibility"* (Zizek's emphasis).[25] And if, as I shall argue, the *impossibility* of Wordsworth's communities can be apprehended in the class-related contradictions inherent in Wordsworth's self-representation, then the result is both fantastic and material in the sense that it is an idealization or misrecognition of social relations that succeeds in establishing itself as the basis of an extensive and consequential set of representational practices. Hence the poem's originality appears precisely in Wordsworth's profound engagement with literary tradition, its strong effect on the way the poems it engages will later be read, and its influence over the way poetry will come to be written.

But to call Wordsworth's discursive engagement in "Tintern Abbey" literary rather than political is only to beg the question. What, after all, does it mean to be literary? The right way to frame this question is not to locate a text's historical dimension in the presence or absence of its references to contemporary objects or topics, but rather to ask what kind of social action it performed. To seek its originality, then, would mean to ask in what way it has shaped its own reception and our own habits, conventions, and institutions of reading.[26] Thus the fourth theme, that of the significance of Wordsworth's achievement in literary history, is only the third writ large. The question of the poet's individual contribution here enters the context of widespread, long-lasting changes in the collective character of poetry. At the same time the upper-case version of the theme of contemporaneity involves not only recovering the norms and conventions that framed and conditioned Wordsworth's emergence as a major poet, but also a careful inquiry into how those conventions were linked to institutions in such a way as to dominate aesthetic production and reception. This strategy obviously will raise once again the question of how one articulates Wordsworth's poetry with other contemporaneous discourses. Now, however, such contextualization bears the goal of distinguishing the specific privilege or singularity of literary value and literary labor within a general framework of social conventions, their emergence, and their functions. I do not propose to initiate such a general inquiry here, but rather to suggest how the reading of Wordsworth might fit into this larger framework.

There is no shortage of recent hypotheses about the specific qualities and effects of Wordsworth's invention. Marilyn Butler stresses the way an atmosphere of political defeat permeated Wordsworth's poetic innovations and therefore communicated itself to our dominant, apolitical sense of literary value.[27] David

Simpson assigns the power of Wordsworth's poetry to its singularly rich and yet indeterminate evocation of the tensions of current political and ethical debates, and he seeks to restore to Wordsworth's poetry its lost sense of social relevance.[28] Jon Klancher delineates Wordsworth's project against the background of the growth of mass reading audiences. Klancher argues that Wordsworth's praise of imagination as the key both to successful composition and to worthy interpretation represents a humanist fantasy of triumphing over the barriers of social class, and he concludes that it is precisely this fantasy that has most often shaped academic interpretations of Romantic poetry.[29] Several recent critics, including Clifford Siskin, Jonathan Arac, and Alan Liu have speculated that Wordsworth's importance has to do with his new and peculiarly modern sense of selfhood.[30] Siskin, for instance, argues that Wordsworth invented a prescriptive version of the self under the imperative to "feel" and be sympathetic as a cure for the urban malaise described in the "Preface to *Lyrical Ballads*," and that this version of the self is in its turn a central determinant of the sense of duty and value we know today as professionalism. Don Bialostosky makes the similar but more ameliorative claim that modern literary criticism represents the common enterprise of understanding that Wordsworth called for in his 1815 "Essay, Supplementary to the Preface".[31]

The primary point that needs to be repeated in the face of these hypotheses is that the singular quality of literary labor and value must have something to do with the way in which poetry gives pleasure. If Wordsworth's invention taps into a peculiarly modern sense of selfhood or exercises any considerable influence over the institutional practices of teaching and scholarship that nowadays preserve, exalt, isolate, or distort literature, it does so much less by repressing desires than by gratifying them. Does a literary convention achieve dominance by silencing certain voices and excluding certain topics (as in the romantic ideology's erasure of social reality or its delegitimation of political interests); or, on the contrary, by seducing our desires, perhaps confusing or momentarily neutralizing antagonistic interests? The repressive effects of a dominant literary convention, while they may be quite forceful, remain at best only the bare preconditions for a text's being read and reread. To draw readers into the spell of a specific text and the conventions it bears requires a positive inducement, a reward, fantastic though it may be.

I do not mean to deny the potential oppressiveness of literary conventions, but rather to argue that their survival—and therefore, *a fortiori,* their strategic convenience in a scheme of class hegemony—depends crucially on their primary and positive quality of eliciting pleasure. Certainly social and institutional practices encourage and perpetuate the dominance of some sources of pleasure rather than others. Such practical desires and interests have no doubt collaborated with Wordsworth's texts to produce an ideologically comforting way of recognizing the self and the world that exercises its seductive power within the boundaries of what one might call, by analogy to Foucault's theorization of bourgeois sexuality, a discipline of literary pleasure.[32] In the case of Wordsworth, one of the most engrossing vehicles of this pleasure is a fantasy of community, a fantasy based on a radical confusion of participation and detachment. But the confusion of discipline and pleasure, participation and detachment, or historical contingency and subjective universality is not merely a problem to be overcome by an analysis of the differential class functions of poetic convention, nor by specifying Wordsworth's misrepresentation of some "real" social order. On the contrary, this set of antagonisms and paradoxes is itself at the core of Wordsworth's achievement, because it structures the space where his poetry crafts its version of freedom and pleasure from the materials of contingency and impotence.

To invoke a term from Lacanian analysis, Wordsworth's confusion of participation and detachment can be likened to the "kernel of the real" in its stubborn dissonance as well as its persistent centrality to Wordsworth's fantasy of community. This problem unfolds most clearly in *The Borderers,* where the community's sense of coherence depends precisely upon its symbolic appropriation of the outcast, excluded member. But the site of this traumatic construction of the coherent self persists, for instance, in Wordsworth's turn to the paradoxical assertion of authentic community in visionary solitude. This thematic pattern may well reveal its historical specificity in its misrecognition of contemporary class relations. Nonetheless its ideological power seems to me to be something more slippery, a protean quality that can turn even the unveiling of its error into another version of its call to the pleasures of recognition.

THESIS: COMMUNITY, VIRTUE, AND VISION

The thesis this book means to explore can now be advanced in more detail. It concerns three major topics in Wordsworth's writing during the 1790s.

1) *Community*. The most general form of the argument is that the concept of community, and particularly the ideal of an authentic community, holds a central place in Wordsworth's poetry throughout his career, and especially during the crucial phase beginning with his return from France in 1792 and culminating in the major achievements of 1798–99. This study therefore contributes to a growing list of interpretations of Wordsworth that stress the fundamentally political and social quality of Wordsworth's interests.[33] Several apparent and obvious differences separate the social and political tenor of the pieces that stand at either end of this study, the *Letter to the Bishop of Llandaff* and "Tintern Abbey." For instance, the early text takes on public themes in a polemical manner, while the later one dwells upon private affairs in a lyrical meditation. Nonetheless the argument to be developed here begins from their common ground, that is, from their shared, fundamental concern with a sense of community.

More specifically, I will argue that the concept of community is the site of a central contradiction in Wordsworth. This contradiction is by no means an individual or idiosyncratic one, however unique its expression becomes in Wordsworth's poetry. Rather, it resides within a class discourse, the self-representation of the "middle rank," which will be detailed in chapter 2. The contradiction has to do with the simultaneously historical and natural constitution of the middle class, and it enters Wordsworth's writing in the context of the heteroglossic explosion of political discourse in the 1790s. Michael Friedman, in *The Making of a Tory Humanist,* has interpreted Wordsworth's changing notion of community as one that moves from concern with an effective (legal and political) community to an affective community of shared feelings and values. While recognizing the descriptive accuracy of Friedman's dichotomy between effective and affective notions of community, I propose to explore its basis in a more complex network of discourses, where the discourse of community finds its various and overlapping paradigms in politics, economy, or psychology, that is, in the operation of law, the market, or the passions. These paradigms will be explored in two major contexts: the political debates centering on the French Revolution and the English response to it (in chapter 2); and the debate over the English Poor Law (in chapter 3). The crucial point at which the debates and Wordsworth's notions of community intersect is in the problematic figure of social totality and cohesiveness.

2) *Virtue*. Different notions of social cohesion predicate different relations between the individual and society, psychology and poli-

tics, or the public and the private. Each of these oppositions is crucial to the interpretation of Wordsworth's poetry because each of them links the concept of community to notions of virtue that pose the problem of social cohesion at an individual and ethical level. Thus the *ethos* of Wordsworth's *personae* shifts in ways closely related to changing ideas of community throughout the poetry and prose of the 1790s. A detailed account of the interdependence of notions of virtue and community in the Salisbury Plain poems, *The Borderers, The Ruined Cottage,* and "Tintern Abbey"[34] will bear the burden of demonstrating that politics seems to gradually disappear from Wordsworth's poetry because Wordsworth's way of representing a sense of community and his authority within it radically alters the articulation of politics and morality with one another.

As explicit political concerns fade from view, Wordsworth's political hope increasingly resides (and to some extent secludes itself) within his ideal of authentic community. But what is true of virtue is also true of fear and anxiety. As the figures of social cohesion change, so do the aspects of disorder and alienation. The problem of popular, revolutionary violence, for example, emerges most strongly in conjunction with paradigmatically related notions of republican virtue and political representation. In the same way, Wordsworth's most characteristic anxieties about his vocation— for instance, anxieties about voyeurism and indolence in *The Ruined Cottage,* about the reliability of signs in *The Borderers,* about isolation in "Tintern Abbey"[35]—surface when the presiding quality of virtue becomes sympathetic and when political or legislative activities give way to figures of exchange and recognition. Thus Wordsworth's project of representing an ideal community is increasingly crossed and shadowed by a sense of the poet's solitary detachment.

3) *Vision.* At this point, Wordsworth achieves his most characteristic originality and power by means of—or at the cost of—making visionary solitude become a figure for authentic community.[36] "Tintern Abbey" is Wordsworth's most splendidly wrought version of this equivocal triumph. The utopia of individual visionary experience in "Tintern Abbey" completes a development begun in the antithetical and critical exposition of Mortimer's corrupted sense of community in *The Borderers.* There the figure of the "face" of recognition, although it is wholly defeated by theatricality, provides the kernel of Wordsworth's later glorification of natural presence. *The Borderers* explores a nightmarish version of the social contract. In *The Ruined Cottage* and "Tintern Abbey," by means

of Wordsworth's figurations of a privileged vision of nature, the poems themselves become virtual embodiments of a more subtle and more fantastic form of community.

One implication of this argument is mirrored in this book's organization. The "triumph" of "Tintern Abbey" is not a matter of Wordsworth's having mounted a step on the ladder of poetic growth, for example, of having left behind *The Borderers* to press on toward *The Prelude*. It is rather that in "Tintern Abbey" Wordsworth achieves a solution to a set of anxieties that reiterate themselves throughout his career; but, because it is a purely poetic solution to political, social, and personal problems, it does not necessarily carry over to the next poem and the next. Nonetheless "Tintern Abbey" suggests a recurrent strategy that leads to other, similarly equivocal "triumphs," and in this sense can be called a breakthrough. The business of the first half of this book is to take note of Wordsworth's reiterated anxieties, along with some paradigmatic shifts in their expression, within the span of about half a decade both before and after "Tintern Abbey." The second half of the book zeroes in on that extended episode of trauma which Wordsworth calls his crisis of despair in *The Prelude,* and which is represented here primarily by *The Borderers* and the tale of Margaret, and on Wordsworth's attempts to heal or close it, particularly in the various frames of *The Ruined Cottage* and in "Tintern Abbey." This entire episode, I take it, comprises the emergence of Wordsworth's mature poetic practice.

One further implication of this argument, which has already been mentioned along the way, can bear repeating here. The didactic element in Wordsworth's concept of community, for instance, his praise of the Lake District, was largely doomed to irrelevance by the course of English economic and social development. Yet Wordsworth's writing became enormously influential, not by virtue of the agrarian community it envisioned, but rather by virtue of the literary form of community it modelled and produced in its dissemination. This literary form of community is deeply implicated in modern Anglo-American culture, and it is largely held in place by the academic institutions within which literary pedagogy and criticism most typically now take place. In this specific sense the present interpretation of Wordsworth aspires to the status of critical self-knowledge.

2

Wordsworth's Ethos: Violence, Alienation, and Middle-Class Virtue

WORDSWORTH'S SUSPICIOUSLY SELF-SERVING VERSION OF THE counter-revolutionary turn in his career could be paraphrased thus: I stood, within myself, perfectly still, while the world turned about me. For instance, in the sonnet "Composed near Calais, on the Road Leading to Ardres, August 7, 1802," Wordsworth reported that, having returned to France after an absence of ten years, his own revolutionary sympathies came fresh upon him, but left him now sadly out of tune with the land where revolution had died:

> Jones! when from Calais southward you and I
> Travell'd on foot together; then this Way,
> Where I am pacing now, was like the May
> With festivals of new-born Liberty:
> A homeless sound of joy was in the sky;
> The antiquated Earth, as one might say,
> Beat like the heart of Man: songs, garlands, play,
> Banners, and happy faces, far and nigh!
> And now, sole register that these things were,
> Two solitary greetings have I heard,
> "*Good morrow, Citizen!*" a hollow word,
> As if a dead Man spake it! Yet despair
> I feel not: happy am I as a bird:
> Fair seasons yet will come, and hopes as fair.
>
> (P2V 156–57)

Although "Citizen" has become a hollow word in Napoleonic France, Wordsworth keeps alive the May festival of liberty in his memory and hope. He assures us, then, that he is still Citizen Wordsworth, still at one with the songs, banners, and happy faces of the early revolution and that he can still, therefore, speak to public issues in 1802 with the character of uncorrupted virtue manifested in his constancy to this good old cause.

But what kind of constancy can be attributed to Wordsworth's notorious itinerary, in the previous decade, from the militant, republican virtue of the *Letter to Llandaff* and *Salisbury Plain,* to his absorption in sympathy for the poor, the marginal, and the outcast in *Adventures on Salisbury Plain, The Borderers,* and *The Ruined Cottage,* to sympathy with "inarticulate things," mere "nature," in "Tintern Abbey" and the introspective lyricism associated with it, and back, finally, to the political issues of the great sonnet sequence of 1802? Wordsworth's sonnets of 1802 represent a kind of return to the beginnings of his ten-year journey; and this revisitation of the site of a former political commitment, like his tour of the Wye in 1798, provides an opportunity for meditating upon how much he has changed and how much he has stayed the same. For Wordsworth's *ethos* in the 1802 sonnets has indeed changed, and changed drastically, from that of the *Letter to Llandaff.* Yet the class affiliation on which that *ethos* is based remains solid as a rock.

THE PROBLEM OF VIOLENCE IN *A LETTER TO THE BISHOP OF LLANDAFF*

Wordsworth probably wrote his *Letter to the Bishop of Llandaff* in February and March of 1793, during the first flush of his outrage at England's declaring war upon France.[1] Wordworth's uncompleted pamphlet, a fervid reply to Richard Watson, the Bishop of Llandaff's homiletic attack on the French Revolution and defense of the British Constitution, includes scalding commentary on such topics as the proper qualifications for voting and holding office, aristocratic corruption and the law of primogeniture, legislative regulation of wages, and the inflammatory nature of Burke's rhetoric. Admiring Priestley, disdaining Burke, and heavily indebted to Paine and Rousseau, it is in all respects typical of, and thoroughly immersed in, the furious political debate of the early 1790s.

Wordsworth's speaker refers to himself in the pamphlet's title simply as "a republican" (PrW1 29), and he addresses himself at various times to "a philosopher" (38), "an enlightened legislator" (37), "a sensible republican" (37), and "the friends of liberty" (49), presumably a collective identity including all of the others.[2] Wordsworth enlists himself, in short, in the party of reason, a group whose qualifications are presented as universal principles. The situation turns out to be less straightforward than that, however, since Wordsworth's party enjoys its quasi-natural perspective due to historical and restricted privileges.

The unselfconscious complexity of Wordsworth's republican *ethos* emerges most clearly, perhaps, when the pamphlet takes up the defense of violent means to overthrow monarchic oppression:

> You [Watson] say "I fly with terror even from the altar of liberty when I see it stained with the blood of the aged, of the innocent, of the defenceless sex; of the ministers of religion, and of the faithful adherents of a fallen monarch." What! have you so little knowledge of the nature of man as to be ignorant, that a time of revolution is not the season of true Liberty. Alas! the obstinacy & perversion of men is such that she is too often obliged to borrow the very arms of despotism to overthrow him, and in order to reign in peace must establish herself by violence. (33)

Political violence appears in this passage to be not only the product of a peculiar set of historical circumstances ("a time of revolution"), but also a natural, inevitable occurrence arising from the "obstinacy & perversion of men." The problem therefore lies in imagining how peace, the "season of true Liberty," will emerge from the exercise of revolutionary despotism. When is depotism not despotism? What distinguishes the violence of the friends of liberty from that exercised by the political order they seek to overthrow?

Wordsworth's answer turns on a distinction between two types of virtue:

> This apparent contradiction between the principles of liberty and the march of revolutions, this spirit of jealousy, of disquietude, of vexation, indispensable from a state of war between the oppressors and oppressed, must of necessity confuse the ideas of morality and contract the benign exertion of the best affections of the human heart. Political virtues are developed at the expence of moral ones; and the sweet emotions of compassion, evidently dangerous where traitors are to be punished, are too often altogether smothered. But is this a sufficient reason to reprobate a convulsion from which is to spring a better order of things? (34)

The difference between moral and political virtue arises first of all from the problem of representation. Acting politically means acting as the representative of a class of people rather than acting as an individual, that is, morally—a conventional distinction Wordsworth shares with James Mackintosh in *Vindiciae Gallicae* (1791):

"In the few remarks that are made on the Nobility and Clergy of France, we confine ourselves strictly to their *political* and *collective* character: Mr. Burke, on the contrary, has grounded his eloquent apology on their *individual* and *moral* character."[3] Thus Wordsworth's key assertion here is that in the current "state of war between the oppressors and the oppressed . . . political virtues are developed at the expence of moral ones." The crux of his defense of violence is that the friends of liberty wrest the means of oppression away from the despots on behalf of the oppressed. Political virtue, then, involves acting as a proper representative of the social order's best interests and, therefore, understanding the historical and political necessity for deploying discretionary violence in the public interest. In the "state of war between the oppressors and the oppressed," the use of violence devolves upon the friends of liberty precisely insofar as they become the representatives of the oppressed.

The ability to act as representatives of the public interest implies a vantage point from which the men of reason can view the oppressors, the oppressed, and the "better order of things" they strive for. This vantage point enables Wordsworth to ground his demand to sacrifice moral to political virtue in the long-standing abuse of violence by the rulers and its dehumanizing effects on those they have ruled. Wordsworth quotes Rousseau to this purpose: *"Tout homme né dans l'esclavage nait pour l'esclavage: . . . les esclaves perdent tout dans leurs fers, jusqu'au desir d'en sortir; ils aiment leur servitude, comme les compaignons d'Ulysse aimaient leur abrutissement"* (36). The *abrutissement* of the oppressed guarantees that their liberation will be accompanied by mob violence:

> The coercive power is of necessity so strong in all the old governments that the people could but at first make an abuse of that liberty which a legitimate republic supposes. The animal just released from its stall will exhaust the overflow of its spirits in a round of wanton vagaries, but it will soon return to itself and enjoy its freedom in moderate and regular delight. (38)

The metaphor of "the animal just released from its stall" hints, however, that the populace will return to being happily guided by their natural rulers rather than becoming full participants in the republic. At what point would the freed animals become men—or, more to the point, friends of liberty, men of reason, philosophers, enlightened republicans? The weakening of coercive power into republican law can perhaps be trusted to undo the extraordinary corruption of the ruling class. Wordsworth's "grand objection to monarchy," he declares, echoing Algernon Sidney, is that "the office of king is a trial to which human virtue is not equal" (41).[4] But it is less than clear how the "obstinacy and perversion of [common] men" will conform itself to the "moderate and regular delights" of the republic.

The people's return to moderation is not to be left to the mere exhaustion of the mob's animal spirits, either. The friends of liberty are precisely those who have been tainted neither by the corrupting influence of court and aristocratic privilege nor by the oppression it generates and who therefore are left to carry the banner of reason at the head of the revolution. Their mission is the humanization, so to speak, of the brutalized populace. Wordsworth concludes the passage on revolutionary virtue superseding "the benign exertions of the best affections of the human heart" with a call for education to wipe out the contradiction that presently exists between political necessity and the principles of liberty: "It is the province of education to rectify the erroneous notions which a habit of oppression, and even of resistance, may have created, and to soften this ferocity of character proceeding from a necessary suspension of the mild and social virtues" (34).

Two pertinent questions might be put to Wordsworth here concerning the character he has constructed for his *persona*. First, what grants the friends of liberty their position as representatives of the oppressed and masters of the "province of education"? Second, from what source will the friends of liberty draw the "mild and social virtues" into their program of social renovation? The answers to these questions appear more clearly as issues of contention in Wordsworth's milieu than as explicit arguments in his pamphlet. In both cases property is the central theme: in the first place, because the friends of liberty emerge onto the stage of history due to their position within a certain stage of the development of commercial relations; and second, because the mild and social virtues are implicated in the same historical development.

Even though the most visible or explicit topics of the English political debates surrounding the French Revolution pertain to forms of government (monarchic, aristocratic, democratic) and their legitimation (by tradition or constitution, nature or history), the status of property is arguably the central issue throughout them. Burke and Paine, along with most other writers on political matters in the 1790s, share the assumption that the basic function of government is to protect the rights of property and the conduct of its production and exchange. The difficulty comes in deciding exactly what protecting property means. For the concept certainly refers not only to items of material wealth such as real estate, finance, or the moveable commodities exchanged in commerce, but also, and sometimes primarily, to the social relations constituted by such production and circulation. Both the class origins of the friends of liberty and the practical basis of the mild and social virtues comprise important topical moments in the discursive articulation of these social relations.

Property and social class are obvious centerpieces of Burke's attack on the French Revolution. As J. G. A. Pocock comments, anyone reading Burke's *Reflections on the Revolution in France* "with both eyes open" will realize that the central crime of which he accuses the French revolutionaries is not the assault upon Marie Antoinette's bedchamber, but their having seized French church lands and used them as security for issuing a new paper currency.[5] A few years later, in the first of his *Letters upon a Regicide Peace,* Burke would define Jacobinism as "the revolt of the enterprising talents of a country against its property" (5.309).[6] In the *Reflections,* his analysis of the class make-up of the French National Assembly and his tirades against paper money share an extreme, even hysterical, evocation of the dangers of uncertainty and volatility that may accompany the reign of "enterprising talents." Putting the sale of confiscated lands under the management of financiers, for instance, will mean that

> the spirit of money-jobbing and speculation goes into the mass of land itself, and incorporates with it. By this kind of operation, that species of property becomes, as it were, volatilized; it assumes an unnatural and monstrous activity, and thereby throws into the hands of the several managers, principal and subordinate, Parisian and provincial, all the representative of money, and perhaps a full tenth part of all the land in France, which has now acquired the worst and most pernicious part of the evil of a paper circulation, the greatest possible uncertainty in its value. (3.485)[7]

The veritable sublimation of solid land into insubstantial credit is one epitome of Burke's critique of French innovation. What makes the specter of a financial oligarchy and its "monstrous activity" so horrifying to Burke is the role he accords to landed property as the anchor of the social hierarchy and political stability. Burke's emphasis on counterbalancing the extravagant tendencies of "ability" with "property" (3.298) results in an almost ludicrously defensive portrait of the character of the aristocracy and landed gentry. Property, which for Burke ought properly to mean the country's "natural landed interest" (3.289), is a principle as "sluggish, timid, and inert" as its enemies are protean and incendiary, and a principle that "must be represented, too, in great masses of accumulation, or it is not rightly protected" (3.298). Even granted that the inert accumulation of property represents the inestimable value of tradition and precedent for Burke, his bizarre rhetoric may well suggest that energy and ability possess a stronger claim on him than he is willing to admit.

Burke's exaggerated solicitude for the aristocracy was certainly one of the quirks in his polemic that drew upon him some of the heaviest invective and ridicule from his opponents. Burke's rhetorical centerpiece, his description of Marie Antoinette's defilement and his lament for the death of chivalry, inspired many a witty rejoinder concerning knight errantry and the swinish multitude. Paine's "He pities the plumage, but forgets the dying bird" (1.260)[8] was the most often-quoted reply. A less economic, more typical example would be Mackintosh's parody of Burke's chivalry: "[Burke wishes] to deliver the peerless and immaculate Antoinetta of Austria from the durance vile in which she has so long been immured at the Tuileries, from the swords of the discourteous knights of Paris, and the spells of the sable wizards of democracy."[9]

Burke's distrust of "ability," however, drew more substantial replies. After all, no less respectable and influential a writer than Adam Smith had argued that the possession of "rank and distinction" tends to actively discourage the acquirement of the extraordinary virtues necessary for leading a country through difficult times. Smith concludes, "In all governments, accordingly, even in monarchies, the highest offices are generally possessed, and the whole detail of the adminisitration conducted, by men who were educated in the middle and inferior ranks of life."[10] In the hands of a skilled polemicist like Paine, the accession of talent and ability to governmental posts became a central point of the argument for "representative" government: "As the republic of letters brings forward the best literary productions, by giving to genius a fair and universal chance; so the representative system of government is calculated to produce the wisest laws, by collecting wisdom where it may be found" (Paine 1.367).[11] "Where it may be found," it turns out, is in the middle class. Wisdom is unlikely to develop too high in the social order ("What is called the splendor of a throne, is no other than the corruption of the state. It is made up of a band of parasites, living in luxurious indolence, out of the public taxes" [1.392]) or too low ("Bred up without morals, and cast upon the world without a prospect, [the poor] are the exposed

sacrifice of vice and legal barbarity" [1.405]). However, the workings of commerce are producing a new order of men in the middle
rank who must be allowed to step forward and take the reins of
government away from the aristocracy on behalf of the lower
classes.

Wordsworth's class of educators may well emerge directly from
the second part of Paine's *The Rights of Man,* where Paine depicts
the relation between the democratic movement and the beneficent
workings of commerce. Paine equates monarchic and aristocratic
corruption with pensions and excessive taxation, and he consistently praises the virtue and prosperity of progressive commercial
society in contrast to the economic dependence of European monarchies upon military adventurism. Instead of incendiarism confronting rooted stability, Paine presents the current conflict in
terms of productive citizens confronting corrupt governmental
parasites. Paine blames popular violence, as well, on governmental
interference with the naturally beneficent workings of commerce:

> Excess and inequality of taxation, however disguised in the means,
> never fail to appear in the effects. As a great mass of the community
> are thereby thrown into poverty and discontent, they are constantly
> on the brink of commotion; and deprived, as they are, of the means of
> information, are easily heated to outrage. (1.359–60)

Because Europe's present governments, according to Paine, origi-
nated in a precommercial, warlike society and have retained their
military character, they are now being superseded by "a morning
of reason rising upon man, on the subject of government, that has
not appeared before. As the barbarism of the present old governments expires, the moral condition of the nations, with respect to
each other, will be changed" (1.396). Reason's new dawn promises,
in fact, to eclipse the old version of political power and light the
way to a new alliance of moral virtue and commercial
interdependence:

> If commerce were permitted to act to the universal extent it is capable
> of, it would extirpate the system of war, and produce a revolution in
> the uncivilized state of governments. The invention of commerce has
> arisen since those governments began, and is the greatest approach
> toward universal civilization, that has yet been made by any means not
> immediately flowing from moral principles. (1.400)

The emergent commercial order supplies the large number of
independent and prosperous citizens necessary to carry forward

the revolution and educate the debased masses.[12] More than this, however, Paine's version of commerce seems to be the veritable essence of the progress of government away from a military posture similar to the "coercive power" Wordsworth's republicans are forced reluctantly to exercise in the early stage of the revolution and toward the mild and social virtues they look for in the better order of things to come. The crucial topic in this connection becomes the status of the family, and the counterpart of Burke's notorious defense of chivalry and inheritance is the republican concern for encouraging domestic virtue by protecting the subsistence of the common worker.

In Wordsworth's *Letter,* for example, the most important form of "property" that Wordsworth calls upon legislators to protect is the social relation of a laborer to his family: "[Our legislators] have unjustly left unprotected that most important part of property, not less real because it has no material existence, that which ought to enable the labourer to provide food for himself and his family" (43). Wordsworth's immediate point is to attack laws that force the laborer to accept "arbitrary wages," but his emphasis on encouraging virtuous domesticity is a more significant indication of his place in the context of contemporary political discourse. Relations of subsistence, domesticity, and national economy would form one nexus within which questions of policy and law were very often united with antiwar and humanitarian themes by the opponents of Pitt's war on France. Nicholas Roe argues, for instance, that "the 1790s saw an alteration in the structure of feeling for the poor and disenfranchised among articulate liberals, radicals, and dissenters," which resulted in a much stronger "sympathetic emotional identification with social victims." A typical example, according to Roe, is that of Thomas Cooper, whose *Reply to Mr. Burke's Invective against Mr. Cooper and Mr. Watt* proceeds from the usual Paineite connection between aristocratic government and military expenditure to a greater emphasis on the "human cost of war" and especially on the "disruption of 'peaceful habitation and domestic Society.'"[13] Wordsworth in the *Letter to Llandaff* is at the earliest stage of this development, and, while Roe is clearly correct in saying that this is the idiom of protest that links the *Letter* to the Salisbury Plain poems, the question here concerns the basis for the commonplaces that link political and domestic turmoil. The dual signification of material goods and social relations by property forms one mode of connection, and a second, congruent ambiguity troubles the notion of law, which alternately refers both to governmental legislation and to common usage. Perhaps the best way to grasp the intersection of politics and the household is to detail the ways these concepts cohere in the republican version of "political economy."

Take for instance the opening paragraph of Paine's *Rights of Man, Part Two:*

> Great part of that order which reigns among mankind is not the effect of government. It had its origin in the principles of society and the natural constitution of man. It existed prior to government, and would exist if the formality of government was abolished. The mutual dependence and reciprocal interest which man has upon man, and all parts of a civilized community on each other, create that great chain of connection which holds it together. The landholder, the farmer, the manufacturer, the merchant, the tradesman, and every occupation, prospers by the aid which each receives from the other, and from the whole. Common interest regulates their concerns, and forms their laws; and the laws which common usage ordains, have a greater influence than the laws of government. In fine, society performs for itself almost every thing which is ascribed to government. (1.357)

Notice how easily the "mutual dependence and reciprocal interest" that bind together the parts of the "civilized community" turn into the "great chain" of the circulation of commodities among farmer, landholder, manufacturer, and merchant. A similar ambiguity appears even more explicitly and insistently in the distinction between law as "common usage," on the one hand, and "the laws of government," on the other. The emphatic doubling of law points to Paine's polemical intentions: since governmental laws are only "ingrafted" upon the principles of common interest that regulate society, Paine will condemn government precisely insofar as it "assumes to exist for itself" (1.359). The question that then arises concerns the proper role of government, and it leads to Paine's famous proposals for redirecting tax income from military to social programs.

Thus Paine's "political economy" insists on nothing more vehemently than the essential distinction between the political and the economic; and yet the discursive struggle over the legal enactments of the *polis* does resolve itself into the ambiguity residing in the term "economy." For economy is already the juncture of the *oikos* or household, constituted both by household virtue and by the active distribution of private property, and *nomos,* the concept of order, which here looks both toward a political community bound together by the force of legislation and toward that natural, spontaneous community of "common usage." Paine characteristi-

cally vacillates between the poles of this ambiguity, shuttling between demands that the government stop interfering with
commerce and its socially cohesive effects, and proposals that government intervene and redistribute wealth in order to undo the
effects of aristocratic usurpation upon natural rights. This vacillation has less to do with a contradictory attitude toward government
than with the radical ambiguity of economy, which Paine both in-
strumentalizes as public taxation and idealizes in the goal of his
social program—the encouragement of stable, self-sustaining domestic arrangements, or household virtue, among the poor.

Yet the problem of violence, "the cause and apprehension of
riots and tumults" in Paine's phrase (1.431), remains the driving
force that impels the political debate to continue engaging the
theme of property with concepts of political and moral virtue. What
accentuates the problem of violence in the *Letter to Llandaff* is
the relation between property and political representation. Wordsworth presses for the most radical form of citizenship in natural
rights ideology, a citizenship without any property qualification
and based solely upon the human exercise of rational self-direction
(38). In doing so he is directly answering Watson, who had written
that "Peasants and mechanics are as useful to the state as any
other order of men; but their utility consists in their discharging
well the duties of their respective stations; it ceases when they
affect to become legislators."[14] The inclusion of "peasants and mechanics" into the ranks of the citizenry makes it necessary for
Wordsworth and the friends of liberty to unite demands for economic justice with the republican political program.

The energy carried by the theme of violence in the *Letter to
Llandaff* finally testifies to the fact that here the ambiguity of economy gathers into itself the force of a social contradiction. This
contradiction can be registered within political theory by the simple but crucial observation that property both ties people together
and sets them against one another. If, on the one hand, an unequal
possession of property arises in the course of nature and necessitates the formation of governments and the citizens' surrender of
some portion of their freedom to legal constraints,[15] then, on the
other hand, property also seems to create and reinforce social relations of mutually beneficial dependency, and therefore to be intimately involved with the formation of a sympathetic community.
That the threat of mob violence arises in the pamphlet literature
of the 1790s alternately as the effect of continuing to exclude the
propertyless from political representation or as the result of their

improper intrusion into the political process highlights the fact that competing versions of social cohesiveness itself are at stake.

The same tension between social interdependence and distributive law shows up as the ideological crux of Wordsworth's republican *ethos*. The poor are the subjects of equivocal metaphors and programs of education because they lack the material basis for commanding the perspective necessary to a fully participating citizen. The aristocracy, conversely, are politically incompetent because they do not work, and their idle parasitism must devise warlike means of perpetuating itself.[16] But the competent men of the middle rank are neither so indolent as to be corrupted by leisure nor so industrious as to be stultified by labor. Their cultural privilege, the peculiarly clear perspective on affairs of state that they command, thus rests upon a material, economically determined base. But at the same time their moral position is precisely what is *not* culturally or economically determined. It is the free exercise of the natural birthright of any group of men uncorrupted by the extremes of wealth or poverty. Thus Wordsworth's posture is marked in contradictory fashion by the class division it straddles. Facing the aristocracy, the party of reason is a discreet group determined by economic privilege as the statesmen of a new order; facing the suffering poor, the same group espouses the universalistic, prepolitical rhetoric of sympathy that submerges class differences in simple "humanity." But the important point is that both rational statesmanship and humanitarian sympathy articulate the *same* class position.

VIRTUE IN THE WEB OF COMMERCE

The interpretation just offered of Wordsworth's class position in the *Letter to Llandaff* implies that the clearcut change in his predominant tone between 1793 and 1798 does not necessarily correspond to any drastic difference in his ideological orientation or political commitment. The stern republican indignation of the *Letter* or of the earlier Salisbury Plain poem may well speak from the same political position and class affiliation as the humanitarian concern voiced in *The Ruined Cottage* or "Simon Lee." Canning and Frere's well-known parody of Robert Southey, "The Friend of Humanity and the Knife-Grinder," for instance, seizes upon precisely this dichotomy of tone in radical discourse, and the same feature struck Francis Jeffrey as the hallmark of Southey and Wordsworth's new school of poetry in 1802:

They are filled with horror and compassion at the sight of poor men spending their blood in the quarrels of princes, and brutifying their sublime capacities in the drudgery of unremitting labour. For all sorts of vice and profligacy in the lower orders of society, they have the same virtuous horror, and the same tender compassion. While the existence of these offences overpowers them with grief and confusion, they never permit themselves to feel the smallest indignation or dislike towards the offenders. The present vicious constitution of society alone is responsible for all these enormities. . . . While the plea of moral necessity is thus artfully brought forward to convert all the excesses of the poor into innocent misfortunes, no sort of indulgence is shown to the offences of the powerful and rich. Their oppressions, and seductions, and debaucheries, are the theme of many an angry verse; and the indignation and abhorrence of the reader is relentlessly conjured up against those perturbators of society, and scourges of mankind.[17]

Yet Wordsworth's change in tone does accompany a shift in emphasis away from the political and legislative problems that preoccupy him in the *Letter* and toward the educational and cultural program mentioned more briefly there. By May 1794, in a letter outlining his hopes for publishing a politically committed periodical, he writes, "I should principally wish our attention to be fixed upon life and manners, and to make our publication a vehicle of sound and exalted Morality" (LEY 119). A few weeks later, in the same connection, he declares himself "a determined enemy to every species of violence" (LEY 124). This is not, however, the political realignment it may appear to be, as his next sentence shows: "I see no connection, *but what the obstinacy of pride and ignorance renders necessary,* between justice and the sword" (my emphasis). Wordsworth still acknowledges that the "obstinacy and perversion of men" (PrW1 33) may make political violence necessary. He has changed his emphasis rather than the substance of his politics.

At some point, however, Wordsworth's shift of emphasis becomes so irreversible and so central to his poetics that he seems to have abandoned the party of reason altogether. He appears to abdicate his place in the "effective," legal and political, community in order to devote himself to healing an "affective," social and cultural, one; and so his *ethos* ceases to involve an appeal to reason or philosophy and calls instead upon feeling and passion.[18] The appeal to "elementary feelings" and "the essential passions of the heart" in the "Preface to *Lyrical Ballads,*" for instance, accompanies Wordsworth's firm disavowal of "the selfish and foolish hope of *reasoning* [the reader] into an approbation of these particular poems" (PrW1 124, 120). The curious, brief fragment now called the "Essay on Morals," composed in Goslar during the winter of 1798–99 (CEY 34), makes the point even more clearly: "I know no book or system of moral philosophy written with sufficient power to melt into our affections[?s], to incorporate itself with the blood and vital juices of our minds, and thence to have any influence worth our notice [on our moral behavior]" (PrW1 103). The mission of correcting a debased populace's "erroneous notions" (PrW 1: 34) has not altogether disappeared in Wordsworth's hope to combat the "multitude of causes unknown to former times [that] are now acting with a combined force to blunt the discriminating powers of the mind" (PrW1 128); but the sometimes condescending rhetoric of the *Letter to Llandaff* has been superseded by the *ethos* of "a man speaking to men." When the political community of reason yields to the community of essential passions, what has changed, and what remains constant?

The problem of Wordsworth's shifting *ethos* between 1793 and 1798 cannot be adequately explained as a simple turnabout within a continuous set of opposed terms, for instance, a shift from the radical to the conservative side in the debate between Burke and Paine. Rather, it involves the tension between two quite different sets of terms, with different hierarchic oppositions structuring them. Where the *ethos* of republican indignation makes reason the essential human trait, Wordsworth's cultural project stresses "humanity" in the form of compassion. Within Wordsworth's earlier, militant posture, nature refers to the universality of rational principles and the rights based upon them. Later, however, nature for Wordsworth often means "second nature," and it refers to "authentic habits and . . . their attendant feelings," that is, to ingrained manners and well-established customs.[19] The first discourse attacks privilege and corruption from the standpoint of the ideal community of rights and just legislation, but the second discourse attacks superficiality from the standpoint of spontaneity and passionate attachment. Problems of violence, in the first discourse, give way to problems of comprehension and persuasion in the second.

I want to suggest that these two sets of terms refer, finally, to different paradigms of social cohesion. The middle ground occupied by the friends of liberty finds itself uncertainly situated in a society that, when one looks toward the corrupt aristocracy, seems to be held together by force, but, when one contemplates the sufferings of the poor, finds its coherence in the power of feeling. The same sort of difference underlies the contradictory functions attributed to property and the diametrically opposed explanations of the effects of popular enfranchisement that have already been noted in the political discourse of the 1790s. Perhaps the proximity of political revolution, a situation that galvanizes not only the debates of the early 1790s but also most of the major political philosophy in the British isles after 1640, explains the prominence within this discourse of the problem of cohesion or social totality. The need to resolve competing interests for the protection of the common good and to articulate the legal and political means of achieving social unity imposes itself as both a conceptual and a practical goal. As Wordsworth's ethos shifts more decisively toward the character of the poet rather than the legislator, it is just such ideological ramifications that determine that alienation will replace violence as the central problem in Wordsworth's project. To a large extent, the problem of social coherence raises the questions that are being answered in Wordsworth's attempt to envision and realize the community of the "man speaking to men."

The metaphor for the social order that looms most impressively over British political thought in the seventeenth and eighteenth centuries is that of Thomas Hobbes's leviathan. Like all theories of social cohesion, Hobbes's *Leviathan* is also a theory of human nature. When Hobbes narrates the foundation of human political communities, his plot is predetermined by the human nature of its characters. This narrative and its motives appear in summary form in the opening sentence of Part 2 of Hobbes's great essay:

> The finall Cause, End, or Designe of men, (who naturally love Liberty, and Dominion over others,) in the introduction of that restraint upon themselves, (in which we see them live in Common-wealths,) is the foresight of their own preservation, and of a more contented life thereby; that is to say, of getting themselves out from that miserable condition of Warre, which is necessarily consequent (as hath been shewn) to the naturall Passions of men, when there is no visible Power to keep them in awe, and tye them by fear of punishment to the performance of their Covenants, and observation of those Lawes of Nature set down in the fourteenth and fifteenth Chapters [of Part 1 of *Leviathan*].[20]

The commonwealth results from human self-restraint in the interest of self-preservation. The political community manifested in and enforced by laws and contracts is therefore the artifact of reason's conscious triumph over the unrestrained passions.

Hobbes's rational commonwealth is a direct embodiment of his humanism, in the sense that the form of human society expresses the difference between human beings and animals. Ants and bees, says Hobbes, "live sociably with one another . . . and yet have no other direction, than their particular judgements and appetites" (225). But this instinctive form of sociability is not to be confused with human politics, because human beings are engaged in a variety of behaviors peculiar to them as a species: competition for honor and dignity; discrimination between public and private good; the use of language; the activities of finding fault, assigning blame, and thinking themselves wiser than others (225–26). The final difference, which encompasses all the others, is that human covenants are artificial, unlike the natural agreement of the social animals with one another. Thus the Hobbesian narrative of human nature is the story of the public contractualization and restraint of men's private, emulative, judgmental, hierarchizing, and garrulous passions. Natural competition between private individuals is overcome by the rational fear of violence, and this fear is the natural agent of the artificial sociability of the political human.

The next century produced a series of writings that more or less explicitly rejected Hobbes's narrative. In order to do so, they were forced to contradict his characterization of human nature.[21] The keynote of these counternarratives is that in the place of the triumph of rational fear over passionate violence they put a providential design that gives humans, like ants and bees, an innate disposition to community: "Nature works by a just Order and Regulation as well in the Passions and Affections, as in the Limbs and Organs which she forms; . . . it appears withal, that she has so constituted this *inward Part,* that nothing is so essential to it as *Exercise;* and no Exercise so essential as that of *social* or *natural Affection.*"[22] Shaftesbury's crucial polemical strategy here is his synonimization of "natural" and "social." Rather than the armed leviathan repressing natural warfare, Shaftesbury's social body is one that finds health and harmony in "common usage."

If Hobbes and Shaftesbury can be made to stand for the theories of social cohesion that motivate, on the one hand, the friends of liberty's militance, and on the other, their humanitarianism, then a third figure must intrude itself before the ground of middle-class virtue can be surveyed. This third figure will be one who locates the nexus of social coherence not in the imposition of law or the disposition of human nature but in the workings of the marketplace. It makes a rather spectacular entrance onto the scene with Bernard Mandeville's moral paradoxes concerning "private vices" and "publick benefits" in *The Fable of the Bees:* "What renders [man] a Sociable Animal, consists not in his desire of Company, Good-nature, Pity, Affability, and other Graces of a fair Outside; but [rather] his vilest and most hateful Qualities are the most necessary Accomplishments to fit him for the largest, and, according to the World, the happiest and most flourishing Societies."[23] What appears here in embryonic form is not really a third position on human nature (Mandeville is basically with Hobbes and against Shaftesbury), but rather a reconceptualization of the social order that replaces the roles of sovereignty or benevolence with the unintended, cumulative effects of a "natural" system of economic exchange.[24] This new figure of social coherence comes to maturity in the four-stage theory of history elaborated in the works of Scottish writers like Adam Ferguson, John Millar, and, above all, Adam Smith.

The way that Wordsworth and the friends of liberty articulate their class position turns upon this concept of economic totality and the historical narrative it generates. The figure of economic totality presents social coherence as a kind of unity of disunity or *concordia discors*. Richard Payne Knight's *The Progress of Civil Society* provides a particularly clear rendering of the conventional scheme. Knight portrays the development of "the soft intercourse of commerce"[25] as the inevitable formation of social harmony out of purely self-interested impulses of desire:

> Yet still where'er it [desire] leads, its windings tend,
> Through ways discordant, to one general end;
> For though each object of pursuit be vain,
> The means employ'd are universal gain.
> Through various ways, as various talents press
> The general prize of riches to possess;
> Though partial losses frustrate schemes deplore,
> All tend alike to swell the general store;
> All fill the streams of industry, and art,
> Which through the whole their vital powers impart;
> And as one prospers, and another fails,
> Degrees are form'd, and order just prevails.[26]

Thus in another conventional figure, natural self-interest—that is, economically rational behavior—spins out of itself, like a spider its web, that delicate network of beneficent human interaction called the social division of labor. The protest poetry of the 1790s often notices that the threads of this commercial network of co-dependence conduct the disturbing effects of warfare or corruption into the lives of the suffering poor, yet the inevitability of the web itself is never called into question.[27]

The uneasy concurrence of the historical and the natural in the constitution of republican virtue marks the tension that inheres in this powerful paradigm between the workings of universal human nature and the historically specific effects of "second nature."[28] Adam Smith's own writings have been best characterized as extraordinarily successful attempts to resolve the conflicting demands of needs and justice or commercial sophistication and patriotic virtue; yet it has often appeared to Smith's readers that a "de-politicized view of individual morality [that is, human nature] and a de-moralized view of politics [that is, second nature]" stand in mutual contradiction in his work.[29] Lukacs might say that a double reification is involved: of the social and economic from the perspective of the private and psychological, and of the private or psychological from the perspective of the economic. From each perspective the other becomes an inevitable and "natural" lawlike determination of human possibilities, and thus the discourse of economic totality absorbs both Hobbesian sovereignty and Shaftesburian sociality as alternate moments.[30]

The crux of the issue as it impinges on Wordsworth is that the middle rank's doubly reified vantage point is also liable to disintegrate into a doubly undermined quagmire of ethical scepticism. Smith, for instance, concedes the morally neutral possibility that "society may subsist among men, as among different merchants, from a sense of its utility, without any mutual love or affection; and though no man in it should owe any obligation, or be bound in gratitude to any other, it may still be upheld by a mercenary exchange of good offices according to an agreed valuation."[31] For Wordsworth, however, such an affectless aggregation of monetary interests seems to radically destabilize the value of any "exchange of good offices." What common ground does such mercenary cooperation offer to a man trying to speak to men "not as a lawyer, a physician, a mariner, an astronomer or a natural philosopher, but as a Man" (PrW1 139)? *The Borderers* explores at length the nightmarish possibility that legal order is based upon, and therefore inevitably corrupted by, the way the deliberate deceptions of self-interest infect and pervert the communication of authentic passions. The same horrific images of human nature and social order appear again in *The Prelude* when revolutionary Paris seems to degenerate into "a wood where tigers roam" (10.82), and Wordsworth monumentalizes the effect of such fears in the crisis of moral despair (10.805–904).

Even in Wordsworth's apparently more confident assertions about community during the *Lyrical Ballads* period, the specter of the inauthentic or mercenary community haunts the formation of the *ethos* of "genuine feeling." The "Essay on Morals" provides a particularly clear example:

> A tale of distress is related in *a mixed company,* relief for the sufferers proposed. The vain man, the proud man, the avaricious man &c., all contribute, but from very different feelings. Now in all cases except that of the affectionate & benevolent man, I would call the act of giving more or less accidental. (PrW1 101)

The apparent unanimity of compassion is specious because this community is in fact united only by the untrustworthy sign of "contribution," behind which a myriad of contradictory motives assume a bland, treacherous uniformity. The "tale of distress" fails to forge this "mixed company" into any more vital union, and from the example of such a failure Wordsworth derives the need for a language that can "incorporate itself with the blood & juices of our minds." If the problem of representation here has shifted decisively away from the exercise of political virtue and toward the deployment of a therapeutic poetics, the basis for that repositioning is the economic formation that so disguises or mediates the passions as to alienate them altogether from their presumed expression in social interaction.

Given such an ethical problematic, it is not very surprising that politics, with all its confusion of motives, complexity of interests, and demand for showmanship, should fade into the background of Wordsworth's project. The "Essay on Morals" implies a position toward politics similar to the one Coleridge avows, perhaps too strenuously, in his letter to his brother George of 10 March 1798.[32] There Coleridge decries the moral deterioration that has attended the revolutions in France and America, where "the morals & domestic habits of the people are daily deteriorating: & one good consequence which [Coleridge] expect[s] from revolutions, is that Individuals will see the necessity of individual effort; that they will act as kind neighbours & good Christians, rather than as citizens & electors" (STCL1 395). Coleridge asserts that governments are merely the effects, rather than the causes, of "what we are," and party politics are therefore merely superficial; he declares himself of no party: "no Whig, no Reformist, no Republican" (395–97).[33]

The disavowal of "party" is a thoroughly conventional gesture that hardly forms a decisive separation between the poets and the friends of liberty, however. Whatever distance Wordsworth reaches from London in poems like *The Ruined Cottage* and "Tintern Abbey," he has not entirely left politics behind, but rather has chosen a different way of addressing himself to political issues. For instance, when Wordsworth sent Charles James Fox a presentation copy of the *Lyrical Ballads* in January 1801, the accompanying letter addressed Fox not as an opposition Whig but as a member of the party of humanity:

> In common with the whole of the English people I have observed in your public character a constant predominance of sensibility of heart. Necessitated as you have been from your public situation to have much to do with men in bodies, and in classes, and accordingly to contemplate them in that relation, it has been your praise that you have not thereby been prevented from looking upon them as individuals, and that you have habitually left your heart open to be influenced by them in that capacity. This habit cannot but have made you dear to Poets; and I am sure that, if since your first entrance into public life there has been a single true poet living in England, he must have loved you. (LEY 313)

Wordsworth's emphasis upon individuals rather than "men in bodies, and in classes" apparently corresponds to the poet's proper concern with moral rather than political virtue. His concern with moral virtue itself, however, expresses the paradigmatic dilemma of the middle rank. Wordsworth worries about the "rapid decay of domestic affections among the lower orders of society" and points primarily to economic causes: "the spreading of manufactures, . . . the heavy taxes upon postage, . . . the increasing disproportion between the price of labour and that of the necessaries of life" (LEY 313). In a democratized version of classical political theory, he attributes healthy household virtue to the independence enjoyed by "proprietors of small estates" as opposed to "hired labourers" or "the manufacturing poor" (LEY 314). Yet domestic virtue preoccupies Wordsworth precisely because it is at the point of intersection between the lower order's economically determined realm of competence and the political problem of reconciling the interests of "men in bodies" with the good of men "as individuals." Wordsworth's project inevitably strives to bridge the gap between class and humanity, second nature and nature: "The poems are faithful copies from nature . . . and may in some small degree enlarge our feelings of reverence for our species, and our knowledge of human nature, by shewing that our best qualities are possessed by men whom we are too apt to consider, not with reference to the points in which they resemble us, but to those in which they manifestly differ from us" (LEY 315). His use of the first-person plural, unfortunately, reaffirms the very distance he wants to over-come. One point in which "they" do "manifestly differ from us," it appears, is that they are not as likely to read Wordsworth's poetry.

ON WESTMINSTER BRIDGE

It would seem that in Wordsworth's political sonnets of 1802 he finally achieved the kind of public utterance he had projected for the *Letter to Llandaff* and *The Philanthropist* and at least hoped for, according to the letter to Fox, in the *Lyrical Ballads*. Certainly the militant republicanism that predominates in the *Letter to Llandaff* and that was mostly submerged in the poetry of the following decade becomes once again outspoken and explicit in Words-worth's 1802 contributions to *The Morning Post* and in the associated sonnets published among the "Sonnets Dedicated to Liberty" in his 1807 *Poems, in Two Volumes*. But there is a difference. Wordsworth's republicanism in 1802 has lost its earlier Paineite ring. Instead he falls back on the older and safer rhetoric of civic humanism and "country" ideology.[34] He invokes Milton repeatedly, along with other Commonwealth examples of steadfast virtue: "The later Sydney, Marvel, Harrington, / Young Vane, and others who call'd Milton Friend" (P2V 166).[35] In a pair of sonnets be-moaning England's present corruption, he declares that the na-tion's abiding strength resides in "manners, virtue, freedom" and "Plain living and high thinking. . . , / The homely beauty of the good old cause" (P2V 165).

All of this country republicanism is subordinated, in its turn, to Wordsworth's emerging nationalism, an ideology he would elabo-rate far more fully a few years later in *The Convention of Cintra*. What is most striking in 1802 is the way Wordsworth grafts the class tensions of his earlier writing onto the opposition of England and France. Thus, where outrage against aristocratic corruption once stood, one finds in 1802 Wordsworth's contempt and indigna-tion toward Napoleonic France (for example, "Calais, August, 1802" or "Calais, August 15, 1802" [P2V 156, 158–59]). In a comple-mentary movement, Wordsworth's humanitarian sympathy for the suffering poor seems to be largely displaced by nationalistic fervor for English land and the English people. Thus the synthesis of nature and second nature that Wordsworth elsewhere sought in the imagery of domestic virtue here finds a political expression in lyr-ics of patriotic love for the mother country such as "Composed by the Sea-side, near Calais, August, 1802" or "Composed in the

Valley, near Dover, on the Day of landing" (P2V 155, 162–63). Some sort of dialectical and almost surely defensive transposition has taken place. If, in the 1790s, Wordsworth assuaged a moral scepticism based on a political crisis by recurring to the relative verities of familial and personal obligations, he now seems to respond to the demands of a domestic crisis (his impending marriage to Mary Hutchinson, combined with the lucky coincidence of the Peace of Amiens, occasioned his trip to France to confront the consequences of his earlier liaison with Annette Vallon) by staking out the relatively firmer ground of patriotic eloquence.[36]

The fulcrum of this vacillation between public and private utterance, however, remains the uncertain basis of economic community. In keeping with Wordsworth's "country" sentiments, commercial England receives an overwhelmingly negative depiction in a number of powerful sonnets. "Written in London, September, 1802" calls England a society of "Rapine, avarice, expense," where "The wealthiest man among us is the best" (P2V 165). "When I have borne in memory" claims that "ennobling thoughts depart / When Men change Swords for Ledgers, and desert / The Student's bower for gold" (P2V 167). One counterpart of this vision of England as "a fen / Of stagnant waters" (P2V 165) is the image of a community rooted in household economy and domestic virtue. "I griev'd for Buonaparte," for instance, the earliest of the political sonnets, asks how the "vital blood" of Napoleon's mind, untempered by "Thoughts motherly, and meek as womanhood," can ever produce wise and good governance. Wordsworth's sonnet portrays a version of second nature ("Books, leisure, perfect freedom") ideal for the training of a governor and plants the "stalk / True Power doth grow on" in the soil of a nurturing maternal figure: "Wisdom doth live with children round her knees" (P2V 157–58).

Yet British commerce itself is capable of coalescing with the power of nature by way of its implicit representation of an organic social whole. Consider, for instance, the ambiguous status of the metaphor of the "flood" in the sonnet which declares that "It is not be thought of that the Flood / Of British freedom . . . in Bogs and Sands / Should perish" (P2V 166–67). The identity of the flood of British freedom with the commercial traffic on the Thames becomes almost literal here: "Road by which all might come and go that would, / And bear out freights of worth to foreign lands." The figure of free circulation as a way of maintaining the economic and political health of the social body is, of course, very widespread. Paine, in *The Rights of Man, Part Two,* writes of "the unceasing circulation of interest, which, passing through its million channels, invigorates the whole mass of men" (1.358). But there is no stable relationship between the network of trade and republican politics. On the contrary, the use of the figure of circulation to identify commercial prosperity with social well-being has quite bipartisan possibilities, as evidenced by Burke's deployment of it in the conclusion of the third *Letter on a Regicide Peace*. There Burke triumphantly portrays the port of London as the heart of Great Britain's healthy wartime economy:

> When we see the life-blood of the state circulate so freely through the capillary vessels of the system, we scarcely need inquire if the heart performs its functions aright. But let us approach it; let us lay it bare, and watch the systole and diastole, as it now receives, and now pours forth the vital streams of all the members. The port of London has always supplied the main evidence of the state of our commerce. (5.498–99)

The trope of healthy circulation receives an interestingly different turn, however, in the hands of Thomas Erskine. In his *View of the Causes and Consequences of the Present War with France,* an antiministerial polemic against England's war with France that we know Wordsworth had in his possession in 1797,[37] he writes:

> Until there was a just and legitimate representation of the [French] people, controulling the other modifications of government, no matter how constituted, clubs and knots of men spread terror and confusion, and the people supported them; because they were represented in those clubs and factions, or not represented at all. They had no other security against tyranny than by a general organization of their authority, and the public humours therefore settled into factions. For this state of society there was no possible cure but legitimate power proceeding from the people. . . .
> It is the free circulation of that, which constitutes substance throughout all the parts which compose them, that alone can preserve them.
> The humours of the human body, which occasionally deform its beauty, and impair its strength, are not in themselves diseases, but indications that the body is generally diseased: they are but the poisoned symptoms of imperfect circulation.[38]

Here circulation refers to political representation rather than economic exchange, and therefore the figure of social cohesion elicits themes of violence, corruption, and legitimacy rather than wealth, interest, and prosperity. This rhetoric is certainly more congenial to the discourse of moral and political virtue in Wordsworth's 1802 sonnets than the commercial implications of Paine's or Burke's versions of healthy circulation. Yet, perhaps because the "freights of worth" borne on Wordsworth's flood remain uncertainly poised amid the quasi-natural benefits of free trade, the fruits of imperial domination, and the salutary effects of a "just and legitimate representation," the sonnet's sestet articulates a familiar contradiction:

> In our halls is hung
> Armoury of the invincible Knights of old:
> We must be free or die, who speak the tongue
> That Shakespeare spake; the faith and morals hold
> Which Milton held.—In every thing we are sprung
> Of earth's first blood, have titles manifold.

In the injunction to live up to Milton's "faith and morals," the second nature of hereditary privilege and literary tradition coalesces with the less distinctive status of merely speaking the English language. Yet the language that Shakespeare spoke would have to become Adamic in order to justify the claims about "earth's first blood" in the final line. Nature and history here provide England the same sort of contradictory privilege as earlier constituted the political and humanitarian virtues of the middle rank.

Wordsworth's most striking realization of the various dichotomies that radiate from the topic of economy comes not in a political sonnet, however, but rather in one of his most haunting lyrics, the sonnet "Composed upon Westminster Bridge, September 3, 1803" (P2V 147):

> Earth has not anything to shew more fair:
> Dull would he be of soul who could pass by
> A sight so touching in it's majesty:
> This City now doth like a garment wear
> The beauty of the morning; silent, bare,
> Ships, towers, domes, theatres, and temples lie
> Open unto the fields, and to the sky;
> All bright and glittering in the smokeless air.
> Never did sun more beautifully steep
> In his first splendor valley, rock, or hill;
> Ne'er saw I, never felt, a calm so deep!
> The river glideth at his own sweet will:
> Dear God! the very houses seem asleep;
> And all that mighty heart is lying still!

Alan Liu has given a compelling account of the range of topical ambiguity this sonnet brings into play, including its delicate balance between love poem and epitaph or epithalamium and satire, and the tension between London as both a New Jerusalem, wedding country and city under the name of English nationalism, and as Babylon, a shadow-world of commercial corruption ceding itself to Napoleonic dominion.[39] What brings the sonnet into its close proximity with what I have called Wordsworth's counterrevolutionary turn, however, is the profound calm or *stasis* it imposes upon the scene. Don Bialostosky catches this tonal quality in his observation that "the shock to the speaker's assumptions is so great that he seems to cast off his identity and to stand for the moment outside it, ecstatically rejecting that dull-souled perspective that could pass this experience by and testifying to an experience of calm in this vision deeper than any he has ever seen or felt."[40] This is the Wordsworth Hartman calls "the halted traveller,"[41] whose loving observation of minute particulars deepens into the sublime claims of imaginative vision. The question here is how this ecstatic moment reshapes and rearticulates the poet's identity within the communities of country, city, and nation.

The dullness of soul that could fail to be touched by the "majesty" of this scene recalls (or anticipates)[42] those "men of prostrate mind" paying homage to Napoleon in "Calais, August, 1802:"

> Lords, Lawyers, Statesmen, Squires of low degree,
> Men known, and men unknown, Sick, Lame, and Blind,
> Post forward all, like Creatures of one kind,
> With first-fruit offerings crowd to bend the knee
> In France, before the new-born Majesty.
>
> (P2V 156)

Clearly this is a nightmare of levelling in which all ranks reach an equal abjection beneath the tyrant. Yet the way the French press forward "like Creatures of one kind" also recalls the bland uniformity of gesture that masks the chaos of conflicting motives in the amoral community of economic exchange. If the French have all been reduced to Napoleon's creatures, the fear that comes home to Wordsworth is that commerce is playing the same trick upon the English. The poet's extraordinary response to the majestic sight of London introduces a moral and aesthetic hierarchy that overcomes a sense of difficulty concerning, first, what is "fair," but even more, what kind of "show" the city of London enacts.

The metaphor of the garment in the fourth line makes more explicit the theme of the unreliability of commercial show. In "Written in London, September, 1802," Wordsworth renders as an ethical imperative what appears from Westminster Bridge as an epiphanic gift:

> our Life is only drest
> For shew; mean handywork of craftsman, cook,
> Or groom! We must run glittering like a brook
> In the open sunshine, or we are unblest.
>
> (P2V 164–65)

How is it that the dawn prospect of London "bright and glittering in the smokeless air" can so effortlessly achieve the guileless purity that at other times commercial society seems to preclude? The answer has to do with the dynamics of representation. The panoramic catalogue of the city's features—"Ships, towers, domes, theatres, and temples"—implies an integrative social scheme. The professions of mariner, statesman, clergyman, artist, and lawyer merge into a compelling, heaven-blest unity "Open unto the fields, and to the sky" that is markedly antithetical to the "one kind" shared by Napoleon's creatures. The city achieves this coherence, however, only by virtue of the compelling perspective that focuses their manifold appearances in the sweeping gesture of the speaker's gaze. Bare, open, bright, glittering, smokeless: the adjectives stress clarity, lack of obstruction; but the foremost quality of the scene's presentation is its enfolding silence. The absence of urban commotion and dirt here crosses over, by way of the exclusively visual imagery, from an accident of diurnal rhythms to an unconscious effect of internalization. It is London's silence that conducts the scene into the associative realm, supplied by the speaker, of valleys, rocks, and hills; and it is the speaker's testimony that represents that associative act as a moment of social integration. The climactic synthesis of public and private, vision and association, comes in the conflation of sight with feeling: "Ne'er saw I, never felt, a calm so deep!"

The final tercet not only plumbs, but also complicates that achievement. Beauty sinks into portentous sublimity, and, as in "A slumber did my spirit seal," the notions of calm and sleep verge dangerously upon a deathlike union with the inanimate. The trope of circulation is the almost inevitable vehicle of this progress. It is as if the river's freedom to follow "his own sweet will" debouched from privacy and solitude into a more impersonal realm of dream, perhaps hallucination, and finally emptied into an oceanic integration with the "mighty heart" of things that is hard to distinguish from annihilation.

The complex figure of the stilled heart recapitulates the lyric victory of vision over the tensions resident in the themes of virtue and community. "Heart," in the sonnet's final line, is both a metonymy of virtue and a metaphor of community. As metonymy, it indicates the domestic and patriotic sympathies invested in the speaker's visionary experience. As metaphor, it refers to London's commercial, imperial centrality, that is, both to a totalizing economy of exchange and to the potentially untrustworthy might of its political and military sovereignty. This multiple, private and public, play of references continues in the speaker's awestruck declaration of the heart's stillness. On the one hand, virtue expands into the ideal community of a London stripped bare of its venal or vainglorious show. On the other hand, the poet's vision virtually creates a new form of community by momentarily halting the antagonistic motions set astir by the city's rhetorical and material significance as a nexus of economic and political power. Yet Wordsworth achieves this visionary totalization of the social world only against and in spite of the notions of social coherence the figure of the heart evokes, for Wordsworth's voice is seldom more haunted by his profound detachment and even alienation from what he apparently means to celebrate. The poem sets the poet both at the center of things and, at the same time, outside of them. The community he convenes is not, finally, either London or the English nation, but rather a series of spectators who silently share his solitary gaze.

There can be little question, now, of the great power of Wordsworth's poetic achievement. Nonetheless, Wordsworth himself seems to have suffered recurrent anxiety about its equivocal nature, that is, its production of a paradoxical community of isolates. Perhaps solitude and *stasis* are the price of visionary experience precisely because of the defensive, compensatory emphasis on industry and personal attachment that is nicely, and conveniently, combined in the cottage economy of many of Wordsworth's common men and women. He tries to approximate his poetic efforts to commoner and more obviously useful work, for instance, in another famous sonnet where he hopes to ply "the Sonnet's scanty plot of ground" in the same way as "Maids at the Wheel, the Weaver at his Loom, / Sit blithe and happy" (P2V 133). The same sonnet goes on to claim that he seeks in this project to shed "the weight of too much liberty." Although that liberty has obvious political and formal references, the next chapter takes up the argument that Wordsworth's burdensome freedom relates primarily to the economic anxieties inherent in Wordsworth's sense that poetic vocation involves a class responsibility.

3

The Economy of Vision

WHEN WORDSWORTH WRITES IN THE ADVERTISEMENT TO THE 1798 *Lyrical Ballads* that "the following poems . . . were written chiefly with a view to ascertain how far the language of conversation in the middle and lower classes of society is adapted to the purposes of poetic pleasure" (PrW1 116), what kind of common ground does he presume the "middle and lower classes" share? How similar is his project, for instance, to the call for class alliance in the 1798 prospectus of his friend James Losh's periodical *The Oeconomist?*

> The inferior ranks of society are particularly interested in maintaining the welfare and independence of the middle ranks. The middle ranks are true barriers for defending the liberty and property of the common people, against the weight of the higher orders of every state. . . . It is therefore the interest of the lower orders to regard the middle orders with friendship and respect. They are their natural guardians and allies.[1]

If the continuity between antiaristocratic political virtue and humanitarian sympathy for the "inferior ranks" is as real in Wordsworth as it is apparent in *The Oeconomist,* Wordsworth's counterrevolutionary turn may look a good deal more like a strategic choice than a political turnabout. At the same time, however, the "language of conversation" and the project of therapeutic poetics that seeks to employ it may also turn out to be quite unevenly available to the "common people" and their "natural guardians and allies." One might ask, for instance, what kind of work it is to experiment with this language and note that Wordsworth's project, in yearning for class alliance, inevitably expresses a class division. I want to argue for the importance of this class division by showing how its presence at the foundation of his poetics determines the ambivalent tonal quality of Wordsworth's visionary moments and profoundly shapes the possibilities of the theme of community in his work. My exhibits are the workings of Wordsworthian sympathy in the context of the debate on the Poor Law, and the anxieties Wordsworth represents himself as suffering because of his poetic vocation.

SYMPATHY AS AN ARTICULATION OF SOCIAL CLASS: WORDSWORTH AND THE POOR-LAW DEBATES OF THE 1790S

Wordsworth's subject matter in the mid-1790s emerges directly from the Paineite background of the *Letter to Llandaff*, and particularly from Paine's extensive proposals for economic legislation in the second part of *The Rights of Man*.[2] The brief section of the *Letter to Llandaff* on economic justice, where Wordsworth shares Paine's enthusiasm for the potential social effects of legislation intended to better the condition of the poor, touches most closely on the concerns that will increasingly predominate in his poetry:

> Your lordship tells us that the science of civil government has received all of the perfection of which it is capable. For my part, I am more enthusiastic: the sorrow I feel from the contemplation of this melancholy picture is not unconsoled by a comfortable hope that the class of wretches called mendicants will not much longer shock the feelings of humanity. (PrW1 43)

Wordsworth's faith in the "science of civil government" places him in the party of reason, a posture that, as has already been observed, would prove quite transient. Yet the source of this passage in *The Rights of Man Part Two* still reads almost like a catalogue of Wordsworth's concerns in the Salisbury Plain poems, *The Ruined Cottage,* and a number of the *Lyrical Ballads.* After enumerating the particulars of his proposals for redistributing national income to social programs, Paine writes:

> By the operation of this plan, the poor laws, those instruments of civil torture, will be superseded, and the wasteful expense of litigation prevented. The hearts of the humane will not be shocked by ragged and hungry children, and persons of seventy and eighty years of age begging for bread. The dying poor will not be dragged from place to place to breathe their last, as a reprisal of parish upon parish.
> Widows will have maintenance for their children, and will not be carted away, like culprits and criminals; and children will no longer be considered as increasing the distress of their parents. The haunts of the wretched will be known, because it will be to their advantage; and

the number of petty crimes, the offspring of distress and poverty, will be lessened. The poor, as well as the rich, will then be interested in the support of government, and the cause and apprehension of riots and tumults will cease. (Paine, 1.431)

Between Paine's arguments and Wordsworth's composition of poems like "The Old Cumberland Beggar" and "The Last of the Flock," which specifically address some of the shortcomings of the Old Poor Law, there intervenes one of the major episodes of a far-reaching and momentous debate concerning such topics. Arguments about the Poor Law were hardly a new thing in the mid-1790s, but they received an enormous charge of fresh energy when bad harvests caused a severe shortage and a sharp rise in the price of basic foodstuffs in 1795 and 1796. The disastrous effects of the scarcity upon the lower classes and the resulting rise in the poor-rates paid by the middle and upper classes provoked an outpouring of pamphlet literature concerning the causes and remedies of the situation. Much of this literature debated the merits of some abortive attempts to legislate a minimum wage and to overhaul the Old Poor Law. The most notable practical development in poor relief during the years of scarcity was the development of the Speenhamland system, that is, the widespread practice of allowing local Justices of the Peace to supplement inadequate wages with doles from the poor rates. While this kind of local, discretionary aid was very much in tune with the paternalistic parish system of relief, it would soon become one of the most vilified aspects of the Old Poor Law because of its improper interference with the self-regulatory mechanisms of the market. The entire episode constitutes a significant prelude to the controversies that would surround the formulation of the New Poor Law in 1834, when the old parish system of poor relief, based on the Elizabethan Poor Law and loaded with all the mass of revisions and attempts at reform accumulated in more than two centuries of tinkering, was abolished in favor of a centralized and nationalized administration.[3] The significance of this epochal institutional transformation may well be rivalled by its ideological impact. Between the debates of 1795–96 and the reforms of 1834, according to one commentator, "The figure of the pauper, almost forgotten since, dominated a discussion the imprint of which was as powerful as that of the most spectacular events in history."[4] According to Polanyi, the fruit of this debate was no less than the modern concept of society, grasped first and incompletely here as the workings of the market.

The figure of the pauper owes its centrality in this discourse less

to the real concern of some British citizens for the welfare of the poor than to the way it condenses the themes of parasitism, dependency, and productivity into the urgent question of distinguishing between moral and legal duties. Wordsworth's most explicit contribution to the debate, "The Old Cumberland Beggar," enters the discussion at precisely this last point.[5] The argument of the poem concerns the correct method of relieving the poverty of a very old, feeble beggar who has wandered the roads of a Cumberland neighborhood for some years past. Wordsworth directs his polemic explicitly against overactive legislators who would deal with the beggar by confining him to a workhouse: "ye / Who are so restless in your wisdom, ye / Who have a broom still ready in your hands / To rid the world of nuisances" (67–70).[6] The debate over the usefulness and morality of confining the poor to workhouses was one of the most persistent and insistent arguments concerning the Poor Laws throughout the eighteenth and early nineteenth centuries. The poet proposes that rather than sheltering the old man in a so-called house of industry, he should be allowed to continue to roam his accustomed district and to die, as he has lived, "in the eye of Nature" (189)—that is to say, shelterless and outdoors. The reasons offered for the poet's wish are equally curious. Wordsworth argues that the beggar, useless as he seems, is nonetheless productive of social good because his presence in the district fosters a sense of community among those who give him alms and assistance. Rather than a merely legal community, where the letter of the law enforces "cold abstinence from evil deeds" (137) and "inevitable charities" (138), Wordsworth uses the beggar as the focal point for representing a community bound together by "a spirit and pulse of good, / A life and soul to every mode of being / Inseparably linked" (77–79). The odd result of this argument, however, is that the old beggar thus becomes the counterpart of a legal document: ". . . the Villagers in him / Behold a record which together binds / Past deeds and offices of charity" (80–82). Thus the entire community participates in a fiction of identity with, or rather *by means of,* the beggar, a situation Cleanth Brooks has aptly described as "inverse scapegoating."[7]

Wordsworth's position resembles, on the face of it, Burke's exhortations in the *Reflections* and elsewhere concerning the importance of encouraging domestic affections and local attachment.[8] In his "Thoughts and Details upon Scarcity," a pamphlet attacking the attempts to legislate a minimum wage that were spurred by the bread shortages of 1795–96, Burke holds that maintenance of the poor ought to be left to individual benevolence rather than the state. The state ought to confine itself to "everything that is *truly and properly* public—to the public peace, to the public safety, to the public order, to the public prosperity" (Burke, 5.166). The rest ought to be left up to citizens in their private capacity:

> As they [statesmen] descend from the state to a province, from a province to a parish, and from a parish to a private house, they go on accelerated in their fall. They *cannot* do the lower duty; and in proportion as they try it, they will certainly fail in the higher. They ought to know the different departments of things—what belongs to laws, and what manners alone can regulate. (5.167)

Burke's argument is diametrically opposed to the Paineite view that inequality of property is maintained largely by political means and is therefore susceptible of political and legal remedies. Wordsworth's own rejection of legal interference with voluntary charity does seem to reverse his earlier faith in "the science of civil government" and might therefore be interpreted as a realignment of his political sympathies with the Pitt ministry rather than the Foxite Whigs.

Wordsworth's resemblance to Burke in "The Old Cumberland Beggar" is really rather superficial, however. Wordsworth emphasizes the dignity those just above the beggar on the social scale achieve by their acts of charity and benevolence: ". . .the poorest poor / Long for some moments in a weary life / When they can know and feel that they have been / Themselves the fathers and the dealers out / Of some small blessings" (140–44).[9] Wordsworth's theme is the maintenance of common decency by a certain kind of empowerment of the common man. Burke is more concerned with maintaining his version of a natural hierarchy, which he identifies with the ascendancy of an agricultural oligarchy: "The whole of agriculture is in a natural and just order: the beast is as an informing principle to the plough and cart; the laborer is as reason to the beast; and the farmer is as a thinking and presiding principle to the laborer" (5.140). Where Wordsworth argues for the usefulness of one indigent old man to the community's sense of coherence, Burke proclaims the necessity of poverty for the continuance of this "natural" social order:

> The laboring people are only poor because they are numerous. Numbers in their nature imply poverty. In a fair distribution among a vast multitude none can have much. That class of dependent pensioners called the rich is so extremely small, that, if all their throats were to be cut, and a distribution made of all they consume in a year, it would

not give a bit of bread and cheese for one night's supper to those who labor, and who in reality feed both the pensioners and themselves.

But the throats of the rich ought not to be cut . . . because, in their persons, they are trustees for those who labor, and their hoards are the banking-houses of these latter. (5.134)

Perhaps it is merely Burke's idiosyncracy that manages to make the rich into a board of trustees and "dependent pensioners" in almost the same breath; yet his glib reversal of the trope of dependence is symptomatic of a widespread conceptual and ideological confusion concerning the relation between productivity and social rank.

A fairly strong consensus is gathering at this time around the idea that labor is society's fundamental source of wealth. Yet the physiocratic belief that wealth flows from the land is still strong, and beyond it lies an even more settled and stubborn notion of society in which wealth flows from above. Gregory King's 1688 table of national population and wealth, for instance, lists and enumerates the various classes who make up the kingdom of England in descending order from top to bottom.[10] On the top half of his table he groups together as the classes "increasing the wealth of the kingdom" those who enjoy an excess of income over the expenditure necessary to maintain and reproduce their families. The corresponding group of classes "decreasing the wealth of the kingdom" will not likely strike a modern reader as uniformly unproductive: "common seamen," "labouring people and out-servants," "cottagers and paupers," and "common soldiers." A century later, even though the role of labor in maintaining the wealthy is generally acknowledged, the logic that equates maintaining the laborers' subsistence economy with securing their proper dependency on the wealthy remains very strong.

In the Poor Law controversies, the difference between procuring a bare subsistence (whether by one's own labor or with the supplementary aid of charity) and possessing the wherewithal to accumulate excess wealth is perhaps the most prevalent means of conceptualizing not only class distinctions but also, more importantly, the duties and obligations that go with them. In this sense Burke's metaphor of the "banking-houses" is altogether typical. For instance, Frederick Morton Eden's massive, and not at all flamboyant, *The State of the Poor* (1797) agrees with Burke that the accumulation of property in the hands of the wealthy represents only a precarious surplus dependent upon the continued labor of a large class of people maintaining themselves at a subsistence level. Eden, like Burke, identifies the accumulated property of the rich with the benefits of civilization as such. Eden spells out these assumptions on the first pages of his study. The one sure universal of human society is the need for subsistence, Eden begins; and a large portion of society is always employed in providing subsistence for the whole. There are in addition some "supernumerary hands . . . occupied in the various arts," to whom mankind is indebted for the refinements of civil society. Finally, there are those who neither toil nor spin. They, according to Eden, "are peculiarly the creatures of civil institutions; which, for the general benefit of society, have uniformly recognized this fundamental principle, that individuals may acquire property by various other means than the exertion of labour, and, under certain prescribed forms, transfer it to their contemporaries, or transmit it to their descendants." The status of the rich depends wholly upon their ability to command the labor of "those, whose daily subsistence absolutely depends on the daily unremitting exertion of manual labour." This arrangement provides society as a whole with a class of people who have the leisure necessary to acquire and exercise the capacity to govern it. Accumulated property, for Eden, is the prerequisite of foresight: "With [the rich], the use of stock previously accumulated, and the anticipation of future resources, often supply the deficiencies of the moment . . . but individuals, in the humbler spheres of life at least, cannot either reason or act in this manner."[11]

The relation between subsistence and accumulation has complex and antithetical implications. The poor's lack of foresight would seem to predicate both paternalistic sentiments and a certain wariness toward these potentially unruly children on the part of the rich. Eden, for instance, is far from blaming the poor for their lack of foresight. On the contrary, he concludes that it is up to those who can plan for the future to help those who cannot. However, since Eden's or Burke's account of the relation between economy and social class argues that property is inextricably involved in the ties that bind together civil society, to be without property, by the same account, is to be a foreign and dangerous presence in society's midst. The notion that an uncertain subsistence economy is the driving force that maintains the propertied class in its civically responsible position would seem to predict a society with a dangerous measure of instability built into it. Thus the literature on poor relief is full of charges of improvidence, intemperance, and indolence against the poor, and the debate shuttles endlessly and irresolvably between assertions that poverty produces criminality and that vice is itself the root cause of poverty.[12]

The capacity for foresight itself has variable consequences that correspond to the disparate meanings of property. Insofar as property denotes material goods, foresight takes the aspect of rational calculation, the ability to quantify and allocate resources according to various contingencies. But those versions of upper-class virtue that emphasize benevolence and philanthropy rest on the idea that the constitutive social relations within which the production and exchange of goods take place are a more important form of property. Foresight, in this context, becomes a matter of habitual regard for upholding virtuous and affectionate social bonds rather than an exercise in financial rationality. "I do not know whether our attachment to *property* be not something more than the mere dictate of reasons, or even the mere effect of associations," writes William Paley:

> Property communicates a charm to whatever is the object of it. It is the first of our abstract ideas; and it cleaves to us the closest and the longest. It endears to the child his plaything, to the peasant his cottage, to the landholder his estate.[13]

The type of paternalism that informs "The Old Cumberland Beggar" usually conflates the exchange of property with the reinforcement of quasi-instinctive social affections. Consider, for instance, the resemblance between Wordsworth's theme and the paternalist, humanitarian sentiments of the conservative reformer William Young. This is Young in 1788 attacking the workhouse system:

> Even the care of the aged and infirm, or of orphan or forsaken children, should not be farmed. Let it not be made matter of contract, but let us have to think—let us have to feel, whether we should eject the old labourer from his ancient cottage, in which his embers of industry, fanned by the proud breath of independence, and sustained with the vigilance which local attachment inspires, may be satisfied with a little aid of fuel. A trifling stipend of alms may be sufficient to support him who is willing, though not wholly able, to support himself. To afford that stipend, is at once the strictest Parsimony, and the Noblest Charity.[14]

Sir William Young's Act of 1796 and the Speenhamland system it sanctioned[15] were ways of affording this "trifling stipend." The economic logic is indeed not far from King's. The stipend makes up the difference between what those "decreasing the wealth of the kingdom" produce (that is, are paid or allowed to retain) and what they need in order to maintain their families. The point, however, is that the laborer's independence, local attachment, and domestic affections are more essential forms of wealth than the money the poor-rates extract from the rich. As the Rev. J. Howlett argued in a 1796 pamphlet in favor of establishing a minimum wage, "How could it discourage industry, to assure a man, if he exerted himself properly, he would be able to maintain himself and his family in decency and comfort? Allowing him the common affections of nature, the common attachments to a wife and children, so far from discouraging industry, it would be a constant spur to the most vigorous exertions."[16]

In "The Old Cumberland Beggar" Wordsworth supports almsgiving rather than outdoor relief, and his beggar lacks both "the common attachment to a wife and children" and the capability of any "vigorous exertions." Yet Wordsworth's argument for the beggar's social usefulness to the community remains more similar to Howlett's or Young's solicitude for "the proud breath of independence" than to the political-economic arguments for voluntary rather than legal relief, even when they adopt the tropes of paternalism. For instance, the political economist Eden (a better Burkean than Burke, according to Gertrude Himmelfarb[17]) writes:

> There seem to be just grounds for concluding, that the sum of good to be expected from the establishment of a compulsory maintenance for the Poor, will be far outbalanced by the sum of evil which it will inevitably create; that the certainty of legal provision weakens the principles of natural affection, and destroys one of the strongest ties of society, by rendering the exercise of domestic and social duties less necessary.[18]

The unfortunate effect of this type of distrust of legal provisions was not a general increase in voluntary charity, but rather a concerted effort to insure that the recipients of public relief would not be encouraged in any way to neglect their "domestic and social duties." Strangely enough, such concern for the morality of the laboring class ended up being allied to the most severe form of rational, quantified calculation, the most dogmatic protection of the unimpeded mechanism of the free market, and the most ambitious and centralized kind of legal provision for the poor.

Jeremy Bentham's "Outline of a Work Entitled Pauper Management Improved" (first published in the *Annals of Agriculture* in 1798) calls for a system of relief that would be mandatorily enforced upon every indigent person in the kingdom, regardless of their moral status. He envisions a system of Houses of Industry, built on the Panopticon model, which would house as many as a million paupers. In order to avoid any interference between the goods produced in the Houses of Industry and the circulation of standard commodities in the market, the whole system of pauper relief must be made to comprise an immense, independent subsistence economy that pays for itself entirely and precisely with the labor of the incarcerated paupers. Bentham's determination to transform the entire problem of poverty into an exercise in good management, combined with the austere demands of the logic of subsistence, sometimes produces a shocking divorce of human values from the calculations of his accounting sheets:

> Is an *average* child at his birth—supposing him certain of not living beyond the age of one-and-twenty complete—worth *more* or *less* than *nothing* to those (himself of the number) who, during that period of legal, as well as natural, subjection, have the benefit of his capacity for labour at command? If more than nothing, at what age does he become so?[19]

The importance of the concept of mere subsistence to Bentham's calculations is one of Bentham's major legacies to Poor Law reform. A central tenet of the reformed Poor Law of 1834, the less-eligibility principle, probably draws upon such formulations in Bentham's "Pauper Management Improved" as his "suitable-fare principle":

> Maintenance at the expense of others should not be made more desirable than *self*-maintenance. Fare consequently the cheapest that can be found, so it be nourishing and wholesome—for, if there be any cheaper in use, it must be among the self-maintaining poor. *Luxury,* being a relative term, is applicable with as much propriety to the diet of the poor as of the rich. Luxury, if it does *not* render the condition of the burdensome poor more desirable than that of the self-maintaining poor, fails of its purpose: if it *does,* it violates *justice,* as well as *economy,* and cuts up *industry* by the roots.[20]

It is most unlikely that Wordsworth was responding directly to Bentham in "The Old Cumberland Beggar." There is no evidence that Wordsworth even knew of Bentham's work.[21] Nonetheless Wordsworth's increasing distance from the party of reason may well have been motivated, at least in part, by a perception that dominance over the discourse of "reason" was shifting away from the defenders of natural rights and toward the application of political-economic principles as a result of the Poor Law controversies.[22] Looking back on "The Old Cumberland Beggar" in his conversations with Isabella Fenwick, Wordsworth said that the poem responded to "the political economists [who] were about that time beginning their war upon mendicity in all its forms & by implication, if not directly, on Alms-giving also. This heartless process has been carried as far as it can go by the AMENDED poor-law bill" (LB 393).[23] In the 1800 *Lyrical Ballads,* Wordsworth's contribution to the Poor Law debate consists largely of a strategic denial of a quantifiable sense of public prosperity. Instead Wordsworth advocates an ethical sense of community, accessible immediately to the sympathetic individual but invisible to Benthamite balance sheets.

The contrast between the emergent laissez-faire version of rational calculation and the older identification of property with social bonds may well inform the odd portrait of the beggar's meal at the opening of "The Old Cumberland Beggar":

> from a bag
> All white with flour the dole of village dames,
> He drew his scraps and fragments, one by one,
> And scann'd them with a fix'd and serious look
> Of idle computation. In the sun,
> Upon the second step of that small pile,
> Surrounded by those wild unpeopled hills,
> He sate, and eat his food in solitude;
> And ever, scatter'd from his palsied hand,
> That still attempting to prevent the waste,
> Was baffled still, the crumbs in little showers
> Fell on the ground, and the small mountain birds,
> Not venturing yet to peck their destin'd meal,
> Approach'd within the length of half his staff.
>
> (8–21)

The beggar's "fix'd and serious look / Of idle computation" and the way the "waste" of his crumbs turns into the birds' good fortune may amount to a parody of the "political economists" whose attacks upon almsgiving were, according to the elderly Wordsworth, the occasion for the poem. At the same time, the distribution of the "scraps and fragments" of bread from the villagers to the beggar to the birds enacts a scene of social cohesion and binding affections "in the eye of Nature."

Wordsworth's idealizations of rural society in general, and of the Lake District in particular, are not unusual features of the Poor Law literature. A preference for agriculture and for encouraging the cottage economy (see "Michael") is widespread, and a number of writers express approval of the state of social relations in Cumberland over those in the south or the midlands. For instance, Eden notes approvingly that "a man in the county of Cumberland can, and does, earn nearly as much by his labour, as one in the same sphere of life in Hertfordshire; whilst his expenditure, (more especially in the articles of diet and apparel,) is comparatively insignificant. . . . And yet, with all his apparent rusticity, the peasant of the North is as intelligent, as ingenious, as virtuous and as useful a man, as his less provident neighbours" (1: vii–viii). From the perspective of the twentieth century it is not difficult to discern in this geographical bias the contemporary perception of that enormous social crisis by which agrarian capitalism was laying hold of southern England and turning its peasantry into an incipient proletariat. In this context, unemployment and poverty were assuming unfamiliar forms, ones that the political economists' grasp of the market would eventually comprehend, but that made little sense in the more traditional scheme of things.

Wordsworth's entire attitude toward the Cumberland beggar, like much of the Old Poor Law, assumes that poverty is part of a life cycle. Relief is in order for the young, the old, and the helpless, but not the "sturdy beggar." The integrative thrust of Wordsworth's whole argument stems from this older attitude. It appears especially strongly in the poem's insistently repetitive final lines: "As in the eye of Nature he has liv'd, / So in the eye of Nature let him die." The rhythm of these lines, as much as anything else, carries the argument that age is part of nature's inevitable process and poverty is a natural accompaniment of age. The same integrative movement runs through many of the poems of the 1800 *Lyrical Ballads*. "The Two Thieves" portrays the bemused tolerance a group of villagers exercise toward another old man who could be called a social nuisance, and "Andrew Jones" voices a villager's resentment at the title character's mistreatment of a crippled old beggar. "The Idle Shepherd-Boys," with its very specific Lake District setting, combines the story of recovering a lost lamb with a lesson in pastoral responsibility for the two young shepherds. "Poor Susan" uses the rural community as an idyllic backdrop for a delicate portrait of urban alienation. Even "'Tis said, that some have died for love" (one of the more remarkable instances of a poem showing that "men who do not wear fine cloaths can feel deeply" [LEY 315]), by dramatizing a widower's sense of isolation in his rural setting, illustrates the strong bond between his domestic affections and his sense of attachment to his natural surroundings. Many of the best poems in the volume—the Matthew and

Lucy poems, "Hart-Leap Well," "The Brothers," "Michael"—concern themselves in varying degrees with delineating a coherent rural community that holds together youth and age, nature and humanity, even the living and the dead.

The difference between Wordsworth's sense of property and that of the rising political economy also accounts for the way the image of destitution in Wordsworth's poetry consistently focuses less on material poverty than on the experience of isolation. The greatest instance would be that of Margaret in *The Ruined Cottage*. The Cumberland beggar is also described repeatedly as a "solitary man," and the essential argument of the poem is that this solitude is only apparent. The most blamable crime would be to make it real by consigning him to the legalized isolation of a workhouse. In "The Last of the Flock," the protagonist is a shepherd who is being forced to sell off his flock in order to become eligible for parish relief. Wordsworth renders his loss of property not as a deterioration of his wealth but rather as an impairment of his domestic affection:

> Sir! 'twas a precious flock to me,
> As dear as my own children be;
> For daily with my growing store
> I loved my children more and more.
> Alas! it was an evil time;
> God cursed me in my sore distress,
> I prayed, yet every day I thought
> I loved my children less.

>   (LB 87)

When the shepherd declares that "I care not if we die, / And perish all of poverty" (LB 86), Wordsworth's point is that his poverty consists not in the loss of his goods but in weakening the network of dependence and obligation that binds his affections to his daily labor. For Wordsworth, sympathy and isolation form the poles of an opposition that is similar to, but also pointedly nonidentical with, the opposition of wealth and indigence.

Nonetheless Wordsworthian sympathy does retain the structure of a virtue based on class privilege. "The eye of Nature" can endorse the Cumberland beggar's independence only insofar as the narrator manages to make "Nature" into a projection of his own attitude. In fact, the noncalculating, habitual bonds of Wordsworthian sympathy articulate an idealized version of the ties between social classes. This idealization of class bears the telltale mark of middle-class ideology, in that it conflates a historical and a natural mode of determination. Wordsworth insists upon his allegiance to natural feeling, but the ties of sympathy simultaneously occupy the position elsewhere accorded to the accumulated surplus that constitutes civilization. The Cumberland beggar, for instance, is more than a little bit like a communal property in his usefulness as a sign of accumulation. Or consider the trope of accumulation the poet uses when he urges his readers to call up sympathy for "Simon Lee, the Old Huntsman" (LB 64–67): "O reader! had you in your mind / Such stores as silent thought can bring, / O gentle reader! you would find / A tale in every thing" (73–76). The poet and the reader, like the Cumberland almsgivers, are to discover their gentleness, their community with one another, in "stores" of contemplation funded by a leisure and distance quite unavailable to the objects of their pity. They exercise their capacity for sympathy on the same kind of basis as Eden's rich exercise their foresight.

The class difference across which sympathy operates appears with unusual clarity in Wordsworth's call for the "gentle reader" of "Simon Lee" to help the poet construct a community of recognition. This call holds together a poetic structure that strikingly justifies Wordsworth's claim in the "Preface to *Lyrical Ballads*" "that the feeling therein developed gives importance to the action and situation and not the action and situation to the feeling" (PrW1 128). The poem begins with sixty-eight lines describing Simon Lee's vigorous youth as a huntsman in the service of the master of Ivor Hall and his poverty-stricken old age as the "sole survivor" of his master's household. In the poem's final three stanzas, the narrator helps Simon Lee by severing the root of a stump for him, and the old man responds with tears of gratitude. Description and incident are joined by the poet's exhortation to the reader to respond contemplatively and productively to the poem: "It is no tale; but should you think, / Perhaps a tale you'll make it" (79–80). Making a tale, it turns out, enacts the dominance of feeling over action in this poem; and it emerges from a confrontation between economies of subsistence and accumulation.

When the poet urges his readers to respond with deep feeling to an apparently trivial incident, he is foreshadowing the way feeling overpowers action in the poem's final stanza. After the narrator severs with a single blow the root at which Simon Lee had been working "long / And vainly," the old huntsman thanks the younger man:

> The tears into his eyes were brought,
> And thanks and praises seemed to run
> So fast out of his heart, I thought
> They never would have done.
> —I've heard of hearts unkind, kind deeds
> With coldness still returning.
> Alas! the gratitude of men
> Has oftner left me mourning.

The poet is mourning, apparently, because Simon Lee's tearful gratitude has so forcefully brought the old man's situation home to him. On the one hand, he feels embarassed about provoking such thanks; perhaps he should not have cut the root so quickly and effortlessly. The contrast between Simon Lee's vain labor and his own dispatch, he realizes, has only made the old man more painfully aware of his helplessness.[24] On the other hand, the old man's excessive thanks bring a social tragedy into view. They bespeak Simon Lee's isolation as the "sole survivor" (along with his wife) of Ivor Hall, where, one suspects, an old man would have been spared the indignity of attempting a task he was no longer able to perform.

The poet's address to his readers appeals to their sympathetic understanding on several levels. First, he calls upon them to exercise such understanding in order to realize the complex necessity of offering relief to the needy without damaging their self-respect. Beyond this, however, the poet urges the gentle reader not only to repeat his own attempt to make a tale of the incident, but also to resolve or complete the poet's endeavor. As Bialostosky argues, the narrator "urges on his reader a thoughtful kindness that, in recovering Simon's meaning, redeems the narrator's deed and his tale".[25] The poet asks the reader to repeat the work he has brought to bear on the incident insofar as the poet has already made a tale of it, the tale that occupies the poem's first sixty-eight lines. Given the resource of this prior narrative, the cutting of the root becomes a striking metaphor of Simon Lee's own dislocation and of the ease with which the organic, rooted community represented by Ivor Hall can be thoughtlessly, unintentionally destroyed. But by presenting the making of the tale as the reader's moral responsibility and at the same time providing the ready-made narrative-description as the ground for fulfilling that responsibility, the poem renders the relation between natural feeling and social history somewhat problematic. A familiar pattern reappears; both nature and history constitute the basis for sympathetic virtue. "Simon Lee" is remarkably self-conscious about this situation. The poet's sense that the poem is unresolved and in need of the reader's supplementary aid precisely represents the gap between natural feeling and sympathetically constituted, healthy community.

The poem's self-consciousness causes the issue of social class to take the form of a relation between poetic genres. It is not unusual that the lower-class character Simon Lee should be responsible for introducing natural feeling into the poem. The task enjoined upon the gentle middle-class reader, however, is a progressive accomplishment that transforms the stuff of popular ballad into the modern lyric. The opening of "Simon Lee" clearly invokes the manner of the popular ballads in Percy's *Reliques of Ancient English Poetry*.[26] The narrator's final response, "I've heard of hearts unkind," echoes the poem's opening, "I've heard he once was tall" (4). The distance between what the narrator has heard and what he makes into poetry involves both the distance between Simon Lee's youth and his old age and the distance between the reader's expectation of balladlike entertainment and the dominance of feeling over incident in the poem's closure. But the description of Simon Lee's youth also alludes to the popular ballad: "No man like him the horn could sound, / And no man was so full of glee" (17–18). These lines can be glossed by Bishop Percy's etymology of "glee" and the relation of its derivatives to the Anglo-Saxon "gleemen" or minstrels in his "Essay on the Ancient Minstrels in England": "The arts [the minstrels] professed were so extremely acceptable to our ancestors that the word 'glee', which particularly denoted their art, continues still in our language to be the most expressive of that popular mirth and jollity, that strong sensation of delight, which is felt by unpolished and simple minds".[27] The narrator's sympathy for the old man establishes a continued access to the native fund of "simple and unpolished" pleasure, but also transforms it into something polished and gentle.

The difference between Simon Lee's history and the narrator's reflection upon it has its basis in the economic difference between subsistence and accumulation. Simon Lee appears to be firmly, and perhaps constitutionally, limited to the possibilities of a subsistence economy. The young Simon Lee is the very type of the man wholly caught up in action:

> He all the country could outrun,
> Could leave both man and horse behind;
> And often, ere the race was done,
> He reeled and was stone-blind.

(41–44)

Simon Lee combines splendid vitality with a lack of vision or fine discernment, and it is hard to avoid the suspicion that this combination has partly determined his descent into liveried poverty. His life repeats the pattern of the races he ran in his youth. His strength causes him to outlive his social milieu, and yet he finishes half-blinded ("he has but one eye left" [15]) and without resources. He and his wife own a scrap of land, but its value cannot take the form of an accumulated surplus. Rather, it is only valuable to them as an opportunity to work: "What avails the land to them, / Which they can till no longer?" (63–64) Their lives run in the narrow track of work and nourishment: "You with your utmost skill / From labour could not wean them" (53–54). They occupy a position of childlike dependency in a fairly rigid social hierarchy that dictates certain obligations and rewards. Far from having been set free by their master's death, that event deprives them of the relationship that protects their dignity and even their survival. Without the paternal benevolence of the master of Ivor Hall, they seem to be orphaned, as it were, in the maternal embrace of labor.

This is the situation which dictates Simon Lee's response to the narrator's attempted kindness. But the narrator reacts to Simon Lee's gratitude with a complex, antithetical mourning that enacts the possibilities opened by accumulation, that is, by his access to the "stores of silent thought." The eyes of the narrator transform Simon Lee from a commoner to a "common man." The narrator's sympathy rests on "elementary feelings," "the essential passions of the heart"; and the story of the low and rustic man's life becomes the narrator's and the "gentle reader's" access to the primary elements of human nature. The way the incident works upon the narrator and he works upon it allows him to gain far more from the encounter than Simon Lee does. The poem itself represents his profit, so to speak, the valorization of his experience by reflection and contemplation upon it.

The narrator's sympathy does not transcend social differences but rather translates them into the project of Wordsworth's therapeutic poetics. He calls upon poetry to repair his damaged sense of community, and he offers the poem itself as the means of doing so. "Simon Lee" can thus stand as a paradigm for all of those other, mostly later, lyrical ballads that try to forge an alliance of common feeling between the middle and lower classes. No doubt the community of recognition forged in this poem is also supposed to translate the ideal bonds of literary sympathy into more practical forms of social improvement. Probably social history itself, rather than some intrinsic quality of Wordsworth's poetics, in the long run turns this project into something more exclusionary and disciplinary than Wordsworth envisioned. Nonetheless, what Heinzelman has called Wordsworth's "labor theory of poetic value"[28] here offers the reader, rather than the place of a colaborer, something more like that of a stockholder sharing the poet's metaphysical dividends.

The blind beggar episode in *The Prelude* (7.589–623) also translates social differences into a poetic community of recognition. None of Wordsworth's encounters with the poor claims a greater metaphysical profit than this one does when the poet's visionary rapture turns the sign explaining "The Story of the Man and who he was" into "a type, / Or emblem, of the utmost that we know, / Both of ourselves and of the universe." The entire verse paragraph works through this transformation in an extraordinarily compelling way. The scene moves quickly and forcefully through five stages: 1) Wordsworth's reflection, as he passes through the thick urban crowd, that "The face of every one / That passes by me is a mystery"; 2) a deepening estrangement from the figures on the street as the dreamlike "shapes before my eyes became / A second-sight procession," where "the ballast of familiar life . . . / Went from me, neither knowing me nor known"; 3) his being "smitten with the view / Of a blind Beggar," the sight of whom causes the poet's mind to "turn round / As with the might of waters"; 4) a bout of profit-taking, when the poet apprehends the spectacle of the beggar as a "type, / Or emblem" of the human condition; and 5) a descent, finally, back through the sight of the beggar's shape and face to a reconstructed sense of awe: ". . . on the shape of this unmoving Man, / His fixed face, and sightless eyes, I look'd, / As if admonish'd from another world."

The episode's most remarkable accomplishment, however, is the way Wordsworth here fuses alienation and community in the act of reading. The poet gathers humankind together in a community that is precisely antithetical to the scene of urban alienation from which it emerges. On the London streets the closeness of the crowd only accentuates the city-dwellers' isolation from one another, but the way the poet's mind works upon the "written paper" on the beggar's chest figures forth a community of readers whose solitude and separation are exactly what establishes their essential identity. When the scene rounds itself out with the admonishing gaze of the beggar's "fixed face and sightless eyes," it is almost as if the human face has taken on the character of a written paper itself, mediating communication and recognition but at the same time interposing its uncomprehending and, at least in this instance, uncanny silence into the project of the "man speaking to men."

Perhaps Wordsworth's sympathetic alliance with the lower class confesses its limits here. The visionary moment's paradoxical achievement of communal solitude may be the only way Wordsworth's literary sophistication can entirely embrace or internalize the beggar's reality. "These, chiefly, are such structures as the mind / Builds for itself" (7.625–26), he says in the next verse paragraph; and the cost of the mind's efforts, in this case, seems to be the estrangement and devitalization of the urban crowd. The poetic structure ends up being so expensive, so extravagant, that the poet's encounter with the beggar can be represented as an otherworldly event. Yet what is this other world but a name for the poetic process itself, or for the place it gives to the middle-class poet's distanced, spectatorial gaze?

Everything depends upon the poet-reader's interpretive grasp, as Wordsworth next admits: ". . . things that are, are not, / Even as we give them welcome, or assist, / Are prompt, or are remiss" (7.643–45).[29] Behind this kind of difficult sympathetic achievement there still lies the possibility of a different sort of solidarity:

> What say you then
> To times when half the City shall break out
> Full of one passion, vengeance, rage, or fear,
> To executions, to a Street on fire,
> Mobs, riots, or rejoicings?
>
> (7.645–49)

At this point in *The Prelude*, Wordsworth chooses to launch a magnificent description of Bartholomew Fair, setting Wordsworth's community of literary recognition in explicit antithesis to the commercial grotesque.[30] But the passionate unanimity he allows us to glimpse beforehand surely recollects the "mobs, riots, or rejoicings" of revolutionary upheaval. If, as Jonathan Wordsworth comments, the episode of the blind beggar "shows most clearly the terror that underlies Wordsworthian optimism,"[31] that is because the implicit, still antithetical double of poetic understanding remains the potentially violent sense of purpose offered by political and social revolution.

THE PROBLEM OF INDOLENCE: PROVIDENTIAL ECONOMY AND POETIC VOCATION

The blind beggar episode draws out to a sublime conclusion the visionary possibilities offered but then comically foreclosed by

Wordsworth's encounter with the leech-gatherer in "Resolution and Independence" (P2V 123–29). Both pieces explore the dynamics of inclusion and exclusion, but instead of urban alienation, the poet's ecstatic integration with the natural scene in the beautiful opening stanzas of "Resolution and Independence" seems by its very power to isolate him from the human community. This isolation then rebounds upon the poet and calls his vocation into question:

> I heard the Sky-lark singing in the sky;
> And I bethought me of the playful Hare:
> Even such a happy Child of earth am I;
> Even as these blissful Creatures do I fare;
> Far from the world I walk, and from all care;
> But there may come another day to me,
> Solitude, pain of heart, distress, and poverty.
>
> My whole life I have liv'd in pleasant thought,
> As if life's business were a summer mood;
> As if all needful things would come unsought
> To genial faith, still rich in genial good;
> But how can He expect that others should
> Build for him, sow for him, and at his call
> Love him, who for himself will take no heed at all?
>
> I thought of Chatterton, the marvellous Boy,
> The sleepless Soul that perish'd in its pride;
> Of Him who walk'd in glory and in joy
> Behind his plough, upon the mountain-side:
> By our own spirits are we deified;
> We Poets in our youth begin in gladness;
> But thereof comes in the end despondency and madness.
>
> (29–49)

The poet's anxiety concerns three forms of rationality, each of which his poetic vocation threatens to disrupt. The poet doubts his ability to provide for himself; he doubts his ability to love or to properly engage in family relations; and he fears madness, a fear that seems to justify itself by its very intensity.

The basis for all of these fears is the sheer irrationality of the poet's vocation. He seems to be dependent, even parasitic, relying on others to "Build for him, sow for him, and at his call / Love him." This formula alludes, of course, to the Sermon on the Mount:

No man can serve two masters; . . . Ye cannot serve both God and
mammon . . .

Take no thought for your life, what ye shall eat, or what ye shall drink;
nor yet for your body, what ye shall put on. Is not the life more than
meat, and the body than raiment?

Behold the fowls of the air: for they sow not, neither do they reap, nor
gather into barns; yet your heavenly father feedeth them. . . .

Consider the lilies of the field, how they grow; they toil not, neither do
they spin:

And yet I say unto you, That even Solomon in all his glory was not
arrayed like one of these. (*Matthew* 6:24–29; King James version)

The poet, like a lily of the field, toils not, neither does he spin, and
yet he finds himself arrayed in more glory than Solomon. The
poet's fears turn upon the fact that he reaps what *others* sow. A
perpetual child of earth, who has not grown up, has not become
a father or established a household, he accuses himself of being
economically irresponsible in every sense. But the allusion to the
Sermon on the Mount also invokes on the poets' behalf a supremely
authoritative counterrationality. The poet offers his service to God
rather than Mammon, and therefore he operates within a providential economy based on his faith in the infinite abundance that God
or Nature will place in his way-wandering path.

The problem is that Wordsworth's poetic strength seems in some
way to derive itself from the very opposite of labor. Indeed Wordsworth's fears about his own sanity may be grounded in the hyper-
bolization of dependence or passivity in some of the most sublime
moments in his poetry. A famous entry in Dorothy Wordsworth's
journal, written on 29 April 1802, just a few days before she first
mentions the earliest version of "Resolution and Independence"
(known as "The Leech-Gatherer" at this point), tells of a curious
and fanciful wish her brother made:

William lay, & I lay in the trench under the fence—he with his eyes
shut & listening to the waterfalls and the Birds. There was no one
waterfall above another—it was a sound of waters in the air—the voice
of the air. William heard me breathing & rustling now and then but we
both lay still, and unseen by one another—he thought that it would be
as sweet thus to lie so in the grave, to hear the *peaceful* sounds of the
earth & just to know that ones dear friends were near. (GJ 92)

What makes this story so impressive is not just the clear relevance
of its "sound of waters," as either a source or an echo, to a "Leech-
Gatherer" perhaps already in progress or perhaps just about to be

composed. Beyond this, the poet's odd fantasy about death bears a striking resemblance to two of the great moments in "Tintern Abbey:" the poet's being "laid asleep / In body, and become a living soul," and his projection of his sleeping body's abdicated life onto that of his dear sister. Thus a childlike moment, something like a game of hide and seek, opens quite startlingly onto that weird blending of the animate and the inanimate that will characterize Wordsworth's sublimity in the Westminster bridge sonnet and in his description of the leech-gatherer as well.

In his more confident moods (for example, in the spring of 1798) Wordsworth would no doubt have called his posture beneath the waterfalls "wise passiveness" (LB 108). But in the spring of 1802, facing the prospect of his impending marriage, he would more likely have called it indolence. On 9 May 1802, a day on which Wordsworth "worked at the Leech gatherer almost incessantly from morning till tea time" (GJ 97), he also began composing the "Stanzas Written in My Pocket-Copy of Thomson's *Castle of Indolence*" (P2V 581–83). Wordsworth's playful stanzas imitate Thomson's idea of representing himself and his friends as residents in a kind of fool's paradise. The whole of Thomson's Spenserean allegory makes a *felix culpa* argument in which Adam's curse becomes the stimulant to civilized progress and economic rationality. What Wordsworth probably found most congenial in the *Castle of Indolence* is the way it uses the tension between "false luxury"[32] and dutiful labor as a frame for representing the poetic vocation, so that the poet in pursuit of his art becomes entrapped in a morally equivocal realm at the edge of the larger social community.

One of the highlights of *The Castle of Indolence* is the wizard Indolence's song of temptation. The wizard uses the "lilies of the field" text as one of his authorities:

> Behold the merry minstrels of the morn,
> The swarming songsters of the careless grove,
> Ten thousand throats that, from the flowering thorn,
> Hymn their good God, and carol sweet of love,
> Such grateful kindly raptures them emove!
> They neither plough nor sow; ne, fit for flail,
> E'er to the barn the nodding sheaves they drove;
> Yet theirs each harvest dancing in the gale,
> Whatever crowns the hill, or smiles along the vale.

(1.10)

Indolence goes on to equate labor with alienation from nature, and blames all vice on the "savage thirst of gain" (1.11). He advocates instead a posture of repose and receptivity, in which one lets "soft gales of passion play, / And gently stir the heart, thereby to form / A quicker sense of joy" (1.16). But when the wizard grabs a victim, it becomes clear that what he calls "pure ethereal calm" (1.16) has much in common with a scene of sexual aggression and surrender:

> For whomsoe'er the villain takes in hand,
> Their joints unknit, their sinews melt apace;
> As lithe they grow as any willow-wand,
> And of their vanished force remains no trace:
> So when a maiden fair, of modest grace,
> In all her buxom blooming May of charms,
> Is seized in some losel's hot embrace,
> She waxeth very weakly as she warms,
> Then sighing yields her up to love's delicious harms.
>
> (1.23)

Wordsworth's self-portrait in the "Stanzas" includes some of that repose and receptivity he and his sister had enjoyed on April 29: "On his own time he here would float away; / As doth a fly upon a summer brook" (6–7). The image of the fly on the summer brook recalls the lines from the Alfoxden Notebook that are probably the source for Wordsworth's praise of "wise passiveness" in "Expostulation and Reply." In the Alfoxden Notebook, amid a series of attempts to delineate the special gifts of the story-telling pedlar of *The Ruined Cottage,* appears this fragment:

> there is a holy indolence
> Compared to which our best activity
> Is oftimes deadly bane
>   They rest upon their oars
> Float down the mighty stream of tendency
> In a calm mood of holy indolence
> A most wise passiveness in which the heart
> Lies open and is well content to feel
> As nature feels and to receive her shapes
> As she has made them.
>
> (RC&P 115)

Indolence, almost always the name of a dangerous vice, here becomes an attitude of effortless reception superior to our best activity. "Holy indolence" allows its practitioners to draw upon the infinite resources of providence. To be a poet is to be able to surrender oneself to nature's feeling and so "receive her shapes."

In 1802 Wordsworth places his emphasis, however, on the impassioned and compulsive wandering depicted in "Resolution and Independence." In the "Stanzas," he combines it with some of the dark sexual undertones of Indolence's song:

> Some thought he was a lover and did woo;
> Some thought far worse of him, and did him wrong;
> But Verse was what he had been wedded to:
> And his own mind did, like a tempest strong,
> Come to him thus; and drove the weary Man along.
>
> (32–36)

Since Spenser's "Prothalamion" stands in the background of "Resolution and Independence"—in fact, its presence there probably accounts for Wordsworth's decision to pick up Thomson's Spenserean imitation just at this time—the poet's being wedded to verse seems to be a guilty gesture in the direction of a prothalamion that is not being written. Whatever the thing "far worse" some might accuse him of doing, the poet's virtual enslavement to his "own mind" implies a refusal of conventional duties and his withdrawal from the sexual and emotional economy they entail. Surely there are hints of onanism in the poet's exhaustion upon his return from his walks: "Ah! piteous sight it was to see this Man, / When he came back to us a wither'd flower; / Or like a sinful creature pale and wan" (19–21). All of this makes it hard to sort out God and Mammon or, more to the point, to decide which of them the luxury of being a poet serves.

The economy of poetic vocation in "Resolution and Independence" and the "Stanzas" is of a piece with the paradox of shared solitude in the blind beggar episode. Why should spreading sympathy and communion through poetry exact the poet's own isolation as its price? A part of the reason Wordsworth feels so little in tune with the hum of everyday productivity is that his poems, at their best, seem to harvest fruits that labor cannot grasp. But perhaps another, more pertinent way to put it is that Wordsworth's project of representing a class alliance ends up falling into a kind of class vacuum instead. Both for better and for worse, the poet's providential economy weds the leisure of the middle or upper classes to the noncalculating improvidence of the poor. The ambivalent, uncanny tone of the Wordsworthian sublime points to the troubled cohabitation there of Wordsworth's insistent middle-class origin and his utopian, universal goal. The sublime moment's uncertain poise between trancelike elevation and effete marginality can be called, with apologies to Harold Bloom, the anxiety of indolence.

The central section of "Resolution and Independence" dramatizes the tension between elevation and marginality, as the poet's
extravagant imagination competes with the voice of a very common man. The poet's mind drives the image of the leech-gatherer
along, playing meanwhile with the boundaries between things and
persons: "As a huge Stone is sometimes seen to lie . . . Like a
Sea-beast crawled forth . . . Such seem'd this Man, not all alive
or dead" (64, 69, 71). The poet eventually turns the leech-gatherer
into another second-sight procession, "Wandering about alone and
silently" (138). But the leech-gatherer's livelihood is, after all, that
of putting parasites to use, and his persistence finally manages to
humble the poet and bring the poem to its comic resolution.

Yet the tension between an indolent but sublime seclusion and
responsible integration with the community of labor is not something that can stay resolved for long. Wordsworth's identity as a
poet is constituted neither by his genuine participation in the flock
of common industry nor by his isolated, wayward sensitivity, but
rather by the play between the two. Consider two more examples
of the topic of indolence. The first, taken from Coleridge, establishes one of the major and enduring images of the Romantic artist,
the figure of the aeolian harp.

In Coleridge's "The Eolian Harp" (STCPW 100–102), the harp
is a metaphor not so much of the character of the artist as of
his characteristic posture of receptivity, sensitivity, and
responsiveness:

> on the midway slope
> Of yonder hill I stretch my limbs at noon,
> Whilst through my half-clos'd eye-lids I behold
> The sunbeams dance, like diamonds, on the main,
> And tranquil muse upon tranquillity;
> Full many a thought uncall'd and undetain'd,
> And many idle flitting phantasies,
> Traverse my indolent and passive brain,
> As wild and various as the random gales
> That swell and flutter on this subject Lute!
>
> (34–43)

The abeyance of conscious control over his interior discourse
("Full many a thought uncall'd and undetain'd") recalls the voluptuous sexual play associated with the image of the harp earlier in
the poem: ". . . by the desultory breeze caress'd, / Like some coy
maid half yielding to her lover" (14–15). In just this way the re-
clining Coleridge coyly half-yields to pantheistic speculation before

restoring himself to chastened orthodoxy, that is, returning from his intellectual flirtation to his wife: "But thy more serious eye a mild reproof / Darts, O beloved Woman! Nor such thoughts / Dim and unhallow'd dost thou not reject, / And biddest me walk humbly with my God" (49–52).[33] He rouses himself from his withdrawn, spectatorial attitude and from lazing around at noon back to matrimonial and doctrinal duty—back, as he puts it in the closely related poem "Reflections on Having Left a Place of Retirement" (STCPW 106–8) from "slothful loves and dainty sympathies" to the "bloodless fight / Of Science, Freedom, and the Truth in Christ" (59, 61–62).

The opposition between indolence and duty involves a parallel opposition between kinds of discourse in "The Eolian Harp": on the one hand, the "shapings of the unregenerate mind," his vain philosophical speculation; and on the other, the earnest words of "Faith that inly *feels*" (60). The image of the aeolian harp suggests not only indolence but also superficiality. The glittering play of the sunbeams on the water becomes the metaphor for the discourse of the indolent poet in the moment he dismisses his speculations as "Bubbles that glitter as they rise and break / On vain Philosophy's aye-babbling stream" (56–57). The situation becomes more confusing in the later version of the poem (published in 1817). When Coleridge adds the most famous passage, the eight lines beginning: "O! the One Life within us and abroad," the "One Life's" interpenetration of surface and depth robs the contrast between a superficial aeolian discourse and "Faith that inly *feels*" of all its force.

By 1798, in fact, the image and posture of the aeolian harp had developed precisely in the direction pointed to by the interpolated "One Life" passage. The aeolian harp became an image of depth, of the poet's internal reservoirs of feeling, while at the same time it remained an image of spontaneity. Coleridge's most programmatic use of the posture of indolence as access to spontaneity and depth comes in one of his contributions to the 1798 *Lyrical Ballads,* "The Nightingale" (STCPW 264–67). There the song of a nightingale makes Coleridge think of the poet who first called the nightingale's song melancholy:

> And many a poet echoes the conceit;
> Poet who hath been building up the rhyme
> When he had better far have stretched his limbs
> Beside a brook in mossy forest-dell
> By sun or moon-light, to the influxes
> Of shapes and sounds and shifting elements

Surrendering his whole spirit, of his song
And of his fame forgetful! so his fame
Should share in Nature's immortality.

(23–31)

Once again the posture of indolence serves to represent the opposition between a superficial and a more profound discourse, but with a startling reversal of its value. Coleridge's version of indolence now articulates the argument against mechanical repetition of worn-out figures of speech that Wordsworth would later repeat in his attack on poetic diction. The issue, in both Coleridge's and Wordsworth's texts, is not just spontaneity but also and pre-eminently a sense of community. In the 1802 appendix on poetic diction, Wordsworth advocates a language that arises from "passion excited by real events," whereas poetic diction is merely an attempt to impress upon others a "notion of the peculiarity and exaltation of the Poet's character" (PrW1 160, 162). "The first Poets," he says, "spake a language which, though unusual, was still the real language of men. This circumstance, however, was disregarded by their successors. . . . They became proud of a language which they had invented, and which was uttered only by themselves; and, with the spirit of a fraternity, they arrogated it to themselves as their own" (PrW1 161). Wordsworth's false poets, striving after fame rather than taking what nature gives, are clearly cognate with Coleridge's "youths and maidens most poetical, / Who lose the deep'ning twilights of the spring / In ball-rooms and hot theatres" (35–37) in "The Nightingale." Against them Coleridge sets both the "surrendering" poet and the small, close-knit group of friends with whom he shares his conversation. Strangely enough, then, the posture that signified withdrawal into solipsistic idleness in 1795 had become by 1798 the way to lead poetry back to an unaffected familiarity and ease based on, and representing, an authentic sense of community.

Whatever sort of privileged access indolent receptivity affords to a natural, spontaneous sense of belonging in the world, however, the posture of indolence just as consistently includes a guilt-ridden awareness of singularity and dereliction of duty. It is as if the goal of finding oneself fitted to nature, as Wordsworth puts it in his "Prospectus to The Recluse," cannot ever be squared with the historical and material bases of republican and even humanitarian versions of middle-class virtue. One final example of the topic of indolence can illustrate the perpetually unresolved and vacillating character indolence gives to the poetic vocation.

This final exhibit begins, once again, with Coleridge. Indolence is on the whole an overwhelmingly negative topic for Coleridge. It seems possible that Thomson's *Castle of Indolence* was in his mind in November 1794, when he wrote his brother George an early installment in what would prove to be a long series of disavowals of radical politics. After professing his determination to "Talk not of Politics—*Preach the Gospel*," he expresses his anxiety about having perhaps forfeited his brother's affections. The problem, he explains, is his indolence:

> There is a Vice of such powerful Venom, that one Grain of it will poison the overflowing Goblet of a thousand Virtues. This Vice Constitution seems to have implanted in me, and Habit has made it almost omnipotent. It is INDOLENCE! Hence whatever Web of Friendship my Presence may have woven, my Absence has seldom failed to unravel. . . . Like some poor Labourer, whose Night's sleep has but imperfectly replenished his overwearied frame, I have sate in drowsy uneasiness— and doing nothing have thought, what a deal I had to do! But I trust, that the Kingdom of Reason is at hand and even now cometh! (STCL1 125)

If it is pathetic to listen to such a brilliant young man as the Coleridge of 1794 pleading to his duller and more conventional brother to leave open a place for him in the web of his affections and the kingdom of reason, then it becomes heart-wrenching to find Coleridge twenty years later suffering the same doubts, but now about a far more serious problem, his opium addiction. Opium, in 1814, becomes the demonic embodiment of indolence:

> My Case is a species of madness, only that it is a derangment, an utter impotence of the *Volition,* & not of the intellectual Faculties. (STCL3 919)

> I used to think St James's Text, "He who offendeth in one point of the Law, offendeth in all", very harsh; but my own sad experience has taught me it's aweful, dreadful Truth.—What crime is there scarcely which has not been included in or followed from the one guilt of taking opium? Not to speak of ingratitude to my maker for the wasted Talents; of ingratitude to so many friends who have loved me I know not why; of barbarous neglect of my family. . . . And yet *all* of these vices are so opposite to my nature, that but for this *free-agency-annihilating* Poison, I verily believe that I should have suffered myself to have been cut to pieces rather than have committed any one of them. (STCL3 927)

Wordsworth's life mainly spared him from such tortured self-inquisition. Yet he launches his autobiographical masterpiece from a similar kind of guilt, and with the same accusation of "wasted Talents." I am referring, of course, to the lines that conclude the prefatory episode Wordsworth inserted into the 1805 version of the "Poem to Coleridge" (as he usually called it):

> This is my lot; for either still I find
> Some imperfection in the chosen theme;
> Or see of absolute accomplishment
> Much wanting, so much wanting in myself,
> That I recoil and droop, and seek repose
> In indolence from vain perplexity,
> Unprofitably travelling towards the grave,
> Like a false Steward who hath much receiv'd
> And renders nothing back.
>
> (1.264–72)

The similarity of Wordsworth's guilt to Coleridge's is limited in a significant way. Whereas the problem of indolence seems all too frequently to have inundated Coleridge's entire sense of well-being, for Wordsworth it remains a specific feature of his sense of poetic vocation. Rather than an all-embracing psychological and medical problem, Wordsworth's indolence is no more or less than an integral feature of his ideological currency. It has more to do with the way his literary practice explores his class position than with the personal tragedies invoked by the topic of indolence in Coleridge's letters.

Nonetheless the problem of indolence in Wordsworth is still quite an intimate one. The question his allusion to the parable of the talents introduces in the 1805 *Prelude* is the same one that began his autobiography in its first major incarnation (Ms. JJ, written in Goslar in the winter of 1798–99): "Was it for this." "This," in 1799, has no proper antecedent. It refers, apparently with an almost triumphant glow, to the poem being written and to the act of writing it. Yet Wordsworth's question also has something to do with the plot of his life. He is asking whether the vivid childhood experiences he goes on to recount were *for* something, whether there is a message to be deciphered in the murmurs of Derwent stream that blended with his mother's voice, or in the strange loud utterance of the wind that blew through his ears when he stole eggs from the raven's nest. "This" points to those experiences as an emblem of their inarticulacy as well as a reference to their power. Finally, and especially since he is writing "this" reminiscence instead of *The Recluse,* the question also sounds like a self-reproach. Perhaps above all, in recalling the natural abundance that blessed his childhood, he is wondering whether these gifts were wasted upon him.

The episode that introduces the question "Was it for this" in the 1805 *Prelude* does not stabilize the previously absent antecedent of "this" at all. Rather, it unfolds more explicitly the anxieties that polarize its significance and energize its play. The poet begins by receiving the blessing of a breeze. The aeolian visitation develops into a figure of depth, as the breeze that blows upon his body becomes a corresponding mild creative breeze felt within. The figure of depth leads on to the complex duties of poetic vocation: "Of active days, of dignity and thought, / Of prowess in an honorable field, / Pure passions, virtue, knowledge, and delight, / The holy life of music and of verse" (1.51–54). But the poet's plot cannot be one of simple progress. The moment of reception, because of its very effortlessness, does not allow itself to become the first step in the rational accomplishment of a duty. On the contrary, it simply keeps reiterating itself as a counterpoint to poetic striving or ambition.

Wordsworth epitomizes the incompatibility of ambition and reception when he accuses himself of being a "false Steward" of his poetic talent. Some of the competing antecedents of "this" in the 1805 *Prelude* include his having received nature's blessing, his "vain perplexity" at being unable to set forth on "The holy life of music and of verse," and the way he "seeks repose / In indolence" from his frustration. Indeed the question is to some degree itself the indolent or receptive counterpart of the "rigorous inquisition" (1.160) he undertakes a bit earlier in order to ascertain his preparedness for undertaking an epic composition. One way to survey and, hopefully, explain Wordsworth's economy of industry and indolence is to describe how it takes its shape from the alternating versions of virtue that rule the poet's epic preparations.

The poet's "rigorous inquisition" turns out to reveal an embarrassment of riches: "Time, place, and manners; these I seek, and these / I find in plenteous store; but nowhere such / As may be singled out with steady choice" (1.170–72). His failure to make a firm choice may stem from the fact that the epic schemes he considers fall into three different kinds, each of which corresponds to a distinctly different notion of poetic virtue. He contemplates a number of historical and semimythic plots (1.180–220). These stories share a focus on republican virtue, invoking martial and patriotic valor, strong continuity of purpose, and the underlying theme of "independence and stern liberty" (1.220). His inability to settle on any one of these projects may be accounted for by their inadequacy to the more dominant, humanitarian mode of virtue in Wordsworth's therapeutic poetics. Thus he turns from the historical schemes to consider "Some Tale from my own heart, more near akin / To my own passions and habitual thoughts" (1.222–23). But this project, too, meets "deadening admonitions" (1.226). Humanitarian virtue without the political and historical grounding of the prior schemes lacks epic scope, and so Wordsworth rejects the heart's tale as "Shadowy and insubstantial" (1.229). The third type of project corresponds to *The Recluse* itself: ". . . some philosophic Song / Of Truth that cherishes our daily life" (1.231–32). This is the *real* project, the one proclaimed in the ringing declamations of the final section of *Home at Grasmere* (the lines published in 1814 as the "Verse Prospectus to *The Excursion*"). Nevertheless the project of synthesizing republican heroism and humanitarian lyric in "philosophic Song" presents itself to the poet here as an "awful burthen" (1.236) that precipitates him into a downward spiral of guilt and self-doubt, fueling and fueled by his inactivity.

Wordsworth wants to compose a philosophic song that transcends class differences, reconciles man and nature, and marries visionary poetry to everyday life. However, as his poetic ambition mounts, so too does the poet's isolation and the poem's abstraction. At the other pole of Wordsworth's poetic economy from ambition is the posture of indolence, where the poet's receptivity dissolves the context of social responsibility, envelops the poet in nature's abundance, and provides a quasi-sexual comfort beyond, or beneath, the reach of vision. The prefatory episode of *The Prelude* contains perhaps Wordsworth's finest rendering of that posture:

> Thus, long I lay
> Chear'd by the genial pillow of the earth
> Beneath my head, sooth'd by a sense of touch
> From the warm ground, that balanced me[, though lost]
> Entirely, seeing nought, nought hearing, save
> When here and there, about the grove of Oaks
> Where was my bed, an acorn from the trees
> Fell audibly, and with a startling sound.
>
> (1.87–94)

All of history and philosophy cannot quite counterbalance the "sense of touch" with which Wordsworth takes to himself the substance of the very earth. At the same time, his individuality and volition disappear as well, and all intimations of republican, humanitarian, or philosophic song contract into the seminal but preverbal "startling sound" of the dropping acorns. Eventually Wordsworth's epic project will, like the acorns, come unbidden.

The posture of indolence is incommensurate and incompatible with the types of virtue that inform Wordsworth's therapeutic poetics, yet it seems equally indispensable to the poet. One could say that this situation reiterates a fundamental ideological contradiction, that Wordsworth must receive as nature's gift what history and society have already afforded him as a class privilege. His guilt and misgivings attest to the inevitable pathos of distance that afflicts his sympathy. Yet it is precisely by pursuing none of Wordsworth's epic schemes that *The Prelude* does succeed in being a hymn to liberty, a triumphant tale of Wordsworth's own heart, and even a philosophic song.

The paradoxical structure of Wordsworth's community of recognition also has its roots in his class situation. The material community forged by his poetic practice resembles both his intimacy with Coleridge and with Dorothy Wordsworth and his utter solitude before the unyielding mystery of the blind beggar. It feels as close-knit as a family, yet remains as dispersed as the London crowd. The remainder of this book will attempt, through close readings of major poems written in the crucial years from 1795 to 1798, to describe in detail the emergence of Wordsworth's mature literary practice and the community it projects.

4

Civic Virtue and Social Class at the Scene of Execution: The Salisbury Plain Poems

When Wordsworth moved from London to Racedown in the fall of 1795, he also crossed a watershed dividing the writings that assume the *ethos* of the "friends of liberty" from those addressing the sympathetic community of "humanity." An emblem of this transition appears in a letter to William Matthews dated 24 October 1795, less than a month after his move to Racedown. In it Wordsworth offers to trade Matthews a copy of Gordon and Trenchard's *Cato's Letters* for Matthews's copy of volume 10 of John Bell's *Classical Arrangement of Fugitive Poetry,* which Wordsworth desires particularly because it contains Beattie's *The Minstrel. Cato's Letters,* a classic of English republicanism and London political journalism, belongs to the London Wordsworth was leaving behind, along with his attempted collaborations with Matthews on *The Philanthropist* and with his Cambridge friend Francis Wrangham on an imitation of Juvenal's eighth satire.[1] *The Minstrel,* a narrative of "the progress of a Poetical Genius, born in a rude age, from the first dawning of fancy and reason, till that period at which he may be considered capable of appearing in the world as A MINSTREL,"[2] points in the direction Wordsworth was heading.

Even more significant than the strong likeness Dorothy and William Wordsworth recognized between William and Edwin, the main character of *The Minstrel,*[3] or than the obvious similarity of its plot to Wordsworth's greatest poem, is the way Beattie's poem rehearses the eighteenth-century commonplaces of sympathetic, domestic, and rural virtue. Its hero, "deaf to mad Ambition's call," is one of those who consider themselves "Supremely blest, if to their portion fall / Health, competence, and peace" (1.2). Beattie enjoins the urban reader to "Fret not thyself, thou glittering child of pride, / That a poor Villager inspires my strain" (1.4). Because Edwin's parents enjoy the health that springs from labor, they are content with their humble lot and live together in ideal domestic concord (1.13). The foremost moral lesson imparted from father to son is the duty of universal sympathy: "All human weal and wo learn thou to make thine own" (1.29).

These kinds of postures had been allied to republican and "country" sentiments throughout the century.[4] Nonetheless Beattie's emphasis accords far better with the "perfect solitude" (LEY 154) and tranquil housekeeping William and Dorothy enjoyed at Racedown than does the activist rhetoric of the London projects. In March 1796, Wordsworth described his distance from London in the last surviving letter to Matthews: "We plant cabbages, and if retirement, in its full perfection, be as powerful in working transformations as one of Ovid's Gods, you may perhaps suspect that into cabbages we shall be transformed. Indeed I learn that such has been the prophecy of our London friends" (LEY 169). This chapter will trace the movement from the environs of political debate and satiric declamation to a less explicit, if not quite cabbagelike, idiom of social protest in Wordsworth's transformation of *Salisbury Plain* into *Adventures on Salisbury Plain*.

FROM ADVOCACY TO MIMESIS

Wordsworth composed *Salisbury Plain* (SP) mostly in 1793 and completed it by the spring of 1794. The first major piece of composition Wordsworth undertook after his move to Racedown was to revise this poem into *Adventures on Salisbury Plain* (ASP).[5] One of the most easily noticed and striking differences between the two versions is the shift in the narrator's stance from that of a polemical orator in SP to that of an inconspicuous spectator in ASP.[6] The opening stanzas of the earlier poem exploit a politically charged commonplace, comparing the physical suffering of savages to the more thorough misery of those who fall destitute in the midst of civilization; and the poem closes in a similar vein, militantly exhorting the "Heroes of Truth" to introduce the rule of reason over monarchic superstition and error: "Heroes of Truth pursue your march, uptear / Th'Oppressor's dungeon from its deepest base" (61).[7] The later poem allows its characters to speak for themselves. It begins with an old man and a young one meeting, and the old man telling the young one the sad story of his life. ASP derives its power throughout from fleeting moments of sympathy and shared suffering between poor, outcast men and women against a backdrop of social and natural catastrophe. This fading away of explicit political argument in ASP is concomitant with, an effect of, the recession of the narrative voice into a less obtrusive role, as if the poet were now listening to his characters rather than exhibiting them as evidence in a brief against the state.

One could say that Wordsworth's mode of representing the poor shifts from advocacy in SP to mimesis in ASP. In contrast to SP's indignant orator, the narrator of ASP no longer addresses himself to a party, and no longer makes explicit the relation between the sufferings of the humble characters and the need for rational political action. Gone, too, is the global perspective of the last fourteen stanzas of SP (for example, "Lo! where the Sun exulting in his might / In haste the fiery top of Andes scales" [51]). ASP, for the most part, shows the reader only what the characters can see. The new poem correspondingly gains remarkably both in the specificity of its social content and in its dramatic power. All of these changes indicate a partial displacement of the paradigm of political virtue operating in SP by that different set of virtues associated with the sympathetic passions rather than rational judgment. The question is precisely what this displacement of one kind of virtue by another indicates.

The counterpart of ASP's lack of explicitness is a stronger tension between alienation and comprehension. This tension emerges quite strikingly, for example, in the concluding stanzas of ASP, where Wordsworth juxtaposes legal violence, its deleterious effects on popular morality, and the possibility of moral regeneration. The central character, a sailor whose desperate poverty upon his return home from the war has led him to commit a murder, has had his guilty conscience heightened beyond endurance by the sight of his abandoned, dying wife. He therefore resolves to turn himself in to be executed for his crime:

> Confirm'd of purpose, fearless and prepared,
> Not without pleasure, to the city strait
> He went and all which he had done declar'd:
> "And from your hands," he added, "now I wait,
> Nor let them linger long, the murderer's fate."
> Nor ineffectual was that piteous claim.
> Blest be for once the stroke which ends, tho' late,
> The pangs which from thy halls of terror came,
> Thou who of Justice bear'st the violated name!
>
> They left him hung on high in iron case,
> And dissolute men, unthinking and untaught,
> Planted their festive booths beneath his face;

And to that spot, which idle thousands sought,
Women and children were by fathers brought;
And now some kindred sufferer driven, perchance,
That way when into storm the sky is wrought,
Upon his swinging corpse his eye may glance
And drop, as he once dropp'd, in miserable trance.

(91–92)

These stanzas show the spectacle of execution functioning in two radically different ways. On the one hand, the execution signifies the coercive threat that founds the power of those in the "halls of terror." In this sense the legal spectacle becomes the center and occasion of a seriously deformed commercial community, where the "unthinking" and "dissolute" exploit the attractive power of the execution upon the "idle thousands." The crowd, moreover, is made up of families, "Women and children . . . by fathers brought," so that terror and dissolution are being conveyed not only from the ruling centers of society out to the general populace but also from the public realm into the private and domestic. Against all of this, on the other hand, is set the meaning of the execution to the sailor and the "kindred sufferer" of the closing lines. For them the significance of the execution strikes to the heart. They identify themselves both with the punished man and with the sense of right and wrong that ordains punishment. Their reaction to the execution is an exercise in sympathetic understanding, which is precisely what is lacking in the halls of justice and the festive booths, and which the exploitation of spectacular violence tends to destroy in the crowd.

Yet the narrator's sympathy with the characters continues to act from a certain distance. The narrative voice separates itself from the sailor's tale in the final stanzas of ASP, first by the second person familiar address to "Thou who of Justice bear'st the violated name," and then by the description of the sailor's execution. If the vantage point of the latter description is physically impossible for the sailor, the brief address to "Justice" is no less impossible for any of the story's characters. It represents what could be called a vestigial survival of SP's oratory, setting the narrator aside from the crowd, with the rulers of society, in a place where they, too, become spectators to the spectacle of execution. But more than that, it marks the class difference that obtains between the narrator and the characters. A closer look at the complex interplay of class, spectatorship, and sympathy in the two poems will make this clearer.

SPECTATORSHIP AND SELF-CONSCIOUSNESS

Spectatorship plays a key role in the comparison of civilization and savagery with which SP begins. Although the savage undergoes great physical suffering, "his mind / Encounters all his evils unsubdued," because he has never known or seen greater comfort or happiness: "What in those wild assemblies has he viewed / But men who all of his hard lot partake, / Repose in the same fear, to the same toil awake?" (2) Destitution inflicts far worse suffering in the state of civilization:

> The thoughts which bow the kindly spirits down
> And break the springs of joy, their deadly weight
> Derive from memory of pleasures flown
> Which haunts us in some sad reverse of fate,
> Or from reflection on the state
> Of those who on the couch of Affluence rest
> By laughing Fortune's sparkling cup elate,
> While we of comfort reft, by pain depressed,
> No other pillow know than Penury's iron breast.
>
> Hence where Refinement's genial influence calls
> The soft affections from their wintry sleep
> And the sweet tear of Love and Friendship falls
> The willing heart in tender joy to steep,
> When men in various vessels roam the deep
> Of social life, and turns of chance prevail
> Various and sad, how many thousands weep
> Beset with foes more fierce than e'er assail
> The savage without home in winter's keenest gale.
>
> (3–4)

The greater misery of those who suffer in the midst of civilization stems from memory of their past pleasures and reflection upon the comforts enjoyed by others. Both of these figure prominently in the female vagrant's story, for instance, in the repeated "Can I forget" that begins stanzas 27, 28, and 30; and in the pathetic picture of her return to England: "Homeless near a thousand homes I stood, / And near a thousand tables pined and wanted food" (43). Civilization breeds discontent, it seems, in the same process that "calls / The soft affections from their wintry sleep," because it is precisely the sight of "Refinement" and "Affluence" that makes the miseries of poverty heavy enough to "break the springs of joy."

If the self-consciousness of the civilized poor is specific to a

mode of "social life" where "men in various vessels" become painfully aware that their fates are unequally dictated by "turns of
chance," the point of the opening contrast of savagery and civilization is to bring into view the weave of the social fabric that binds
together the unequal fates of the rich and poor. The polemical force
of the poem depends upon Wordsworth's ability to demystify the
"turns of chance" that devastate the female vagrant and the traveller (whose tale of woe is only briefly alluded to, in stanza 45) and
to show that their misfortunes proceed from the civilized brutality
of their rulers. The project of demystification begins by collapsing
the opposition between civilization and savagery into the ruins on
Salisbury Plain, symbols of the continuity of warfare, superstition,
and priestcraft in the progress from rude to civilized society. The
continuity of irrational power, in turn, helps to explain the "turns
of chance" that ruin the life of the female vagrant, and all of this
leads at last to the closing oration's oppositions between reason
and oppression.

The connections Wordsworth makes in SP between war, on the
one hand, and domestic and commercial disorders, on the other,
are typical of the antiwar literature of the early years of Pitt's war
against France.[8] Likewise, Wordsworth's stance as the spokesman
of "Reason" is the typical posture of both Paineites and rational
dissenters. The dissenting minister Joseph Fawcett's 1795 poem,
The Art of War, follows these conventional lines. Here, for instance, Fawcett calls upon the reader to witness the effects of war
upon commerce:

> Nor to the field is the dire rage confin'd . . .
> But complicated Traffic's trembling web
> Shakes, at the trumpet's call, through all its lines. . .
> To the connected, sympathising scene
> The battle's blows their dire vibrations send.
> In other ruins rages there the war;
> There falling fortunes answer falling lives,
> And broken hearts to broken limbs reply.[9]

Fawcett, like Wordsworth, exploits the comparison of rude society
and civilization to the detriment of civilized warfare. Fawcett
claims that the hypocrisy of capital punishment makes his point
for him: "And is this civil life, where civil lands / So scant a sum
of savage violence / Can whip within them, while, without them,
all / Towards each other the barbarian play?" (49). Like Wordsworth, he concludes his poem by calling upon reason to take command of society and end the violence. Fawcett's poem has

sometimes been called upon to help explain the connection between capital punishment and antiwar sentiment in ASP.[10] The polemical voice of *The Art of War,* however, links it more closely to the oratorical Wordsworth of SP, not only in its hortatory directness but also in Fawcett's capacity to take the perspective of a "friend of human kind" who "sits / From the hot combat pensively apart" (49).

What is unusual about Wordsworth's poems is his ability to evoke the poor's tormented self-consciousness when viewing, and in the view of, the rich. ASP certainly lays greater emphasis on the psychology of individual suffering than SP, and a standard account of Wordsworth's career equates this focus upon psychological suffering with Wordsworth's progress toward a more mature art. While tracing the poet's development from the Salisbury plain poems to *The Ruined Cottage,* Geoffrey Hartman writes: "What happens in 1793 seems to have opened to consciousness that break with nature which 'consciousness' as such implies, and the fruits of which are solitude and selfhood";[11] and Mary Jacobus describes the same sequence of poems in terms of Wordsworth's deepening meditation upon suffering, where a "deliberately self-effacing technique" serves to direct his vision "beyond topical issues to the permanent themes of loss, change, and mortality."[12] But the literary value of self-effacement and the thematic centrality of solitude are by-products of Wordsworth's continued focus on topical issues. In ASP (and, *a fortiori,* in *The Borderers* and *The Ruined Cottage*) Wordsworth has certainly moved closer to the heart of traditional literary values. He has found his originality, that is to say, his commitment to a less ephemeral literature than the antiwar pamphlets of the 1790s, and his power to engage that tradition. But this originality has a more local ideological value as well, and its ideological or theoretical bearing on the political and social debates of the 1790s may well have been uppermost in Wordsworth's mind as he undertook his revisions of SP. The increased emphasis in ASP upon the psychological suffering of the characters suggests that war may only bring to light a different social malady, the one that bows down the kindly spirit and breaks the springs of joy and that Wordsworth now considers more fundamental and pervasive than warfare.

This is the possibility within SP that the earliest set of revisions of that poem would seem to have taken up. One of these early revisions has the traveller speaking to the female vagrant at the end of her tale:

> Of social orders all-protecting plan
> Delusion fond he spoke in tender stile
> And of the general care man pays to man
> Joys second spring and hopes long treasured smile
> Sounds that but served her deep breast to beguile.
>
> (Ms. 1, 27v)[13]

These lines expand upon the slight hint of "sweet counsel" the traveller offers the female vagrant in stanza 45 of SP, but in a rather puzzling way. Why put an apology for "social orders all-protecting plan" in the mouth of the traveller, who has shown no interest or capacity for such an abstract and philosophical topic up to now? Further, it is unclear whether his "delusion fond" is simply his belief in such a social order, or whether it also includes his hope that the "care man pays to man" can revive the springs of joy. Perhaps because such questions cannot be answered satisfactorily, this speech received no further attention. But the passage does indicate a train of thought about the poem, which seems to be leading it away from arguments about rights and reason and toward questions about the characters' deluded or redeeming belief in social order and in each other. The poem clearly remains critical of the established order, but now it seems to be defining itself less against a defence of political inequality and more against an apology for social inequality, that is, less against something like the Bishop of Llandaff's attack on the French Revolution that occasioned Wordsworth's *Letter to Llandaff* and more against the piece to which Richard Watson appended it, his sermon "On the Wisdom and Goodness of God, in Having Made both Rich and Poor."

Watson's 1785 sermon shows him responding to fears of popular disorder (widespread in England already in the 1780s, following the Gordon riots) by attempting to talk the people out of their desire for a redistribution of property. He assures the poor that if they "will divest themselves of their prejudices, they will see reason to be perfectly contented with their condition, and be satisfied that things could not have been better ordered" (Watson, 1.453).[14] He makes no attempt to rationalize the unequal distribution of wealth by arguments on the origin of property or on the importance to the stability of the legal and political system of maintaining the rights of property; perhaps he thought that such theoretical or legal issues would have little power to engage laboring men and influence their behavior. Rather, his arguments have to do with the moral effects of property and the forms of social interaction that are encouraged by its unequal distribution: "It must be owned that this unequal distribution of property is a great spur to industry and frugality in the lower classes of life; and habits of industry and frugality bring with them modesty, humility, temperance, indeed so many virtues, that a finer system could not perhaps have been possibly formed, for exalting human nature, for bringing men to a right understanding of their duty, to a reverence of whatever is good and praiseworthy" (1.455). It comes as no surprise that the understanding of one's duty is as asymmetrical as the providential inequality of property. "The Poor owe to the Rich gratitude, thankfulness, and respect, for all the good they receive from them" (1.466); the rich are enjoined to be charitable and to treat their inferiors with "a fellow-feeling kindness" (1.464). Indeed, if the poor ought to be thankful for the ease with which virtue presents itself to their condition, the rich should be no less thankful that the poor are offered to them as occasions for discovering their own moral condition. Inequality seems to be the very atmosphere of virtue: "Were all men upon a level, there would be no room for the exercise of charity and compassion on the one hand, nor of patience and gratitude on the other; the Rich not being called upon to part with his property, would not know whether he was the servant of Mammon or of God" (1.469).[15]

A similar set of arguments was advanced by William Paley in his 1793 sermon, *Reasons for Contentment; Addressed to the Labouring Part of the British Public.*[16] The opening of Paley's sermon brings these arguments closer to the opening of SP:

> Human life has been said to resemble the situation of spectators in a theatre, where, whilst each person is engaged by the scene which passes before him, no one thinks about the place in which he is seated. It is only when the business is interrupted, or when the spectator's attention to it becomes idle and remiss, that he begins to consider at all, who is before him or who is behind him, whether others are better accommodated than himself, or whether many are not much worse. It is thus with the various ranks and stations of society. (3)

Paley's sermon is directed to those spectators from the lower ranks of society whose attention to their own business has become "idle and remiss" through envy of their superiors; Wordsworth's poem, in contrast, assigns the miseries of the poor entirely to unlooked-for interruptions of their laboring and domestic lives. For both of them, however, the crucial problem is the way the poor become aware of their place in society. The manner in which the poor internalize the social order makes the difference between discontent and tranquility for Paley (for whom, indeed, it is best that the poor carry with them as little internality or reflectiveness as possible), and it makes the civilized poor more miserable than savages for Wordsworth.

The problem of self-recognition, or of the way self-consciousness constitutes and is constituted by social relations, becomes much more important in the revision of SP into ASP. Wordsworth's early revisions of SP show him devoting considerable attention to the comparison of civilization and savagery (see 29v and 30v), but, where those revisions most clearly anticipate ASP, he galvanizes the themes of the rhetorical comparison into a character's spectacular confrontation of his relation to the social order: the conscience-stricken sailor contemplating the gibbeted corpse of another murderer. The passages that represent Wordsworth's first attempts to work out the gibbet scene center upon the possibility of "a second spring of joy" coming to the sailor. His capacity for sympathy is clearly a key. Variations upon a set of lines declaring that "Such tendency to pleasure known before / Does nature show that common cares / Might to his breast a second spring restore" (37v) appear in close conjunction with attempts to work out the way the sailor responds to complaints of misery: "His heartstrings trembling with responsive grief / the best of human hearts not more" (37v; compare 38v and 39v). The gibbet scene itself shows how his guilt turns this very sympathy against him: "Yet though to softest sympathy inclined / Most trivial cause will rouse the keenest pang" (39r). In this irritable state the absolutely nontrivial sight of the executed murderer completely overwhelms him. This dilemma is the core of the transformation of SP into ASP. The very sympathetic response that makes the sailor equal to "the best of human hearts" also constitutes his greatest misery, because the same internal power that ties him to his fellow human beings excludes him from society. Such a tormented self-consciousness stands in stark contrast to the animal tranquility recommended to the poor by Paley. Clearly, for Wordsworth in 1794–96, social inequality is not a source of virtue, as Watson would have it, but rather an environment that drives good men to crime and turns their best instincts against themselves. The sailor's situation suggests that the present social order violates the very foundations of healthy community and individual virtue.

War and poverty remain the major public symptoms of class victimization in ASP, but the poem's critical focus turns to private, domestic, and psychological relations. It is not that military and legal "Oppression" become less important, but that they become less visible, a strategic change that testifies to the silencing of the oratorical voice that names "Oppression" rather than to any substantial shift of political allegiance. In ASP the characters' own perspectives regarding their situations take on primary importance, because their sympathies for one another are the very stuff of the social fabric. Thus ASP, like Godwin's *Caleb Williams,* concerns not only "things as they are" but also, even more centrally, things as the characters make them appear to one another. When the passionate interaction of the characters speaking and listening to one another comes into the foreground of the poem, the oratorical narrator and his appeal to "Reason" fade away. The narrator of ASP has *retired* from public view, and this difference between SP and ASP represents precisely the crucial turn that leads Wordsworth away from London, the *Letter to Llandaff,* and projects like *The Philanthropist* or the imitation of Juvenal and toward *The Ruined Cottage* and the *Lyrical Ballads.*

PUBLIC VICES AND PRIVATE VIRTUES

The opening stanzas of ASP interweave the older themes of suffering, social cohesion, and class division with its new emphasis on storytelling. Instead of being presented as the components of a rhetorical comparison, these thematic elements now cohere in a brief encounter between a young traveller—the main character of the new poem—and an old one, who tells him a story. The old man's story concerns his sad lot ("how he with the Soldier's life had striven / And Soldier's wrongs" [3]) and his daughter's wretched circumstances. Just as his story carries on the social protest of SP, the scene through which they travel renews SP's images of "Affluence" excluding the poor. The "gilded door" of the inn they pass by provides no entrance or aid to the needy; and, after the travellers part, the young man finds himself isolated where "dreary corn-fields stretch'd as without bound; / But where the sower dwelt was nowhere to be found" (6). These last lines, retained almost without change from SP, draw new vitality from the image of impersonal wealth and the separation of social effects from their causes presented by the images of the inn and the soldier's suffering.

The sad matter of the old man's tale and its inhospitable setting contrast sharply, however, with the personal ties formed in and around the act of storytelling itself. Two acts of compassion frame the soldier's story: the young man's offer to help the obviously weak and miserable old man and the postboy's kindness in giving the old man a ride. The first of these transforms the old soldier from a picture of disease and poverty—"Propp'd on a trembling staff he crept with pain, / His legs from slow disease distended were" (1)—to one of mental acuity—"The old man's eyes a wintry lustre dart" (2)—and garrulous sociability. The soldier's reception of the ride elevates the pathos of his situation while re-emphasizing the pleasure imparted by a simple act of charity: "The old man then was on the cushion placed / And all his body trembled with delight" (5). These framing acts of compassion and pleasure find their strongest archetype in the bond that motivates the journey itself and is the main import of the soldier's story—his love and compassion for his daughter. Thus the entire incident sets poor men's personal kindness and sympathy against the impersonal world of commerce and political power. If the larger political and economic communities are mediated by violence and self-interest, then the sympathetic community of the poor comes together through their speaking and listening to one another.

The major instance of such storytelling in the poem is, of course, the female vagrant's tale. The talk shared by the sailor and the female vagrant produces "mutual interest" and "natural sympathy" (29), which promises to turn into love (in stanza 66). Although the sailor's resolution to confess his crime precludes such an outcome, the possibility itself highlights both the sailor's predicament, since his reception of the story once again shows his best feelings turned to misery by his guilt, and the association of narrative with passionate bonding between those who share it. In ASP, rather than serving as testimony for the narrator to comment upon, the female vagrant's story serves as a catalyst to the plot. The fact that the story becomes important not only for its thematic content, but also because of the relationship it creates between teller and listener, also changes the story itself in important ways. Wordsworth's revision pays greater attention to the dramatic appropriateness of the tale to its speaker, and this change in perspective crucially alters the story's representation of political and social problems.[17]

One of the most notable changes comes in the female vagrant's description of the way her father loses his property. In SP this is taken care of in seven lines:

> "At last by cruel chance and wilful wrong
> My father's substance fell into decay.
> Oppression trampled on his tresses grey:
> His little range of water was denied;
> Even to the bed where his old body lay
> His all was seized; and weeping side by side
> Turned out on the cold winds, alone we wandered wide."

(29)

"The Female Vagrant" expands considerably upon the "wilful wrong" wrought upon the father:

> "Then rose a mansion proud our woods among,
> And cottage after cottage owned its sway,
> No joy to see a neighbouring house, or stray
> Through pastures not his own, the master took;
> My Father dared his greedy wish gainsay;
> He loved his old hereditary nook,
> And ill could I the thought of such sad parting brook.
>
> "But, when he had refused the proffered gold,
> To cruel injuries he became a prey,
> Sore traversed in whate'er he bought and sold:
> His troubles grew upon him day to day,
> Till all his substance fell into decay.
> His little range of water was denied;
> All but the bed where his old body lay,
> All, all was seized, and weeping, side by side,
> We sought a home where we uninjured might abide."
>
> (35–36)

The later poem is altogether more sensitive to the distinction between what the poet thinks about the situation and what the woman herself knows and feels. Instead of the appeal for sentimental indignation in the final line of the SP version, the later version turns the family's wandering into the woman's search for a new, secure home. The cliched rendition of "Oppression" trampling upon the grey locks of the industrious tenant sounds a good deal more like SP's narrator than like the poor woman telling the story. In ASP the woman sees a new master and his mansion and sees that he has no regard for the community into which he has come. Thus Wordsworth is able to supply the reader with a more detailed account of new wealth invading and "improving" the rural landscape, and, just as importantly, this account is informed by the values and attachments of one who is being uprooted in the process. The shift in perspective that makes the older rhetoric inappropriate also produces a decided gain in pertinent and specific detail.

In the same way that "Oppression" drops out of the revised version of the loss of the female vagrant's childhood home, her account no longer names "War" as the cause of the economic catastrophe that destroys her second household. The value of this change is somewhat less certain than that of the previous one. Compare the SP version:

     "My happy father died
Just as the children's meal began to fail.
For War the nations to the field defied.
The loom stood still; unwatched, the idle gale
Wooed in deserted shrouds the unregarding sail.

   "How changed at once! for Labor's chearful hum
Silence and Fear, and Misery's weeping train.
But soon with proud parade the noisy drum
Beat round to sweep the streets of want and pain"

                (33–34)

to the account in "The Female Vagrant":

     "My happy father died
When sad distress reduced the children's meal:
Thrice happy! that from him the grave did hide
The empty loom, the cold hearth, and silent wheel,
And tears that flowed for ills which patience could not heal.

   "'Twas a hard change, an evil time was come;
We had no hope, and no relief could gain.
But soon, with proud parade, the noisy drum
Beat round, to sweep the streets of want and pain."

                (39–40)

Once again "The Female Vagrant" presents the catastrophe in terms more suited to the woman's perspective. She reacts more believably to her father's death and relates it more pointedly to her family's distress. The idle implements of labor are now those that could have been in her cottage; and, instead of remarking upon the onslaught of war, she tells us of her immediate situation: "We had no hope, and no relief could gain." But she can only see "a hard change, an evil time" where the half-submerged narrator of SP saw a chain of events originating in national politics. If in SP the causal sequence leading from war to commercial disorder to conscription is all too obvious, in "The Female Vagrant" the war seems only to be the last of a string of natural disasters. Even here the political theme is arguably stronger in "The Female Vagrant." The bitter irony with which the "proud parade and noisy drum" provide the "relief" the woman seeks is certainly more poignant in the later version. But the political significance of that irony must, like the "tale" of "Simon Lee," be supplied by the "gentle reader" rather than being made explicit in the poem. Whatever the aesthetic or dramatic benefits of Wordsworth's new strategy,[18] it certainly does not erase the class difference between the poor characters, on the one hand, and the poet and his expected audience, on the other.

When the suffering poor begin to speak for themselves in Wordsworth's poetry, politics inevitably begins to recede from view. Since the characters are excluded from political participation, they are more apt to notice social than political inequality. Their opportunities for exercising virtue or falling into vice are correspondingly foreshortened. Thus problems of corruption appear to the poverty-stricken in the choices offered them in their search for "relief," or in the conflicts that arise in attempting to simultaneously obtain subsistence, hold together one's family, and protect one's virtue. The female vagrant in the latter portions of her story finds herself in a situation similar to that which led to the downfall of the sailor, torn between need and virtue, unable to steal or beg yet unable to live without doing so. Her deepest suffering, like that of the sailor, is a guilty conscience:

> "But, what afflicts my peace with keenest ruth
> Is, that I have my inner self abused,
> Foregone the home delight of constant truth,
> And clear and open soul, so prized in fearless youth."
>
> (61)

Because it expresses the perspective of the poor, "the home delight of constant truth" bears little resemblance to the farsightedness and perspicuity of "Reason" in SP or to the vigilant solidarity of the "friends of Liberty" in the *Letter to Llandaff;* virtue is, instead, located in the narrow circle of the domestic affections.

The crucial turn toward the poem's resolution comes in a scene of lower-class corruption being conquered by sympathy and domestic virtue. The sailor and female vagrant happen upon a family whose father has just beaten his five-year-old child. Although the sailor's remonstrances have no effect upon the enraged father, the sight of the sailor crying for his son awakens his "self-reproach" (73). This is, in fact, a simple repetition of the effect the sight of the bleeding child has just had upon the sailor, whom it reminds of the man he murdered. The sequence enacts a doubled echo of the gibbet scene, then, and its domestic context serves to make visible the effect of the sailor's crime in separating him from, and finally destroying, his family. The sailor's love for his family prompts his murder, fuels his guilty conscience, and makes possible both his sympathetic effect upon the child-beating father and his own moral regeneration.

The final triumph of the sailor's love and virtue must wait for the appearance of his dying wife, a few stanzas further on in the poem; but the speech he delivers upon the reconciliation of the father to his wife and son explains the form virtue can take in this lower-class setting:

> "'Tis a bad world, and hard is the world's law;
> Each prowls to strip his brother of his fleece;
> Much need have ye that time more closely draw
> The bond of nature, all unkindness cease,
> And that amongst so few there still be peace:
> Else can ye hope but with such num'rous foes
> Your pains shall ever with your years increase."
> While his pale lips these homely truths disclose,
> A correspondent calm stole gently on his woes.
>
> (74)

The sailor's "homely truths" disclose a drastic gap between the limited sphere in which the "bond of nature" can assert itself and the "bad world" of legal oppression and commercial rapacity. This chasm between the public and the private is fully borne out by the structure of the poem as well. In ASP public problems find only private solutions, as the entire poem moves progressively from the disclosure of the miseries inflicted upon its main characters in the bad world to a more intimate setting where the characters' virtue is competent. In the sailor's speech, as in the poem, this region of self-determination, so to speak, is first that of the family and finally, in the stanza's final line, contained within the conscientious individual. But to what does the sailor's "correspondent calm" correspond, then? If it is to the truths he has just spoken, then it represents an absolutization of and resignation to the unbridgeable gap between public vice and private virtues.

It would seem, indeed, that the sailor's resolution, the calm that steals upon his woes, internalizes and reconciles him to a divided social order quite as fully and peacefully as a Watson or a Paley could wish. If the purpose of the Bishop of Llandaff's or the Archdeacon of Carlisle's sermons was to stifle lower-class resentment and prevent violent popular rebellion, one must wonder whether Wordsworth's representation of domestic and individual virtue might not have been better suited to achieve those ends. Such a judgment would be anachronistic, no doubt, since the poem clearly does not encourage either deferential gratitude or patriotic fervor, and, had it been published in the mid-1790s, there would have been no danger of the government's censors reading it as an apology for the *status quo*. At the very least, however, the poem's final moments present a contradiction between the critical perspective offered upon public justice at the scene of execution and the complete acquiescence to that same justice—indeed even the salvational power of such acquiescence—in the private judgment of the sailor. The contradiction is even further emphasized by the fact that the sailor's virtuous hosts, as well, decide to turn him in as soon as they realize he must have been the murderous husband of the woman who has died in their home: "'Though we deplore it much as any can, / The law,' they cried, 'must weigh him in her scale'" (90).

Such faith in the law clearly separates the characters' perspective from that of the indignant narrator who can address himself familiarly to "Thou who of Justice bear'st the violated name" (91). The separation marks an important distinction. The familiarity with which the narrator expresses his outrage implies political competence, and, moreover, his capacity for expressing it exercises a kind of political virtue quite different from the passionate sympathy and calm resignation available to the characters. The narrator's apostrophic interjection represents the emergence (or re-emergence) of a *public* voice in which the poet speaks to his audience *about* the characters who speak to one another in the private settings of his poem. But the community to which the narrator speaks is no longer the militant, politically active one addressed in the closing oration of SP. Now he speaks to a diffuse group of meditative spectators who can define themselves in a kind of specular opposition to the sensation-seeking crowd watching the sailor's execution at the conclusion of ASP; it is a community whom the poet would teach to listen to and sympathize with the "homely truths" spoken and felt by his humble characters. The development of Wordsworth's thematics moves from public discords toward their private, individual roots. But this kind of radicalization passes from explicitly addressing itself to political actors to the contemplation of those who *suffer* politics from afar. In the process, Wordsworth's poetry becomes more reflective precisely because the poor lack the competence to understand their problems from the broader perspective available to the poet, and thus the polemical force of representing them derives from their mute objectivity, in which the poet of humanitarian protest finds his own sympathies reflected back to him in a socially pertinent way.

5

The Politics of Theatricality and the Crime
of Abandonment in *The Borderers*

THE CRUCIAL DOCUMENT FOR ANY ASSESSMENT OF WORDS-
worth's thematic and artistic development at Racedown is *The
Borderers*. Conclusions based on *Adventures on Salisbury Plain*
must remain qualified by the fact that the surviving manuscript of
the poem is from 1799, even though it is Gill's considered opinion
that the 1795 poem survives "substantially, if not in every detail,"
there.[1] Beyond that, however, and more importantly, *The Borderers*
is both a more ambitious and a more accomplished work of art
than *Adventures on Salisbury Plain*. The tension between the public exercise of coercive power and private understanding of justice
and humanity receives a fuller, more complex treatment in *The
Borderers*, largely because in the play Wordsworth's shift of emphasis toward sympathetic virtue coheres more strongly with his
radical questioning of the basis of community. Storytelling continues to be an important element of plot and theme, but now also
exposes the disturbing role representation plays in establishing *and*
subverting social life. *The Borderers* raises the problems of isolation and of the inauthentic community to the level of a philosophical engagement with the theme of the social contract. The path of
Wordsworth's development into a major poet lies through this play,
then, and in the interest of tracing that path I offer the following
extended close reading of *The Borderers*.

SUFFERING, PSYCHOLOGY, AND POLITICS

The Borderers is in many ways the least characteristic of Wordsworth's major works. His only extant attempt at drama, it relies
more closely on Shakespearean models than on the Miltonic,
Spenserian, or balladic forms that predominate elsewhere in his
oeuvre. Its characters and incidents are significantly more remote

from the common than would be Wordsworth's wont during the next decade. But perhaps the play's most important singularity is tonal rather than formal, for not only is Wordsworth's tragedy unrelieved by any of the meditative lyricism that would appear in *The Ruined Cottage* and remain at the center of his work from then on; it is equally disconnected from the polemical ardor that invests his more immediate engagement of political issues in the poetry from *Descriptive Sketches* up to *Adventures on Salisbury Plain*.

Nonetheless, *The Borderers* is absolutely typical of Wordsworth's best poetry in the mid-1790s in one crucial respect: its intense foregrounding of psychological suffering, where that foreground represents itself as the site of a more radical engagement of social issues than a broader focus on the play's background of political upheaval would allow. That Wordsworth's poetry derives much of its greatness from shifting its focus to "the mind of man" is one of the most frequently repeated claims of Wordsworthian criticism, particularly in the years since Hartman's *Wordsworth's Poetry* came to dominate the field. That this same shift of emphasis is an ideological maneuver in which some serious revision or repression of political problems takes place has quickly become one of the standard claims of a new generation of interpretation. What one generation of critics has spoken of as a deepening of content, a progress from the superficial to the essential, the other has called displacement, occultation, mystification. Yet both versions share the questionable assumption that psychology takes (over) the *place* of politics. Perhaps the question that needs to be asked, then, is precisely what figurative strategy links politics and psychology in Wordsworth's play. What if psychology neither subsumes politics into humanist universality nor acts as its metaphorical (mis)representation? Exactly how is psychological suffering a political issue?

Consider, for instance, what Mortimer has to say, approximately midway through the action of *The Borderers:*

> we look
> But at the surfaces of things, we hear
> Of towns in flames, fields ravaged, young and old
> Driven out in flocks to want and nakedness,
> Then grasp our swords and rush upon a cure
> That flatters us, because it asks not thought.
> The deeper malady is better hid—
> The world is poisoned at the heart.

$$(2.3.337-44)^2$$

Mortimer's speech here answers one by a member of his band warning him of the approach of the army of Henry III and an intensification of the war between the king and the league of barons—the one place in the play where a specific historical context threatens to have any effect on the plot.[3] Mortimer's speech appears to fend off history, so to speak, by reducing political turmoil and its effects to merely "the surfaces of things." In contrast to these superficial events he posits a "deeper malady" residing at the world's "heart." The band's advocacy of the popular cause, one might argue, is futile, perhaps because it is caught in the cycle of retributive violence, but more certainly because such activism fails to confront or even recognize the essence of human suffering. Or, as Rivers will later put it in a more famous speech, "Action is transitory, a step, a blow— / . . . Suffering is permanent, obscure and dark" (3.5.60, 64). The rhetorical opposition such speeches set up between action and passion, surface and depth, accident and essence would, the argument continues, decisively forestall any intense representation of political and social struggles by diverting the thematic focus instead to the crisis of moral despair suffered by the contemplative individual. If the real core of the human condition is only accessible to thoughtful contemplation, presumably by a spectator not caught up in the vanity of political events, then the essence of the drama lies at the fringes of the action, where the onlooker who sees into the life of things must somehow deal with his burdensome knowledge. Any interpretation of Wordsworth's play would then have to insist upon the vital importance of this movement that places a tortured sensibility rather than a tortured countryside at the center of the play's concerns, because this is precisely where Wordsworth's preoccupation with visionary experience, or the self-conscious imagination, first reaches its mature form. Whether to evaluate the emergence of self-consciousness as an imaginative triumph (Hartman) or an ideological retreat (McGann) appears, at this point, to be a choice between complementary rather than radically opposed theses.

Mortimer's speech cannot support such an interpretation, however, for the simple reason that the relation of surface and depth is more problematic than has been indicated so far. The "deeper malady" Mortimer refers to is the corruption he mistakenly believes Herbert to be working upon Matilda. Thus the poison that has reached Mortimer's heart lies precisely upon the surfaces of things, that is, upon those deceptive surfaces where Rivers scripts his trumped-up charges against Herbert. Mortimer's speech begins a quasi-legal prosecution of Herbert upon charges of pandering, but in the context of the play Mortimer's accusations redound against the trial itself rather than the criminal. The trope of depth is a Sophoclean irony directed against Mortimer's own inability to penetrate Rivers's disguise or to distinguish between true feelings and theatrical contrivance, and therefore Mortimer's exposition of the deep truth propagates and spreads the malady rather than rooting it out. The contemplative individual turns out to be a thoroughly involved political actor, and his tortured sensibility deepens nothing except his immersion in a corrupt society's violent legal forms. Nonetheless, even when Mortimer is forced to recognize his error, he sticks to his position: "We are all of one blood, our veins are filled / At the same poisonous fountain" (4.2.56–57); "Thou must be wise as I am, thou must know / What human nature is, decoyed, betrayed— / I have the proofs" (5.3.58–60). His persistence suggests two quite different conclusions. Either Mortimer's earlier error—mistaking Rivers's perfidy for Herbert's—is inconsequential, the poison at the heart of the world predicates a privileged detachment, and the whole complex of self-consciousness and displacement readily falls back into place; or Mortimer's knowledge of what it is to be "decoyed, betrayed" represents a hard-won recognition based, perhaps, on the uncanny pattern of repetition between Rivers's crime and his own abandonment of Herbert. In the latter case, isolation and self-consciousness are intrinsic, and by no means privileged, elements of such problems as political justice, violence, and the articulation of human nature and social institutions.

Wordsworth himself began the critical tradition of resolving such dilemmas in terms of the play's commentary on the French Revolution. In the note he attached to the play on its first publication in the 1842 *Poems, Chiefly of Early and Late Years,* he writes:

> The study of human nature suggests this awful truth, that, as in the trials to which life subjects us, sin and crime are apt to start from their very opposite qualities, so are there no limits to the hardening of the heart, and the perversion of the understanding to which they may carry their slaves. During my long residence in France, while the Revolution was rapidly advancing to its extreme of wickedness, I had frequent opportunities of being an eye-witness of this process, and it was while that knowledge was fresh upon my memory, that the Tragedy of "The Borderers" was composed. (B 813)

According to the elderly Wordsworth, then, *The Borderers* bears witness to the dark knowledge of human nature Wordsworth gleaned from his French experience. He further explains, in the

Fenwick note of 1843, that the central representative of French Revolutionary corruption is the character named Oswald in 1842, Rivers in the 1797 version:[4]

> While I was composing this play I wrote a short essay illustrative of that constitution & those tendencies of human nature which make the apparently *motiveless* actions of bad men intelligible to careful observers. This was partly done with reference to the character of Oswald & his persevering endeavour to lead the man he disliked into so heinous a crime, but still more to preserve in my distinct remembrance what I had observed of transition in character & the reflections I had been led to make during the time I was a witness of the changes through which the French Revolution passed. (B 815)

The main tradition of interpretation of *The Borderers* has consequently focused on the character of Rivers/Oswald as symbol of corruptibility and on corrupt human nature as commentary and stricture upon revolutionary political ambitions. Differences of interpretation within this tradition have turned largely upon various attitudes regarding the relative priority of politics and psychology, which then motivate sharply divided answers to such questions as: What or where is the first order of corruption? Is Wordsworth's drama directly dependent upon his observation of the perverted passions of the actors in the French Revolution, and does it therefore comprise a condemnation of that grand historical project? Or is human nature the basic and perhaps irredeemable subject of all transient historical crises? Is French political history essential to the play's content, or did it merely provide Wordsworth a peculiarly revealing opportunity to observe human nature? At one end of the spectrum, for instance, lies David Erdman, who has inflected these topics most pertinently toward specific allusions to the revolution's history and to Wordsworth's autobiographical reflection upon his experience in France, but who sometimes treats the play as an allegoric or even merely emblematic code (in saying, for example, that "Herbert is Custom, Law, Ancient Faith, the Constitution [in Burke's sense])".[5] At the opposite end of the spectrum from Erdman lie those critics, led by Geoffrey Hartman, who turn the Satanic consciousness of Oswald himself into the vehicle that lifts the play above local polemic and into the realm of philosophical tragedy. Here a peculiar form of self-consciousness becomes the essence of modernity, and this central preoccupation with the imaginative sublime relegates political or polemical contexts to the margins.[6] Between these extremes lies an important group of critics who have read the play primarily as a variation on the themes of contemporary political controversy, thereby rendering Oswald's perversion of the passions and the understanding as a more or less indirect political and moral critique of Wordsworth's early affiliation with, and subsequent rejection of, English "Jacobin" philosophy and particularly the influence of William Godwin.[7]

There are those who have stepped aside from this controversy entirely, arguing that Wordsworth's 1842–43 remarks about the French Revolution are not relevant to the 1797 play at all and that the early version of the play is most deeply concerned with something other than politics—for instance, the aesthetics of imagination and sublimity.[8] But the freshest challenge to the central tradition of interpretation has come via R. F. Storch's strategy of directing attention away from Oswald/Rivers toward "what the play quite clearly shows to be the beginning, middle and end of the dramatic conflict, namely the mixture of love and hate that Marmaduke [Mortimer] feels towards Herbert, the father-figure."[9] Storch's sensitive Freudian reading forces the articulation of psychological crisis with sociopolitical upheaval to emerge as a fundamental problem in the interpretation of *The Borderers*. Reeve Parker's and Alan Liu's notable recent attempts to turn the reader's gaze to family romance rather than political or philosophical debate may also partake in a fundamental historiographic shift of focus toward family structure rather than, or prior to, political arrangements.[10] Thus Parker reads Herbert's storytelling to Matilda as a hierarchical bond by which he lords over her his own usurpation of the place of the mother, and Liu reads Mortimer's anxieties about legitimacy as the symptom of a middle-class ideology that embraces the nuclear family as its ideal (and fantastic) representation in specular opposition to the illegitimate and violence-prone broods of the poor. Parker and Liu are far from ignoring or minimalizing the play's political context. They both, however, render it secondary, giving priority, in Parker's case, to a theory of narrative linking theater to family romance, and in Liu's case, to the social history of the family.[11]

Yet the project of reading the figural matrix that links politics and psychology without turning one into a code for the other is not successfully realized by locating the heart of things in the family, particularly if one takes seriously Wordsworth's testimony that he meant to be speaking, albeit indirectly, about the French Revolution. It can be shown that the play does address itself, coherently and in detail, to the revolutionary political crisis. But it addresses the revolutionary crisis without erecting a specific allegory of contemporary events; it raises philosophical and moral issues without in any way suggesting that they transcend or marginalize political ones; and, rather than comprising a critique of Godwinism or any other specific contemporary political doctrine, it attempts to re-examine the notion of social contract itself. Wordsworth does grant familial bonds a certain kind of priority over political or legal ones. *The Borderers* does not, however, turn politics into a secondary manifestation of some essential individual or familial set of desires. Rather, psychology in *The Borderers,* perhaps more than in any of Wordsworth's subsequent work, is not only a deeply social but also a thoroughly politicized topic.

"Strange Spectacle": Genre and Ideology

If, as Mortimer's speeches repeatedly imply, *The Borderers* ex-poses the poisoned heart of the world, then the soliloquy opening 3.2 presents an interesting version of how this might be so. Rivers is speaking about Mortimer:

> This stripling's mind,
> It hath been rudely shaken, and the dregs
> Float on the surface—yea, the very dregs . . .
>   We dissect
> The senseless body, and why not the mind?
> These are strange sights—the mind of man upturned
> Is a strange spectacle.
>
> (3.2.20–22, 25–28)

Rivers' deception has a quasi-scientific motive that is also, simulta-neously, a dramatic one, to turn Mortimer into a "strange specta-cle." This clinical view of "the mind of man" anticipates and conforms very nicely to Wordsworth's report, in the 1842 and Fen-wick notes, about the way he observed human nature during the French Revolution. In Wordsworth's memory the revolution pro-duces just such a "spectacle" as Rivers describes; revolutionary turmoil shakes men up and thereby exposes their psychological depths. What are we to make of this correspondence? Maybe there is something about "spectacle" that inevitably conjoins, or perhaps confuses, political struggle, psychological depth, and dramatic superficiality.

The situation Rivers describes is, from another point of view, a revealing efflorescence of the play's hybrid generic structure. The spectacle of Mortimer's fears, confusion, and eventual madness—

a dominant feature of the earliest drafts of the play—is *Gothic* in a specific, conventional sense: normally hidden aspects of nature are forced to make a spectacular appearance due to the pressure of unnatural events. For example, the effect of Rivers's plot on Mortimer or of the French Revolution on its participants resembles that of Catholic monasticism, Inquisitorial tyranny, and demonic temptation on the hapless protagonist of M. G. Lewis's *The Monk*.[12] To read Ambrosio's passionate excesses and dire transgressions as mere abnormality or perversion would be to miss entirely the point and the power of Lewis's fable. The monk's commission of rape and incest represents, on the contrary, the emergence of ubiquitous human desires in a situation that strips the psyche of its customary disguises. This is surely why the novel so gleefully depicts Ambrosio, time after time, shedding the pious demeanor he wears in public to indulge his tempestuous passions in private. The generic expectations raised by the Gothic mode in *The Borderers* involve not only this emergence of "strange spectacle," however, but also the play's strong tendency to displace its psychological investigation from any immediate political and social reference. Perhaps Wordsworth's fascination with the Gothic during the mid-1790s depended partly upon the distance it placed between itself and contemporaneity, but Wordsworth's motives do not seem to have been escapist.

Why is it, for instance, that the fairly large number of stock Gothic elements in the earliest drafts of *The Borderers* almost entirely disappear in successive versions of the play? In the Cornell edition of *The Borderers* Robert Osborn equates the Gothic element of *The Borderers* with an early stage of composition transcended in the later drafts. The play's succesive drafts trace out a generic hierarchy leading from "spectacle" to philosophy in "a fundamental shift from the *Ur-Borderers*' emphasis on the spectacle of action and suffering . . . toward emphasis on the philosophic basis of action and suffering" (15). But the EV remains thoroughly Gothic in its final form, for instance in the decision to render the unholy contract that binds Rivers, the tempter, to Mortimer, the sinner, as a parody of matrimony at 3.5.18–37. Ambrosio's crimes in *The Monk* can likewise be read as a series of grotesque parodies of the healthy marriage his vows forbid.[13] Rather than shedding the Gothic, then, Wordsworth's revisions place his "spectacle" in a bare and almost abstract setting in order to highlight the Gothic's central interest, the psychological struggle that the Satanic tempter foments in the protagonist. He is refining his Gothic fable, distilling the essential sources of its strength from its garish and cluttered popular medium. What Robert Mayo said about Wordsworth's "intense fulfillment of [the] already stale convention[s]" of magazine verse in the *Lyrical Ballads* can be just as aptly said of his appropriation of the Gothic in *The Borderers*.[14]

Although the play's Gothic strain lends unusual emphasis to the way extraordinary incidents can become catalysts for psychological or philosophical revelation, the primary antecedents of Wordsworth's plot of temptation remain Shakespearean—*Othello, Macbeth, Hamlet*. W. J. B. Owen, opposing the older view that the numerous echoes of Shakespeare are a serious flaw in *The Borderers*,[15] maintains that, on the contrary, Wordsworth "intends the whole play to be seen as an imitation of Shakespearean tragedy; . . . he is invoking the authority of Shakespearean tragedy to add weight to his own version of tragedy."[16] Owen bolsters his claim with a reading of Wordsworth's intended preface for the Early Version. This preface's strong emphasis on the dramatic credibility and psychological realism of a problematic character (Rivers) places it in a late-eighteenth-century tradition of Shakespearean criticism whose leading exponents would include Joseph Warton and Lord Kames, among others. In this tradition, literature offers psychology the advantage of rendering the normally ephemeral passions in a permanent, fixed object so that they become susceptible of repeated, scientific observation. Therefore, "by considering the copy and portrait of minds different from our own, and by reflecting on these latent and unexerted principles, augmented and promoted by imagination, we may discover new tints, and uncommon features."[17] Owen's evidence strongly implies that Rivers's soliloquy self-reflexively announces Wordsworth's neo-Shakespearean ambition to make his tragedy a vehicle of radical psychological inquiry.

Such lofty ambitions are also, inevitably, philosophical. In fact, *The Borderers* occupies the peculiar ground whereon moral philosophy conjoins psychological with legal and political inquiries. Two more of Wordsworth's literary sources help us get a fix on Wordsworth's position. The first of these is Schiller's *The Robbers*. Schiller's Charles Moor is Mortimer's closest analogue, just as Schiller's quadrangle of Charles and Francis Moor, their father, and Charles's beloved Amelia directly anticipates Wordsworth's quadrangular entanglement of Mortimer and Rivers, Herbert, and Matilda. Charles Moor, like Mortimer, is seduced into crime by the deceptions of his jealous rival; both characters lead bands of outlaws with ambiguous moral and political status; and both Moor and Mortimer represent themselves as mere instruments of providential justice.[18] The most important similarity, however, is that the piteous spectacle of an abandoned father figure serves in both plays as the focal point for themes of justice, punishment, and vengeance. The deeply ironic trial scene in the middle of *The Borderers* resembles the scene in *The Robbers* where Charles Moor discovers his abandoned father. Moor proceeds to use the hideous sight to provoke a fury of resentment in his band and to procure from them an oath of vengeance against his brother Francis: "See, see there! he faints! A son confined his father in that tower—cold, naked, hungry, and athirst."[19] But Wordsworth also echoes this scene in the declining movement of his play, when Mortimer, having discovered that Herbert is innocent, searches for him: "Have you seen / In any corner of this savage heath / A feeble, helpless, miserable wretch, / A poor, forsaken, *famished,* blind old man" (5.2.1–4)? In both plays, the abandoned father elicits questions about guilt and responsibility and evokes problems of allegiance and social cohesion.

A Shakespearean allusion in Mortimer's speech opening 5.2 (and in Alexander Tytler's 1792 translation of Schiller) directs our attention to a second site of similarity and influence. The archetype of the pathetic but crucial figure of the abandoned father is King Lear, cast out by his daughters, confronting the tempest on the heath: "A poor, infirm, weak, and despised old man."[20] The Gothic impulse to strip the psyche of its customary disguises thus also finds a monumentally authoritative source in the figure on the heath. As Lear himself says to Edgar, disguised as Tom-a-Bedlam, "Unaccommodated man is no more but such a poor, bare, forked animal as thou art. Off, off, you lendings! Come, unbutton here."[21] The spectacle of mad King Lear tearing away his clothing, set against a backdrop of political turmoil, motivated by a passionate familial struggle, in a remote and almost abstract historical milieu: all of this adds up to the specific authority that guides Wordsworth's use of tragedy as a philosophical vehicle. *King Lear* provides the dramatic prototype for the conjuncture of legal, moral, political, and psychological themes in *The Borderers*.[22]

Wordsworth's philosophical ambitions would seem to have dictated the setting of *The Borderers,* which not only copies *Lear's* historical distance and vagueness, but also strives to attain the elemental, timeless quality of the scenes on the heath in *Lear's* third act. The Fenwick note is instructive: "As to the scene & period of action little more was required for my purpose than the absence of established Law & Government—so that the Agents might be at liberty to act on their own impulses" (B 814). The setting approximates a well-exercised convention of eighteenth-century moral and political philosophy, the "state of nature." The state of nature is, as C. B. Macpherson observes, "a logical and not an historical hypothesis," derived by stripping men of legal and governmental restraints and of "manners" in order to isolate the universal "passions" lying beneath them—"off, off, you lend-ings."[23] Rivers is fond of proclaiming that he and Mortimer share the privilege of acting in a state of natural liberty: "Happy are we / Who live in these disputed tracts that own / No law but what each man makes for himself" (2.1.51–53); "A few leagues hence we shall have open field, / And tread on ground as free as the first earth / Which nature gave to man" (2.1.111–13). I will be arguing that such proclamations are caught in a web of complex ironies that both undercut Rivers's assertions and at the same time allow them to retain considerable critical force, particularly when set against Mortimer's assumptions about nature, justice, and law. But the strategy that puts these ironies into play is one that combines Gothicism and Shakespearean tragedy with a philosophical inquiry into the radical, "natural" determinants of legal and political arrangements.

The argument I am advancing here, then, is that *The Borderers* anticipates the philosophical ambitions that Wordsworth would soon announce for the *Recluse* project. The abandoned Herbert belongs next to the other marginalized figures around which Wordsworth's project seems to have crystallized, such as Margaret and the discharged soldier. Moreover, as Alan Bewell has recently argued, the discursive paradigm of contemporary moral philosophy plays a significant part in placing these marginalized figures at the center of Wordsworth's thematic material.[24] Bewell argues that the poems of the *Lyrical Ballads* period are unified by Wordsworth's anthropological interests. *The Borderers,* in contrast, focuses upon a more specifically political problem, that of the *interregnum,* that state of "natural" order, disorder, authority, and equality which persists under the suspension of law and government, as, for instance, in revolutionary France: "To Nature then / Power had reverted; habit, custom, law / Had left an interregnum's open space / For her to stir about in uncontroll'd" (*Prelude* 10: 609–12).[25] The play thus stands at a point of crisis between Wordsworth's faith in the revolution's restoring the "native dignity" of "primaeval Man" in *Descriptive Sketches,* where "Nature, as in her prime, her virgin reign / Begins, and Love and Truth compose her train" (529–30, 784–85, 1793 text), and the account of the revolution in *The Prelude.* This crisis does not take the form of an encoded commentary upon events in France, however; rather, *The Borderers* sets itself the problem of giving literary form to an inquiry concerning the bases of justice, political power, and social cohesion. It is an essay of impassioned reason seeking the form—or discovering the impossibility—of an authentic human community.

The same scene in which Rivers twice urges Mortimer to recover his natural liberty contains another important exchange that both ironizes Rivers's arguments and points toward the more complex framework within which Wordsworth wants to present the theme of natural community. Mortimer, at this point, is convinced of Herbert's guilt and of the justice of executing him and is able with some difficulty to reconcile this action to his instinctual sympathy for the venerable-looking old man: "If I ever knew / My heart, and naked saw the man within me, / 'Tis at this moment" (2.1.87–89). Rivers, however, wants to insist (for obvious reasons) that the execution should be secret rather than public:

> The eye
> Of vulgar men knows not the majesty
> With which the mind can clothe the shapes of things:
> They look but through the spectacles of forms,
> And from success alone they judge of actions.
>
> (2.1.98–102)

Rivers's bad faith is quite obvious. He is intent upon using "the spectacles of forms" to seduce Mortimer into a crime that will force him to recognize that success alone is the judge of actions. The strong contrast between the way the mind clothes things, according to Rivers, and the image of truth as the naked heart, according to Mortimer, is more thematically pertinent than Rivers's explicit argument. The gap between the naked heart and the clothed intellect could be taken as emblematic of the difference not only between spontaneous feeling and discursive reason but also between nature and custom. But these dichotomies are precisely what the exchange calls into question; what is disturbing about it is that Mortimer's naked truth depends so heavily upon the spectacle furnished to him by Rivers's elaborate deception. Indeed, the whole problem of justice in this play is inextricable from the problematics of deception or, more precisely, from the *theatricality* that seems to make it impossible to protect spectacle—for instance, the spectacle of public execution—from mental reconstruction or perversion of its meaning.

Here is the point at which Wordsworth's philosophical tragedy engages the contemporary political debate. Theatricality and public execution receive one of their most famous treatments in a notorious condemnation of revolutionary justice, which moreover alludes to the same passage of *King Lear* as *The Borderers* and *The Robbers*. Edmund Burke's denunciation of the events of 6 October 1789, which signal to him the demise of those "pleasing illusions which made power gentle" by furnishing the "wardrobe of a moral imagination" to "cover the defects of our naked, shivering nature" (Burke, 3.331), sounds unpleasantly similar to Rivers's praise of "the majesty / With which the mind can clothe the shapes of things." In the same famous passage Burke sets up theater as a model for exercising the *natural* emotions that Richard Price and other sympathizers with the Revolution have violated:

> No theatric audience in Athens would bear what has been borne in the midst of the real tragedy of this triumphal day: a principal actor weighing, as it were, in scales hung in a shop of horrors, so much actual crime against so much contingent advantage. . . . In the theater, the first intuitive glance, without any elaborate process of reasoning, will show that this method of political computation would justify every extent of crime. (3.338–39)

Here it sounds almost as if Burke is preparing a *précis* of Wordsworth's villain, who speculates during the soliloquy opening 3.2 that "It were a pleasant pastime to construct / A scale and table of belief," and who asserts later that "every possible shape of action / Might lead to good" (4.2.109–10). Indeed it may be far from accidental that Rivers sounds just like Burke sometimes, and just like Burke's revolutionary villains at others. Both Burke and Rivers believe in the conscious manipulation of theatrical illusion as a proper technique for maintaining political power; that Burke is enamored of such "spectacles of forms" as courts afford, while Rivers is contemptuous of them, may be only an accident owing to their different circumstances. But the intention governing Wordsworth's scattered allusions to Burke's *Reflections* is not the central issue. The point is Wordsworth's deep concern in *The Borderers* with the way that shows and appearances hold together society.

Such a concern with the theatricality of everyday life was the central material of Adam Smith's *Theory of Moral Sentiments,* and thus constituted one pole of the theoretical structure within which Smith sought to encompass the inner and outer, private and public aspects of human social life.[26] Smith, in a move that may well have influenced Burke's exploitation of the theatrical metaphor, derives the "distinction of ranks and the order of society" not, as one might expect, from a sheer inequality of property or of strength, but from the "natural" disposition of mankind to sympathize with the spectacle of wealth and ease and to reject or treat with contempt those who look poor, powerless, or miserable. Monarchic power, according to Smith, draws heavily upon its subjects' "natural" response to courtly *spectacle:* "That kings are the servants of the people, to be obeyed, resisted, deposed, or punished, as the public conveniency may require, is the doctrine of reason and philosophy; but it is not the doctrine of Nature. Nature would teach us to submit to them for their own sake, to tremble and bow down before their exalted station, to regard their smile as a reward sufficient to compensate any services, and to dread their displeasure, though no other evil were to follow from it, as the severest of mortifications" (50–53).

Godwin's *Political Justice,* to come closer to Wordsworth's personal sphere of influence, attributes a similarly great importance to the "splendour of ornament" with which kings surround themselves, since Godwin considers it a "necessary instrument of policy" for maintaining the "imposture" of regal power.[27] For Godwin, such play-acting points to the radical source of all political error: "All the arguments that have been employed to prove the insufficiency of democracy, grow out of this one root, the supposed necessity of deception and prejudice for restraining the turbulence of human passions" (2.124).[28] In Godwin's utopia, theatrical display does not disappear altogether, however. Rather, the daunting effects of regal showmanship are transformed into the coercive power of neighborly censure, which Godwin depends upon to maintain public order in the absence of legal or police authorities:

> The principle object of punishment, is restraint upon a dangerous member of the community; and the end of this restraint would be answered, by the general inspection that is exercised by the members of a limited circle, over the conduct of each other. . . . No individual would be hardy enough in the cause of vice, to defy the general consent of sober judgment that would surround him. It would carry despair to his mind, or, which is better, it would carry conviction. He would be obliged, by a force not less irresistible than whips or chains, to reform his conduct. (2.199)

The extreme importance Godwin lays upon "sincerity" in "social communication" thus bears witness to the power exercised by mere appearance in the present order. The coercive role of utopian sincerity is the theatrical correlative of Godwin's faith in naked reason.

What concerns Wordsworth in *The Borderers* is not simply deference for property and titles or contempt for the poor (although sympathy for the poor is obviously an important theme for Wordsworth throughout his career), but rather the question motivating arguments like Smith's or Godwin's: how does our sympathetic understanding of the spectacles presented to us by the appearances of others form the basis of a community? The immediate occasion for reopening such a question was, no doubt, a widespread crisis in England's sense of community brought about by the combined effects of war with revolutionary France, domestic persecution of "Jacobin" activities, and the disastrous grain shortages of 1795–96. Burke announces this crisis in characteristic terms in his *Letter to Portland,* a copy of which Wordsworth received in a packet of books sent to him by James Losh in March, 1797:[29]

> It is but too easy, if you once teach poor mechanics and laborers to defy their prejudices, and, as this has been done with an industry scarcely credible, to substitute the principles of fraternity in the room of that salutary prejudice called our country—it is, I say, but too easy to persuade them . . . that this war is, and that the other wars have been, wars for kings . . . and that their condition is not likely to be altered for the worse, whatever party may happen to prevail in the war. Under any circumstances this doctrine is highly dangerous, as it tends to make separate parties of the higher and lower orders, and to put their interests on a different bottom. But if the enemy you have to deal with should appear, as France now appears, under the very name and title of the deliverer of the poor and the chastiser of the rich, the former class would readily become not an indifferent spectator of the war, but would be ready to enlist in the faction of the enemy,—which they would consider, though under a foreign name, to be more connected with them than an adverse description in the same land. All the props of society would be drawn from us by these doctrines, and the very foundations of the public defence would give way in an instant. (5.40–41)

The French (with the unprincipled cooperation of the Foxite Whigs) threaten, in Burke's complaint, to draw away the props of English society by appearing under the title of deliverers of the poor and thereby usurping upon the sympathetic identification of the English poor with their proper rulers. *The Borderers* responds to this crisis with an extended meditation upon the problematic status of sympathy and deference as cornerstones of communal identity. Wordsworth is much less intent upon unmasking Jacobinical or royalist sophistry than on understanding how social bonds come to depend so heavily upon masks; one might say that *The Borderers* takes its clue from that unintentional Burkean pun by which the "props of society" is both an architectural and a theatrical metaphor.[30]

Thus the radical psychological inquiry afforded by the "strange spectacle" of "the mind of man upturned" is also, simultaneously, a critical inquiry into the political and social functions of what we would today call ideology. Although most of Wordsworth's preface to the early version of the play is devoted to explaining the character of Rivers, the ultimate significance of his "perverted reasons justifying his perverted instincts" (B 67) is not psychological but social. The real issue is not so much the dark, poisoned heart of man as it is the way that theatrical illusion pervades everyday life and *empowers* base motives. This is the point of two somewhat muddled paragraphs near the end of Wordsworth's preface that have attracted little previous commentary:

> There is a kind of superstition which makes us shudder when we find moral sentiments to which we attach a sacred importance applied to vicious purposes. In real life this is done every day and we do not feel the disgust. The difference is here. In works of imagination we see the motive and the end. In real life we rarely see either the one or the other, and when the distress comes it prevents us from attending to the cause. This superstition of which I have spoken is not without its use, yet it appears to be one great cause of our vices; it is our constant engine in seducing each other. We are lulled asleep by its agency and betrayed before we know that an attempt is made to betray us.
>
> I have endeavored to shake this prejudice persuaded that in so doing I was well employed. It has been a further object with me to show that from abuses interwoven with the texture of society a bad man may be furnished with sophisms in support of his crimes which it would be difficult to answer. (B 67–68)

It is not quite clear how the superstition "which makes us shudder" in the first sentence can also be the agency which lulls us asleep and becomes the engine of our seduction in the final sentences of the same paragraph. Nonetheless, Wordsworth does announce a clear intention of using his "work of imagination" to demystify a prejudice that works surreptitiously and perniciously in "real life." "Moral sentiments to which we attach a sacred importance" are often "applied to vicious purposes," and the work of art affords us a detachment from this process and its effects that allows us to see that which we usually cannot. Instead of being characters embroiled in real life's drama we are granted the luxury of a place in the audience; art, unlike life, sets a clear-cut boundary between spectacles and spectators.[31] The crucial point, however, is that Rivers's sophisms are "furnished" to him by "abuses interwoven with the texture of society." The demystifying effect of aesthetic form must therefore unravel the texture of society sufficiently not only to disentangle the spectator, but also to render visible (at least conceptually or provisionally) the "abuses" woven into society's deep structure. Rivers's perversions are the catalysts of this dissolution.

Let me now offer a more detailed thesis about the political thematics of Wordsworth's concern with "spectacle." *The Borderers* consists of two major actions: the deception of Mortimer and the abandonment of Herbert. The first is Rivers's conscious, perverse project; the second is its unintentional result. Rivers's motivation is clearly revolutionary in a broad sense, but his machinations result in repetition rather than renewal. We can revise our questions about the linkage between psychological suffering and politics in the play, then, as follows: does the irony of repetition primarily attach itself to Rivers's revolutionary ambition, or, on the contrary, is the abandonment of Herbert a spectacular unmasking of the norm? Is the abandoned father the sign of revolutionary transgression, or does his abandonment symbolize the legal and political order that frames and frustrates Rivers's puny, megalomaniacal scheme? Put another way, the question sets up the premise that Mortimer's abandonment of Herbert re-enacts some sort of Primal Scene. Surely the scene has to do with violence and authority— but what kind of authority? Is Wordsworth replaying the fall of man, conceived as the chastisement of human desire to usurp upon divine (or "natural") power? Or is it, rather than the violation of a preordained, cosmic law, the ritual institution of law itself? Could the father's abandonment represent the founding of an order of violent political power?

I shall argue that Herbert's abandonment symbolizes the law and its ritual. Such an argument needs to address the status of ritual and social ceremony in *The Borderers;* to sort out the relationship between Rivers's revolutionary project and Mortimer's ambiguous position in regard to law and the community; to speculate upon the conceptual links between violence, law, and political order; and, finally, to interpret the significance of the peculiar type of violence perpetrated against Herbert. Briefly, however, the argument runs as follows. Rivers attempts to institute a new order by an act of violence. He calls upon nature as an amoral model for the freedom of a new kind of hero. In ironic contrast to his rhetoric of sublimely isolated will, however, he attempts to bind Mortimer to himself by means of seizing the power of death over another, making of that other a sacrificial victim whose execution produces the communal bond of shared guilt. The play lets us know that this procedure is nothing new, that it is, in fact, things as they are. It lets us know, moreover, that Rivers's entire project is a pathetic self-deception. Although the terms in which Rivers conceives of community and law are exposed as entirely specious, however, his unintentional success in causing Mortimer to reproduce his own crime nevertheless constitutes a devastating critique of Mortimer's more authentic sense of community and justice. The source of Rivers's power is not his freedom from moral constraints, but his ability to dupe Mortimer into cooperation. True power, the play tells us, rests less upon violence than upon vision. Or rather, violence usurps upon vision in precisely the way that political power usurps upon the bonds of spontaneous, passionate community through its manipulation of spectacle.

EMPTY SIGNS, COMMERCIAL ART, AND THE FACE

Wordsworth quite deliberately subverts and empties out the meaning of social ceremonies and rituals in *The Borderers*. Weddings, trials, and funerals comprise a significant, if understated, leitmotif in *The Borderers*. The foreground action of 1.2 (the first scene at the inn) fades into a wedding celebration in the background; the brief scene between Matilda and the Old Pilgrim opens with the report of a declaration of Herbert's restoration in a court of law (2.2.5–10); and the sound of "wassellers / Returning from the wake" (4.3.8–9) disturbs Margaret and Matilda just before Robert enters to tell them of Herbert's abandonment. This thin strand of minor incidents becomes more striking when laid alongside a pattern of grotesque or demonic parodies of the same ceremonies in the foreground. Thus the court-ordered restoration of Herbert in 2.2 ironically prefigures the tragically misdirected trial of 2.3, which in turn, once Rivers's deception becomes apparent, suggests druidic, ritual sacrifice to one member of Mortimer's band: "What if he [Rivers] mean to offer up our Captain, / An expiation, and a sacrifice / To those infernal fiends?" (3.4.38–40). The wedding celebration, aside from its obvious contrast to the diverted marriage of Mortimer and Matilda, also receives a grotesque parody in the bond Rivers hopes to substitute for Mortimer's marriage:

"I still will be your friend, will cleave to you / Through good and evil, through scorn and infamy" (3.5.36–37).[32] The wake, finally, not only looks forward to the final scene, where Herbert's corpse lies in state, as it were, in the interior of Robert's cottage, but has also been strangely anticipated by reports in 1.3 and 2.1 of the obsessive funeral ceremony an abandoned woman in the neighborhood performs for her lost infant:

> every night at the first stroke of twelve
> She quits her house, and in the neighbouring church-yard
> Upon the self-same spot, in rain or storm,
> She paces out the hour 'twixt twelve and one,
> She paces round and round, still round and round,
> And in the church-yard sod her feet have worn
> A hollow ring.
>
> (1.3.16–22)

The abandoned woman's obsessive circling round her infant's grave is to mourning much what the trial in the next act is to criminal justice.[33] Instead of helping the woman to dissipate her grief in shared, ritual recognition of her loss, this self-enclosed, quasi-magical ceremony simply perpetuates her sense of isolation and her separation from the community.

Moreover, this vignette echoes throughout the play (and beyond it as well, in *The Ruined Cottage* and "The Thorn") in such a way as to suggest that the abandoned woman's plight is not merely pathetic but somehow archetypal. Mortimer takes her to be "a skeleton of Matilda" (2.1.33), a prefiguration or type of the fate Matilda is about to suffer at the hands of the evil lord Clifford. The type of the Abandoned Woman appears once again in the story of the captain's daughter, who, upon hearing of her father's being marooned by Rivers and his crew, "neither saw nor felt as others do, / But in a fearful world of her own making / She lived—cut off from the society / Of every rational thing—her father's skeleton" (4.2.86–89). Mortimer himself will finally exit the play as the veritable "skeleton" of abandonment and isolation, having been led into "a fearful world of [his] own making" by, in part, the *spectacle* of the Abandoned Woman.

For the woman is not only a type but also a prop in Rivers's theater. The "hollow ring" she traces has a double meaning. On the one hand, it represents her own relentless orbit around the absent child, and so, by inference, it is a sentimental reminder of the power of maternal love. The ring signifies the essential, sustaining form of an authentic community. On the other hand, the mad funeral ceremony empties out the ritual of grief, turning it into a meaningless form that only perpetuates the woman's isolation. In this sense, her pacing simply orbits the endlessly self-renewing thought of her tragedy, and the form of the ring signifies not fidelity but morbid repetition. Her sentimental power lends itself to Rivers's theatrical manipulation because she has emptied a ritual form of its proper function; the same process makes her an uncanny double of the community that has expelled her.

Perhaps the best image of the way abandonment and deception are insinuated into the signs of civil society comes in another apparently minor incident in 4.1. The audience sees Herbert enter the stage searching for help. He is led by "the irregular sound of a bell," which presumably comes from an old chapel visible on a ridge of rocks in the background (4.1.s.d.). In 5.2 Robert has more to say about this bell and chapel:

> On a ridge of rocks
> A lonesome chapel stands, deserted now.
> The bell remains, which no one dare remove,
> And when the stormy wind blows o'er the peak
> It rings as if a human hand were there
> To pull the cord.—I fancy he had heard it,
> And it had led him towards the precipice
> To climb up to the spot whence the sound came.
>
> (5.2.21–28)

This incident clearly doubles Mortimer's betrayal of Herbert, but it also suggests that the crime is much more than simply a personal or individual failing. The ringing bell that Herbert takes as the promise of aid is only the mechanical production of the relic of an institution. The ruined chapel, like the abandoned woman's funeral, has been emptied of the significance it would bear within a healthy community. Yet it still carries a delusive power derived from its institutional form. This power is even more impressive because no stage manager stands by to manipulate the signal or its reception. Rather, the chapel bell survives by the sheer force of superstitious awe: "The bell remains, which no one dare remove." It is a mere prop on a stage without actors, where it nonetheless continues to ring out a hollow summons "as if a human hand were there." The final agent of Herbert's destruction is precisely the empty form of a ritual call to social unity.

It could perhaps be argued that the ruined chapel with its meaningless bell is not a figure for social structure and political theater, but simply the last, pathetic irony sealing Herbert's fate. A careful reading of the illusion Rivers foists upon Mortimer, however, will suggest otherwise. If the perverse motivation of Rivers's crime inevitably suggests that Iago is his precursor, it is no less true that one of the central questions one poses concerning Othello must also be asked about Mortimer: what makes him so vulnerable to the shadowy hints and unsupported accusations of the tormentor? And just as Othello's marginalized status in Venetian society partially determines the emergence and force of his jealousy, so Mortimer's ambiguous legal and political standing provides Rivers with his opening. Mortimer, like Othello, is both an insider and an outsider. He is, more particularly, a sort of inverse Othello: a friend of the community and an enemy of the law. It is precisely into this gap between community and law, insiders and outsiders, friends and enemies, that Rivers wedges his narrative representation of Herbert. The result will be a catastrophic widening of the discrepancy between inside and out until it finally becomes an abyssal chasm separating fantasy and reality. Yet Mortimer's eventual insanity is initiated upon a social, not merely a psychological, ground.

Notice the mixture of psychological, political, legal, and economic themes in Rivers's first extended description of Herbert:

> For that another in his child's affection
> Should hold a place, as if 'twere robbery,
> He seemed to quarrel with the very thought.
> Besides, I know not what strange prejudice
> Seems rooted in his heart: this band of ours,
> Which you've collected for the noblest ends,
> Here on the savage confines of the Tweed
> To guard the innocent, he calls us outlaws,
> And for yourself, in plain terms he asserts
> This garb was taken up that Indolence
> Might want no cover, and rapaciousness
> Be better fed.
>
> (1.1.28–38)

In the opening lines of the speech Rivers likens Herbert's parental possessiveness to a claim that Matilda's affection is Herbert's private property. This shuttling of the metaphor between familial and legal bonds seems casual, but is in fact a first tracing of the "texture of society" that Rivers will unravel. He immediately proceeds to an allegation of "prejudice." Herbert insists on seeing Mortimer in conventional, legal terms as an outlaw, who must therefore be vicious (rapacious) and deceptive (wearing a "garb . . . taken up that

Indolence / Might want no cover"). Alongside Herbert's rooted prejudice Rivers arranges Mortimer's self-conception as leader of a noble band who protect the "innocent" from a "savage" political situation. The nuance of the phrase "savage confines" is symptomatically ambiguous. Does it refer to the noble savagery of the locale Mortimer protects from baronial incursions? Or is the locale made savage by the aristocratic warfare Clifford and his ilk wage for the right of imposing their rule on the people? Savagery is either the undisturbed, prepolitical state of things or it is precisely a political disturbance of that natural social order. This ambiguity resembles not only the well-known paradoxes of Rousseau's *Second Discourse* or the conflict between commercial and political order in the second part of Paine's *Rights of Man,* but also the social theory of no less a representative of the French Terror than Antoine St.-Just: "Saint-Just clearly affirms the autonomy and specificity of the social by contrasting a *society,* an immanent and internally experienced unity, with an *aggregate,* which is an apparent society and a purely formal unity, an externally imposed and not internally experienced cohesion. The political state designates every relation based on force, inequality, and constraint. And Saint-Just unhesitatingly equates the so-called civilized life with savage life."[34] The innocence Mortimer protects is not legal, nor is the society he protects from savagery a political body. The conflict Rivers sets up is not between a radical and a conservative (or ministerial and Jacobin) politics, but rather between Herbert's legal and political conservatism, on the one hand, and what one might call a social and popular conservatism, on the other. That is, Mortimer sees himself as the essentially conservative defender of a society—"an immanent and internally experienced unity"—whose ties (to one another and, one can speculate, to the locale itself) are prior to the power relations enacted in law and politics. He hopes to preserve a society whose constitution is analogous to the "child's affection," whereas Rivers deftly places Herbert among that "aggregate" of those for whom this sort of bond has been reified as Property.

Rivers continues to interweave Herbert with "abuses interwoven with the texture of society," first of all, by associating him with the evil lord Clifford:

> In truth, I think I saw—
> 'Twas at a distance and he was disguised—
> Hovering around Herbert's door, a man whose figure
> Resembled much that cold voluptuary
> The villain Clifford.

(1.1.249–53)

Indeed, corrupt aristocratic power is the primary condition that makes Rivers's deception possible. Aristocratic oppression remains in the background, a crucial but never an active contributor to the plot. Instead, a second, antithetical form of abuse becomes far more intimately engaged in Rivers's scheme. The figure of the dishonest beggar, the mendicant as con man, emerges to act out the themes of property and deception and to represent the venal, commercial community into which Rivers expels Herbert.

Before Rivers associates Herbert explicitly with beggars by introducing his suborned witness, the Female Beggar, into the cast of characters, he has already described Herbert in terms that clearly invoke a stock figure which haunts the widespread and varied literature on poverty and charity, that of the lying beggar:

> To see him thus provoke her tenderness
> With tales of symptoms and infirmities—and yet
> I'd wager on his life for twenty years. . . .
> Matilda has a heart.—It is her virtues
> Of which he makes his instruments.—A man
> Who has so practiced on the world's cold sense
> May well deceive his child.
>
> (1.1.215–17, 220–23)

The fraudulent beggar is a Commercial Artist, a professional actor, but one dedicated to eradicating the difference between theatrical appearance and reality:

> The employment of him who has taken up for life the trade of a beggar, is one routine of hypocrisy. If he were to tell the truth, it would be of no use to him. It would not extort a farthing from the tenderest-hearted man that lives. But his tongue and truth have taken a lasting leave of each other. He scarcely so much as knows what it means. He is all a counterfeit. The melancholy tone of his voice, the forlornness of his gestures, the tale that he tells, are so many constituent parts of one infamous drama.[35]

Rivers's speeches allude most clearly to an especially disturbing quality of the professional beggar that forms a topic of frequent complaint, the way that the beggar preys upon sympathy. The beggar lives upon the pain he causes by presenting a false spectacle of his own suffering. Bentham's telegraphic prose is sufficiently eloquent on this topic:

> Mischiefs produced by the practice of begging—1. In the instance of passengers in general, considered as exposed to the importunity of

beggars—to some, the pain of sympathy:—no pain, no almsgiving;—begging is a species of extortion to which the tender-hearted, and they only, are exposed.[36]

The figure of the dishonest beggar makes a sympathetic "society" into the victim of an avaricious "aggregate."

One of the major complaints against the pushy professional beggar in the Poor Law debate is the accusation that, like Goneril and Regan outshining Cordelia, his loquacity and showmanship obscure the plight of the truly needy: "It is generally found, that modest worth stands at a distance, or draws nigh with faltering tongue and broken accents to tell an artless tale; while the most worthless are the most unreasonable in their expectations, and the most importunate in their solicitations of relief."[37] The conflict between commercial art and true need is not just a struggle of economic competitors, but an opposition between rival economies. For instance, according to an anonymous correspondent to the *Monthly Magazine,* beggars keep alive a veritable countereconomy that parasitically attacks not only the virtue of the almsgiver but the value of honest labor in general: "Thousands of useless mouths are daily fed among us; useless hands are confirmed in idleness; and some hundred pounds-worth of base coin is kept in circulation, to the injury of the fair trader."[38] This same writer sounds the very keynote of the attack upon almsgiving when he concludes that everything depends on making "a wide distinction between the honest laborious poor, and the dissolute idle vagrant" (859).

If the deceptive beggar proved endlessly useful in justifying stern legal measures rather than spontaneous benevolence as the proper response to poverty, the defenders of casual charity, including Wordsworth, often responded by wondering at what price sympathetic responses to suffering would be stifled and concluded by bemoaning the decay of a traditional sense of social responsibility. The debate on almsgiving thus sets in action that more fundamental ideological struggle where the instinctual and spontaneous moral sense that manifests itself in sympathy and pity for beggars is brought up hard against the concept of civil society as a system of restraints upon instinctual aggression or, increasingly, as a system that formally integrates disparate, self-interested economic activities. Rivers's deception of Mortimer draws upon and dramatizes this crisis.

Herbert has indeed been a beggar, as an Old Pilgrim and former companion of Herbert's tells Matilda: "We joined our tales of wretchedness together / And begged our daily bread from door to door" (2.2.18–19). But this type of begging is antithetical to that of the professional, fraudulent beggar, and it implies an antithetical economy. The pilgrim's begging signifies a casting loose from the moorings of property, an act of faith in providential assistance. Providence here takes the form of human sympathy and charity, the pilgrims' dependence upon the goodness of those they chance upon. The play's opening scene, where Rivers first associates Herbert with the beggar as commercial artist, also supplies strong images of this antithetical economy in the interaction of Herbert and Matilda. Matilda's strong sympathy and support for Herbert closes the circle of self-sacrifice begun by Herbert's heroic rescue of the infant Matilda from the flames in Antioch. It is, however, their dependence upon "tales of wretchedness" that provides Rivers the opportunity to reinterpret their relationship by placing Herbert's narrative in a different economic context.[39]

As Rivers manipulates Herbert out of the familial and popular community Mortimer sees himself as serving and defending and into a commercial alliance with the corrupt aristocrat, the figure of mendicancy is transformed, with a certain structural inevitability, from the sacred pilgrim to the con artist. This transformation points to and depends upon Mortimer's sense of a popular and spontaneous economy of trust, generosity, loyalty, and pity—all of which are aptly conjoined in the act of almsgiving. The deceptive beggar's profession not only violates the moral code of almsgiving by its substitution of a profit motive for one of real needs; it also usurps upon the spontaneous economy, drawing entirely upon the power of the virtue and sympathy it redirects to its own vicious ends. The transformation of Herbert from pilgrim to con man, in short, exactly mirrors the threat Rivers earlier posed to Mortimer's sense of himself: an economy of spontaneous affection and freely given service is twisted into one of self-serving calculation. A moral transaction becomes the site of a theft, and the family finds itself confronting the region of public law and its structurally ordained methodology, violence. The beggar's theater will inexorably invoke the theater of justice.

The Female Beggar's performance enacts the rupture between all that almsgiving implies and the venal economy of Commercial Art. At first Mortimer takes the Female Beggar's stories as mere performances of a "babbling gossip" and a "prater" (1.3.34, 61). He gives her money and asks, sarcastically, about the rest of her repertoire: "Pray, good lady, / Do you tell fortunes" (1.3.61–62). But her reply converts his disdain into sympathy.

BEGGAR.   Oh! Sir! you are like the rest.
            This little one—it cuts me to the heart—
            Well! they might turn a beggar from their door,
            But there are mothers who can see the babe
            Here at my breast and ask me where I bought it:
            This they can do and look upon my face.
            —But you, Sir, should be kinder.

MORTIMER.   Come here ye fathers,
            And learn of this poor wretch.

                                              (1.3.62–69)

Why does the beggar's answer have such an effect on Mortimer? We can begin by noticing the division of the community into two factions in her accusation, "You are like the rest." "The rest"— them, not us—are those who cannot tell the difference between the beggar's art and its authentic ground, her need to provide for her infant. They can mistake her baby for a mere prop, a commercially acquired means of enhancing the illusion of need and misery in order to coerce sympathy and money from her audience. "This they can do and look upon my face": they have lost their capacity for shame, that is, their own ground in the sure awareness of what ties together and motivates human beings. They can deny sympathy to a mother's need to feed her infant. It is as if the face should speak a stronger language, one not subject to narrative and theatrical distortion or misconstruction. The beggar implores Mortimer to "be kinder," and he replies in kind, by calling together a familiar and familial group to be instructed by the mother's humanity and by the inhumanity of "the rest." He stands with the nursing mother, inside the family, looking out upon a hostile world.

Into this hostile world that has shut its doors upon true maternal and paternal bonds[40] the Female Beggar immediately begins to install Herbert as its archetype. Her version of Herbert is the con artist without any authentic or passionate ground, a man who really does embody the inhuman figure fantasized by "the rest" in their reproaches, that is, one who really buys a child and fakes familial affection with a purely venal motive. Matilda, Mortimer learns, is not Herbert's beloved daughter but rather a precious commodity, a carefully cultivated piece of capital Herbert plans to valorize by selling it to Clifford. The authentic bond of nurturance projects as its nightmarish double Herbert's use of paternal affection as a mask for pandering. If the authentic community coheres under the sign of the family, the commercial world of Herbert and Clifford meets in the slave market under the sign of woman-as-property.[41]

Herbert becomes the fully articulated symbol of a studied art of deception that, at every step of the way, draws upon and subverts authentic human passion to its own chrematistic ends.

The full extent of the rupture and subversion in Mortimer's sense of things accomplished in 1.3 can be measured by juxtaposing the scene's beginning and its end. It starts with Mortimer's protestation: "I would fain hope that we deceive ourselves: / When I beheld him sitting there, alone, / It struck upon my heart—I know not how" (1.3.1–3). This is one instance of an assertion repeated throughout the play, that Herbert bears such a pious demeanor it could not be a mask for vice. Mortimer, who cannot look upon the face of the Female Beggar and deny the authenticity of her need, also cannot look upon the face of Herbert without believing in his benevolence. When Mortimer slides back from the stern project of vengeance urged upon him by Rivers to resignation of Herbert's fate to heavenly justice, he looks to the incontrovertible evidence of Herbert's face for reassurance: "It must be—I must see / That face of his again . . . / 'Twere joy enough to end me" (2.3.308–10). Matilda will later call upon "the terible pleading of that face" as an unassailable motive for her placing filial obedience to Herbert above her love for Mortimer (3.5.132). Herbert's face seems to possess a natural, spontaneous power, or to constitute a preverbal language comparable to the "fixed and steady lineaments . . . [of] the universal face of earth and sky" (RC&P, 153–55).[42] It communicates a pure, passionate claim to humanity and a guarantee of authentic community.

The Female Beggar acknowledges the pathetic power of Herbert's appearance, but she reinterprets it as sanctimonious hypocrisy:

> Aye, gentlemen, it is a feast to see him:
> Lank as a ghost and tall—his shoulders bent
> And his beard white with age—yet evermore,
> As if he were the only saint on earth
> He turns his face to heaven.
>
> (1.3.86–90)[43]

At the end of the scene, Clifford's lascivious gaze reveals the naked truth of Herbert's intentions: "When he stood by the side / Of the blind man, he looked at the poor girl / With such a look—it makes me tremble, Sir, / To think of it" (1.3.173–76). Rivers's plot perverts the "terrible pleading" of Herbert's blind, white-bearded face into theater, a visual spectacle woven into a narrative texture that doubles and thereby subverts its claim to authenticity. Now Mortimer must confront the shattering possibilities that spontaneity and fidelity are illusions and that the links which bind together the social chain are forged out of mere self-interest. If Herbert's venerability is a mask, fatherhood merely a role, and the community of need and charity only an instrument of the essential relationships of mastery and slavery, then, according to Mortimer, "The firm foundation of my life appears / To sink from under me" (1.3.181–82).

THE SOCIAL CONTRACT AND THE FIGURE OF THE OUTCAST

The play lets us know that Mortimer is wrong about Herbert. It also lets us know that the power Rivers exercises derives from such passionate bonds as those between Herbert and Matilda or Matilda and Mortimer rather than from Rivers's "independent intellect" (3.5.33). But the dark possibility remains that Mortimer's "firm foundation" *can* be subverted by Rivers because it is already untrustworthy. If Rivers's theater can turn Herbert's face into a contemptible mask, perhaps there was something essentially theatrical about it all along. And if that is so, then the attempt to heal or purify society by casting out the criminal may be doomed to failure. The question, as the play turns from the deception sequence of act 1 to the trial and execution sequences of acts 2 and 3, is whether bringing the criminal to justice can restore and protect a primary, preordained social order or whether, on the contrary, the court of justice is only another theatrical doubling of the deception that pervades civil society.

Mortimer proposes a public trial for Herbert not in order to subject him to legal rule—the trial is anything but legal, as a matter of fact—but rather to restore and purify the true community by exposing and casting out falsehood from its midst. Herbert's crime, according to Mortimer, transgresses nature itself: "There is no earthly law / That measures crimes like his" (2.1.34–35). All that is called for, therefore, is a public scene of recognition, which Mortimer characteristically puts in terms of the power of the "face": "From first to last / He shall reveal himself—his punishment / Shall be before her [Matilda's] face" (2.1.41–43). What is important to Mortimer is openness; he wants to arrange a scene of unmasking and truthtelling to undo Herbert's theatrical devices.

The struggle between Mortimer and Rivers in act 2 has to do entirely with openness versus secrecy rather than with justice. When Rivers actually suggests the legal form of a trial, it is only to upbraid Mortimer for lacking the fortitude to take Herbert's execution into his own hands: "Twelve neighbours, / Plain honest men, might set us right. Their verdict / Would fortify your spirit— end this weakness" (2.3.188–90). Quite contrary to Rivers's intentions, this suggestion is more or less realized in the mock trial that concludes the second act. But the project of truth and recognition has been subtly contaminated by a different issue, that of strength. Thus the neighborly community of opinion emerging from the trial represents itself not by the righteous gaze of Matilda's face, but by the ceremonial ring of a public execution:

> To the camp
> He shall be led, and there, the country round
> All gathered to the spot, in open day
> He shall be sacrificed.
>
> (2.3.425–28)

The call for a community centered on public, ritualized violence bitterly undercuts Lacy's assertions, in the same speech, of the band's independence, rationality, and divine favor.

The best spokesman for the band's decision to publicly "sacrifice" Herbert is Rivers, who steps forward to make a decisive speech just when Herbert's age and blindness seem to be causing some doubts about Mortimer's accusations:

> Are we men,
> Or own we baby spirits? . . .
> Wisdom, if Justice speak the word, beats down
> The Giant's strength, and at the voice of Justice
> Spares not the worm.—The Giant and the worm,
> She weighs them in one scale. The wiles of Women
> And craft of age, seducing reason first
> Made weakness a protection, and obscured
> The moral shapes of things.
>
> (2.3.380–81, 385–91)

Rivers's misogynistic equation of crime with seduction craftily insinuates into the notion of strength not only its superiority to the "Giant" but, more importantly, immunity to the individual weakness of sympathy for age, femininity, weakness, "the worm." Strength becomes a concerted identification and casting out of the seductress, and as a re-enactment of Rivers's myth of fall and redemption, it takes the form of ritual sacrifice:

His tender cries
And helpless innocence, do they protect
The infant lamb? and shall the infirmities
Which have enabled this enormous culprit
To perpetrate his crimes serve as a sanctuary
To cover him from punishment? Fie—Justice,
Admitting no resistance, binds alike
The feeble and the strong.—She wants not here
Her bonds and chains which make the Mighty feeble.
—We recognize in the old man a victim
Prepared already for the sacrifice.

(2.3.391–400)

The ironies of the trial, where the deceiver himself ends up presiding over the ritual casting out of deception, bring to a climax the thematic conflict between legal and popular conceptions of community. Not that it clarifies the difference between them: on the contrary, Rivers succeeds in utterly confusing popular solidarity with legal violence and political theater. This is not the climactic triumph of Rivers's scheme, either. As far as Rivers is concerned, the trial is a cumbersome detour. The trial's significance is that it suggests a collusion between theatricality and popular community quite independent of anyone's conscious intention, and this collusion takes the dark form of ritual sacrifice. Rather than being held together by domestic affection and a more general economy of needs and services, the community here seems to base its identity upon the violent expulsion of a symbolic Other. Rivers's scheme of isolating Mortimer by involving him in an unjust crime is only the ironic counterpart of the form of community enacted in the theater of justice itself. The expulsion and sacrifice of the symbolic Other, finally, appears to be a form of self-mutilation, a dismemberment of age, weakness, and femininity from the body politic. The public execution envisioned by Lacy and applauded by Mortimer thus stands as the fullest realization in the play of the model of ritual suggested by the Abandoned Woman's "hollow ring."

Such an execution never takes place, of course. In fact, Mortimer's abandonment of Herbert finally overshadows both Rivers's brotherhood of violence and Lacy's community of ritual sacrifice. The violence at the center of *The Borderers* is not conspiratorial or bloody, neither an execution nor an assassination, but rather a nearly accidental crime, skirting the shadowy margin between will and forgetfulness. Where Rivers and Lacy envision bonds forged by decisive action, Wordsworth substitutes a tragedy about the denial and dissolution of bonds of affection and duty. This substitution of abandonment for murder decisively subordinates Rivers's individualistic rationalizations of his behavior to the play's social dynamics. More specifically, the abandonment elevates the significance of Rivers's narration of his own crime over the rationalistic and cynical theory of social contract by which he attempts to justify his actions.

Rivers's most concise formulation of his social theory—that is, of the relation of violence, nature, and political order—comes at the end of his first, incomplete revelation of his scheme to Mortimer:

> You have . . . taught us that the institutes
> Of nature, by a cunning usurpation
> Banished from human intercourse, exist
> Only in our relations to the beasts
> That make the field their dwelling. If a viper
> Crawl from beneath our feet, we do not ask
> A license to destroy him: our good governors,
> Wise thinkers! have by forms and ceremonies
> Hedged in the life of every pest and plague
> That bears the shape of man, and for what purpose
> But to protect themselves from extirpation?
>
> (3.5.95–105)

Rivers sketches his project onto a broadly Hobbesian canvas. As in Hobbes, natural right is the right to violence for the purpose of self-preservation. Society appropriates the individual's right to violence and monopolizes it. This monopoly constitutes government and political order as such. Rivers adds a few cynical touches to make this portrait of society his own. The governing class becomes a "cunning" conspiracy usurping individual sovereignty, and their self-interested cowardice motivates the legal ban upon, or rather formalization of, violence. What he finds objectionable in all this is the way the superior individual is "hedged in" and encumbered by the weak.

Rivers's ideology of the strong and independent individual is undercut in several ways. First of all, to seize the natural right to self-preservation is, by his own words, to reduce human relationships to those of the beasts in the field. If Rivers wants to set himself up as the new Prince, he succeeds better in portraying himself as a modern Nebuchadnezzar. But the transparent self-deception of his thinking is even more obvious in the fact that his supposedly rationalistic project, as has often been pointed out, is motivated by his passionate desire to make Mortimer "cleave unto" him by inflicting upon Mortimer an isolation similar to his own.[44]

It is, then, Rivers's second unmasking that supplies the play's real Primal Scene. If *The Borderers* proposes a model of the social contract, its paradigm is the repeated crime of abandonment rather than Rivers's theory of justice. The central "spot" of the play's social and political theme is the tiny island on which Rivers abandoned his captain:

> 'Twas a spot—
> Methinks I see it now—how in the sun
> Its stony surface glittered like a shield:
> It swarmed with shapes of life scarce visible;
> And in that miserable place we left him—
> A giant body mid a world of beings
> Not one of which could give him any aid,
> Living or dead.
>
> (4.2.37–44)

The final chilling phrase, "living or dead," serves amply to distinguish this act of abandonment from revolutionary violence *per se*. The crew has not simply deprived the captain of his life. They have also denied him a funeral or burial. Whereas murder, or ritual sacrifice, would have snapped off the captain's consciousness of himself while preserving his corpse as the spectacular symbol of the revolutionary social body, marooning the captain abandons him entirely to himself while denying him any place at all in the reconstituted community. The crew's crime is even more dehumanizing than Rivers's bestial concept of natural right, because they literally expel the captain from the human species. He becomes a "giant body," not in the sense provided by allusion to Hobbes's leviathan, but rather by the precise opposite, the absolute impossibility of any social contract or "aid" delivering him from his natural tormentors. The specific character of this crime, then, decisively shifts the theme of violence away from analogy to regicide (as Erdman would render it) and toward the sphere of social responsibility, the sphere plotted in Wordsworth's contemporary work by the predicament of the poor and the outcast. The marooned captain is far less similar to Louis XVI than to Margaret or the female vagrant.

The captain's isolation also represents the ultimate rendering of the outcast as spectacle. He is abandoned to a world comprised entirely of surfaces. The stony island glitters literally because of its precariousness; the water that glitters on it also threatens to engulf it. But the simile, "like a shield," represents that uncertain surface as a defense against aggression and as a kind of concealment, that is, as precisely what it is not. The shield, like the "giant body," could appropriately allude to a Hobbesian social contract such as Rivers has earlier described, but once again the hint of an allusion is deeply ironic. What the paradoxical simile points to, perhaps, is indeed the social function of abandonment, the constitution of a community (Rivers and the crew) by the spectacular ("glittering") identification of an Other, of the outsider. The simile measures the distance between the spectacle and its spectators, since the island can plausibly be called a "shield" only in the newly born community's reconstruction and legitimation of its foundational act. In this sense, the simile of the shield resembles Rivers's later suggestion that all legitimation is rooted in narcissistic projection: "We are praised by men because they see in us / The image of themselves" (4.2.152–53). The island's glittering, stony surface also reflects the spectators' images; or, more precisely, their construction of its meaning bespeaks both their aggression against the captain and the deception by which the crew masks it and Rivers tries to deny it. The ironically inappropriate simile quite carefully suggests how political violence may entwine itself in the perverse representations of ideological theater.

The paradigmatic power of Rivers's crime has to be confirmed in the play by its repetition. Mortimer's abandonment of Herbert thoroughly undoes Rivers's project and reveals a deeper source of social power and corruption that ambushes Rivers in the very moment of recognition he has so elaborately prepared for Mortimer. At the end of 4.2, Rivers remains thoroughly entrenched in his delusions of grandeur:

> I've joined us by a chain of adamant;
> Henceforth we are fellow-labourers—to enlarge
> The intellectual empire of mankind.
> 'Tis slavery—all is slavery, we receive
> Laws, and we ask not whence those laws have come.
>
> (4.2.187–91)

But his rationalist, individualist concepts of power and law are framed by Mortimer's fascination, not with Rivers's scheme of intellectual liberation, but with the horrible implications of his crime. The strange incoherence of the dialogue in this scene results from the fact that Mortimer barely attends to anything Rivers says after his narration of marooning the captain. Instead he is wrestling

with the awful implications of Rivers's deception at the hands of
the crew, which exacerbates all of his already strong doubts about
the justice of what he has done to Herbert. His own worries are
quite distant from the glories of "intellectual empire." They have
to do with duty, charity, and the reliability of appearances: "Together we propped up his steps, / He leaned upon us both"
(4.2.186–87); "'Twas in his face—I saw it in his face— / I've
crushed the foulest crime" (4.2.194–95). The discrepancy between
Rivers's fantasy of rational power and Mortimer's passionate dependence on the "face" and its authenticity fuels the irony of Rivers's triumphant unmasking: "The seed must be / Hid in the earth
or there can be no harvest; / 'Tis nature's law" (4.2.214–16). Rivers
quickly discovers that the exotic hybrid he thought to raise has
turned out a mere perennial. Yet his declaration of "nature's law"
exercises a strong critical force against Mortimer's faith in the face
of authentic community. What Mortimer saw in Herbert's face was
not spontaneous nature but that which he was prepared to see, that
which would legitimize his own exercise of a violent legal power.
The darkest political implication here is not the failure of rationalist
doctrine but the inexorable, seemingly inevitable (or even "natural") interweaving of spontaneous and passionate bonds with perverted and misconstructed signs. Sociality degenerates into violent
legality in the same moment that vision is corrupted into theater.

But does not the generalization I have just advanced beg the
crucial question of whether Mortimer's misinterpretation of Herbert is really archetypal, comprising a paradigm for the relation of
social or familial bonds to legal and political order as such? Is it
not, on the contrary, simply an extraordinarily perverse mistake,
which measures, by its enormity, the extent of Rivers's degradation
and villainy? The argument advanced here has been that the opposition between the archetypal and the perverse is false to the workings of this play. I have attempted to demonstrate in my exposition
of Wordsworth's use of "spectacle" that he wields Rivers's extraordinary perversity precisely as a way of uncovering an archetypal
"state of nature." The ruling antithesis of the play in this construction of it involves two versions of natural authority: the violent,
individualistic, quasi-Hobbesian brutishness employed in Rivers's
rationalization of his crimes; and the power of Herbert's face and
figure to command sympathy, respect, and assistance. Many readings of *The Borderers* have focused upon the facultative and psychological dimensions of this opposition and have consequently
rendered the play in terms of the moral and political reliability of
intellect versus emotion (for example, as a critique of Godwin) or

as a fable of the emergent self-consciousness of modernity. But the two forms of natural authority correspond to two disparate conceptions of community. This social and political dimension of the play subsumes, without erasing, its moral and psychological argument.[45] Herbert's authority depends upon, even as it predicates, a community of loyalty and an economy of needs and mutual services. Law, in such a community, is given in the very form of its "natural" relationships. Rivers shows Mortimer an economy of rapacious, capitalistic exploitation and greed, and he posits for it an appropriately instrumental concept of law as a medium for the self-interested manipulation and containment of "natural" aggression and violence. The critical force of Rivers's arguments depends not on their validity, however, but rather, first, on the way that his deception is able to distort Mortimer's vision and, second, on the resulting, paradigmatic effects of that distortion. Herbert's fate signifies the insufficiency of the "face" of affection, the nonimmediacy of law, and the intrinsic, perhaps even constitutive, presence of deception, estrangement, abandonment, and isolation within civil society.

When Mortimer abandons Herbert on the heath he means to revert to a primitive form of justice, the trial by ordeal. This notion is consonant with and, in fact, inspired by Herbert's description of himself as a sacred mendicant, relying wholly upon providence for sustenance and strength:

> Like a Mendicant
> Whom no one comes to meet, I stood alone.
> I murmured, but remembering him who feeds
> The pelican and ostrich of the Desert,
> From my own threshold I looked up to heaven,
> And did not want glimmerings of quiet hope.

(3.3.92–97)

Herbert's reliance upon providence acts as a synecdoche for the entire economy of charity and almsgiving and, just as crucially, of familial duty and affection. In a claim that cannot help but recall the equivocal meanings the local housewives assign to the Female Beggar's child, he equates Matilda's "face" with the power of divine assistance: "Her looks won pity from the world—when I had none to help me she brought me food, she was a raven sent to me in the wilderness" (2.3.124–26).[46] Mortimer's decision to abandon Herbert thus implies his full acceptance of such a notion of providence, except, of course, for the truth or falsehood of Herbert's personal claim to God's favor: "My eyes are weak—there is a judge above . . . He heard a voice—a shepherd's lad came / And was his guide—if once—why not again? / And in this desert? If never, then is he damned" (3.3.121, 124–26). The trial by ordeal is, in Mortimer's conception of it, a prelegal form of justice, both antitheatrical in its committing the judical process to the defendant's solitary confrontation of nature and Edenic in its appeal to a face-to-face relationship between man and God. His reliance upon it is a desperate attempt to validate the prepolitical community he professes to protect.

What ends up being put to trial, of course, is more the theory of justice than the criminal. The trial by ordeal is contaminated by legal theater both in its instigation and its result. Mortimer resorts to the trial by ordeal because he cannot decide between Herbert's testimony and Rivers's; that is, he is driven to rely on providence precisely because of the failure in the first place of the "face" as adequate evidence. And what eventuates is, in fact, not providential but rather a predetermined failure of natural affection. This failure is brought about by the status of Mortimer's crime as repetition: Herbert will die, finally, because *Robert* has been incapacitated as a social being.

As Herbert struggles toward the meaningless chapel bell, help does indeed arrive for him, but it comes in the person of Robert, a victim of the violent legal system. Thinking he is casting Herbert onto the mercy of God, Mortimer instead subjects him to the effects of legal justice at the level of their social and emotional crippling of Robert. In Robert the problem of false appearances reaches its most pathetic example. His function is to carry upon and within himself burdens of guilt and isolation that are entirely social in their origin. When Robert re-enters the stage at 4.3 (the first scene at the peasant's cottage) his first concern is to wash the bloodstains from his frock, because he is afraid of being accused of murdering Herbert (4.3.23–24). The blood is not his, the crime is not his, but the blood and the crime define the boundaries of his situation. Robert himself delineates that situation in some of the play's most poignant lines:

> I am in poverty
> And know how busy are the tongues of men.
> My heart was willing, Sir, but I am one
> Whose deeds will not stand by their own light.
>
> (5.2.46–49)

The busy tongues of men bear ultimate responsibility (as well as more immediate responsibility, in the persons of Rivers and the

Female Beggar) for Herbert's abandonment, because they have disfigured Robert's human face. The point of the scene at 4.3.23–102 between Robert and his wife, Margaret, is not just to narrate the way in which Robert has felt himself forced to repeat the crime of abandonment, but even more to show how the man and wife are inexorably set against one another by the effects of his false imprisonment. Public corruption proceeds into the private, just as the execution scene at the end of *Adventures on Salisbury Plain* asserts. Thus Robert interprets Matilda's presence as his wife's betrayal of him (4.3.96): even the reconstitution of the familial bond between Herbert and Matilda seems doomed to repeat the pattern of betrayal and isolation.

The theoretical sequence being sketched and resketched can be constructed as follows, then. In the beginning there is the human community, held together by domestic affection, mutual needs, and sympathy. Social interaction seems inevitably theatrical, however, so that the quasi-natural appeal and authority of the human face is constantly coming into conflict with the busy, often self-interested constructions of the tongues of men. Theatricality generates institutionalized power and ritual ceremony. That is, the community formalizes social interaction in the hope that these rigid forms will perpetuate the true community. But this very formalization necessitates the casting out of falsehood, the purgation of parasites, the identification and spectacular isolation of the Other who contaminates us. Thus the transition from the state of nature to the civil society is predicated upon violence precisely because of the instability that already infects human sociality in the natural community; this is finally the sense in which "The world is poisoned at the heart." Civil order is an institutional form of defense against one's neighbor (Hobbes was right, according to *The Borderers*); but rather than monopolizing violence, it invents violence in order to dismember itself, to make itself strong by excising falsehood and weakness (Hobbes was right for the wrong reasons). Thus the proper symbol of legal and political order is not the prince but the outcast, the scar, as it were, of the violent act that transfers the power of social cohesiveness from its authentic source to its civil representatives.

In act 5, Mortimer achieves whatever heroic stature the tragedy affords by attracting to himself and, so to speak, interweaving all the failures of justice with an absolute refusal to deny the ultimate compatibility of the claims of civil society and natural humanity. Robert's plight repeats itself in a finer tone when Mortimer finds himself unable even to put himself on trial, because Matilda persists in interpreting the evidence of his face in her own way, even against his own confession that he has murdered her father (5.3.97–120). Yet Mortimer walks through the final scene as obsessed as ever with justice and with his demand for the public exposition of truth: "I'll prove it that I murdered him—I'll prove it / Before the dullest court in Christendom" (5.3.180–81). He concludes the play by recasting the scheme of admonitory and purifying public execution he envisioned for Herbert in the trial sequence of 2.3, only with himself as the sacrificial victim: "Raise on this lonely Heath a monument / That may record my story for warning" (5.3.262–63). Meanwhile he condemns himself to an endless pilgrimage centered on the shrine he cannot return to, the monument to his crime. "No human ear shall ever hear my voice, / No human dwelling ever give me food" (5.3.267–68): even as he mimics Herbert's pilgrimage, he will also repeat the isolation of the marooned captain. On the one hand, he monumentalizes and institutionalizes himself in the stony surface of his narrative; and on the other, his attempt to restore social order uncannily repeats the victimization and casting out of the betrayed, deceived carrier of guilt.

6

Framing *The Ruined Cottage*

WORDSWORTH'S CONFIDENCE IN THE POLITICAL VIRTUE OF THE party of reason reaches a crisis in *The Borderers* from which it never recovers. When he eventually returns to the discourse of republicanism, his concern with sympathy, humanitarianism, the domestic affections, and local attachment points the way toward an emergent nationalism rather than back toward radical rationalism. As the reading of *The Borderers* just offered suggests, however, a more difficult philosophical crisis was facing Wordsworth in 1797 than a shift away from the discourse of natural rights and toward the conventions of second nature. The deepest problem presented by *The Borderers* is that sympathetic virtue and the act of storytelling are inextricably enmeshed with theatricality and social alienation there. Although in *The Prelude* Wordsworth attributes his recovery from his crisis of moral despair to the healing influences of nature and his domestic circle, particularly Dorothy Wordsworth, the evidence provided by Wordsworth's first great, mature poem, *The Ruined Cottage,* suggests that such healing was also a difficult process worked out, and to some extent never resolved, in the act of writing itself.

A PROBLEM OF CONTAINMENT

The public result of that long process was *The Excursion,* published in 1814. Wordsworth's most perceptive contemporaries found much to be dissatisfied with in *The Excursion.*[1] Percy Bysshe Shelley closed the preface to his new poem, "Alastor; or, the Spirit of Solitude" (dated 14 December 1815), by quoting Wordsworth's apparent spokesman in book 1: "The good die first, / And those whose hearts are dry as summer dust, / Burn to the socket!"[2] Shelley's deeply antagonistic gesture twists the storytelling Wanderer's exclamation of grief for Margaret, the subject of his tale, into a confession of Wordsworth's spiritual and political apostasy. The "good," in the context Shelley supplies, means primarily "the Poet" who is the central character in Shelley's complex allegory of desire and sympathy; but it clearly refers as well to the poet of the *Lyrical Ballads* and the *Poems in Two Volumes* of 1807. Shelley is accusing the author of *The Excursion* of having allowed what was vital in his poetry to become dessicated. Shelley's *Alastor* volume thus initiates the critical tradition that condemns *The Excursion* as the onset of Wordsworth's anticlimax. At the source of this evaluation lies his identification of Wordsworth's creative decrepitude with political apostasy.[3]

One might be tempted, in the late twentieth century, to broaden Shelley's irony so as to indict Wordsworth's obsessive and ultimately suffocating revisions of *The Ruined Cottage*. The poem's tortured manuscript history was, after all, the immediate occasion of Jonathan Wordsworth's now-famous assertion, "On the whole poets are known by the best versions of their works: Wordsworth is almost exclusively known by the worst."[4] Like Shelley, Jonathan Wordsworth set out to rescue the young Wordsworth from the older one, and *The Music of Humanity* succeeded in canonizing "the good" *Ruined Cottage* text of Ms. D, which is now read far more often than the "dry as summer dust" version in book 1 of *The Excursion*. How far Jonathan Wordsworth's aesthetic judgment coincides with Shelley's political one raises the central issue of much current critical debate: the relationship (for example, of dependence, determinacy, autonomy, homology) between politics and art, or, more generally, the ideological and the aesthetic.

This issue has dominated the best critical discussions of *The Ruined Cottage* over the last decade, because the substitution of Ms. D for book 1 of *The Excursion* has brought *The Ruined Cottage* very much into the center of the attempt to re-evaluate the Romantic ideology by relocating Shelleyan accusations of Wordsworth's apostasy to the crucial moment of Wordsworth's career represented by his work on *The Ruined Cottage* in early 1798. Jerome McGann writes that the poem enacts the "subtle transformation of Wordsworth's 1793–4 world—including the social and political discontents which dominated his life at that time—into the changed world of 1797–8. . . . [T]he story of Margaret produces in the narrator a sense of shame and humiliation before great suffering, and an overflow of sympathy and love for the sufferer rather than, as in 1793–4, a sense of outrage, and an overflow of angry judgment upon those whom Wordsworth at the time held accountable." This displacement of outrage by sympathy is patently and paradigmatically ideological, McGann argues, because of its strong individual-ization of a social and political problem. The poem displaces politics inward into psychology, thereby preventing the reader from considering Margaret's suffering in social or economic terms.[5] James Chandler, comparing *The Ruined Cottage* to *Salisbury Plain,* also stresses the disappearance of explicit political themes. According to Chandler, Wordsworth's strategy is so thorough that Margaret's tragedy finally "leaves us with no sense whatever of human complicity in the causes of her suffering and death." This erasure of politics clears the slate for "the agenda of [Words-worth's] emerging literary program," that is, his advocacy of "natu-ral education" and "natural culture."[6] Alan Liu and Marjorie Levinson both locate paradigmatic strategies of resisting historical reference in *The Ruined Cottage.* Although Liu writes of the "im-age" and Levinson the "fragment," their analyses are remarkably similar: the effect of the poem's central symbol, the overgrown ruin, is to "erase the appearance of labor,"[7] to remake "the relation between persons and artifacts" into "a bond of affiliative vision—of 'convenient' and sympathetic imagery—rather than of labor."[8] Such analyses recast as a political issue what has been a recurrent complaint about *The Ruined Cottage* from Thomas Dequincey to Cleanth Brooks.[9] The complaint, primarily a moral stricture but also an aesthetic one involving the poem's structure and tone, has concerned the pedlar's "humanity" or rather his lack of it—his "capitalization upon inhumanity," as Alan Liu puts it.[10] What comes through all of these readings, from Shelley to Liu, is the cry that Margaret's tragedy is more disturbing, more terrible, than the frame tale acknowledges it to be.

The poem's manuscript history seems to testify that Wordsworth himself felt the same discomfort with his poem. Once the tale of Margaret was completed, Wordsworth left it nearly untouched in all subsequent revisions. But he rewrote the tale's frame over and over, at first expanding the biography of the storytelling pedlar and generating a lengthy philosophical consolation speech, then cutting the pedlar's biography and devising a much shorter scene of in-struction between the storyteller and the poem's narrator, and fi-nally returning biography, philosophical harangue, scene of instruction, in fact everything he had not already transferred to *The Prelude,* to a framework of epic pretentions in *The Excursion.* Something about the tale of Margaret, its power, both resists direct revision and demands that Wordsworth frame it, contain it, tran-scend it. Yet all Wordsworth's attempts to do so prove unsatisfactory.

Wordsworth's work on framing the tale of Margaret was, none-theless, enormously fecund. Passages describing the pedlar (Ms. B, 5r, 147) and declaring his ideas about storytelling (Ms. B, 29r, 223) represent early statements of the poetics of the "Preface to *Lyrical Ballads*."[11] The biography of the pedlar generates some of the earliest and best passages of *The Prelude*. The entire effort to build a philosophical frame around the spectacle of human suffer-ing is intimately bound up with *The Recluse*. Indeed the composi-tional history of *The Ruined Cottage* is a miniature of the compositional history of *The Recluse* as Kenneth R. Johnston re-counts it, in the sense that Wordsworth's attempts to place the problem of social suffering in the framework of his grand scheme more successfully produce a poetry of personal crisis, narrating the poet's struggle with the theme, than a reconciliation of public and private perspectives.[12] Yet so much grows from Wordsworth's struggle to frame the tale of Margaret that it is as if the major projects of the most vital phase of his career are all generated as ways of putting this tragic narrative to rest.

For these reasons, no other poem attests so well as *The Ruined Cottage* to the problem at the core of Wordsworth's social vision. The problem is not adequately articulated in the observations that Wordsworth's earlier political commitments are displaced or that historical reference yields to the blandishments of organicism, be-cause the poem's significance has very little to do with the way political and historical issues are swept into the background.[13] On the contrary, Wordsworth's difficulty has to do with reconciling his intensely conceived social tragedy's implicit, but nonetheless piercing, political theme with the formal demands of his frame, demands that escalate into a veritable ritual. But this tension be-tween the narrative and its frame derives from an interrelated group of social circumstances: from the economy that separates the scene of narration and vision from the sufferings of the poor; from the distance that allows the spectators to sublimate the bitter, hopeless, meaningless suffering of the objects of their sympathy into a scene of self-recognition; and from the fact that two men eventually come together over the dead body of a woman. The poem's tensions attest to the incommensurability of passion and compassion, of tragedy and elegy. The paradoxical success of *The Ruined Cottage* is that, on the one hand, the tale of Margaret virtu-ally apotheosizes the historical class struggle in the humble linea-ments of common, domestic tragedy; but, on the other, the frame tale finds itself endlessly and unwillingly repeating Margaret's own failure to complete the act of mourning her losses.

THE TALE OF MARGARET, 1797

There are three major versions of the poem nowadays usually called *The Ruined Cottage*.[14] The earliest known version, the one Wordsworth read to Coleridge when Coleridge visited Racedown in early June 1797, survives only in fragments. In January–March, 1798, at Alfoxden, Wordsworth expanded the earlier version into a 528-line poem called *The Ruined Cottage,* which is preserved in a fair-copy manuscript, Ms. B. This poem can be called version 2a in order to distinguish it from version 2b, the closely related *Ruined Cottage* of Ms. D, 1799. Before producing 2b in 1799, however, Wordsworth had already, in March, 1798, surrounded 2a with additions that swell it to some 900 lines. This third version, 3a, is the proper ancestor of versions 3b and 3c: *The Pedlar* of 1803–4 (Ms. E) and "The Wanderer" of 1806, book 1 of *The Excusion.* The changing title reflects a shift of emphasis noted as early as 5 March 1798 by Dorothy Wordsworth: "The Pedlar's character now makes a very, certainly the *most,* considerable part of the poem."[15] The difference between the earliest version and versions 2a and 2b probably involves a similar shift of emphasis, away from the balanced portraits of Robert and Margaret and toward a poem that plays the tale of Margaret and Robert against a countermovement in the frame. Version 3 turns this formal symmetry back in the direction of balancing extended portraits of two characters, Margaret and the pedlar, against one another. The entire sequence can be sketched as follows (cf. Appendix):

1 (1797): Robert / Margaret
↻
2a (1798): frame / tale → 2b (1799)
↻
3a (1798): pedlar / Margaret → 3b (1803–4) → 3c (1806)

Any reconstruction of version 1 entails a certain amount of speculation, complicated by the impossibility of saying for sure whether Wordsworth continued to work on the poem between June 1797 and the period of intense composition at Alfoxden that produced Ms. B. Nonetheless, two distinct possibilities present themselves concerning the poem that was the basis for Wordsworth's revisions in early 1798. Jonathan Wordsworth, on the one hand, by simply eliminating from the 528-line text of Ms. B its opening—the history of the Pedlar—and the transition between parts one and two (all of which can confidently be assigned to 1798), supposes that a 370–400-line version was completed in 1797.[16] On the other hand, John Alban Finch guesses at a 174-line poem.[17] Despite the inconclusiveness of the textual evidence, there are important critical and interpretive differences between the speculations positing the longer and the shorter versions. These differences have to do with the narration of Margaret's decay by way of the Pedlar's four visits to the cottage. Either these passages were composed at about the same time as the framing devices of the opening and the transition between parts one and two in 2a, as Finch's theory would imply; or, as Jonathan Wordsworth supposes, the visits were composed earlier and separately and have, therefore, a less intimate relation to the frame. Although the evidence that led Finch to make such a precise estimate of the length of the 1797 version proved to be mistaken,[18] nonetheless the case for a 1797 poem of approximately two hundred lines remains strong because, first, it takes into account all the material that can confidently be assigned to 1797 and, second, it is lent credibility by the fair copy in the Christabel notebook, which consists of two passages of thirty-four and sixty-three lines, with space left between them for "perhaps 74"[19] more, and with some space left at the beginning as well. In fact, there is no direct evidence for positing the longer version prior to the revisionary work of early 1798; and to do so tends to obscure the full political and ideological force of those revisions. It is important, then, to try to imagine what the shorter 1797 poem might have looked like.

If we arrange the surviving materials of 1797 so as to fill the central lacuna in the Christabel notebook fair copy,[20] the result is a poem that opens with an encounter between an "old man" and a "stranger" at the ruined cottage (Christabel NB, 3r, Coleridge's letter to John Estlin, 10 June 1797). The old man mournfully compares the ruin's present state to the domestic happiness of its former inhabitants, and then he tells their story (Christabel NB, 3r–3v; Ms. A). He gives about equal time to the mental decay and desertion of Robert and to the mental decay and death of Margaret. (There are about fifty lines on Robert in Ms. A, to which we must add the lines on the desertion drafted in the Racedown NB; nearly sixty lines on Margaret's decay can be inferred from Christabel NB, 4v–5v). The story has the structure of a diptych. The left panel, devoted to Robert, illustrates, first in a general way, how the poor are uprooted and scattered abroad by economic and political causes: "Two blighting seasons" and "the plague of war" bring on "hard times," so that "of the poor did many cease to be / And their place knew them not" (Ms. A, 83, 87). The picture is completed by the excruciating close-up of Robert's unemployment, disease, and nervous imbalance, climaxing in his selling himself to the army (Ms. A; Racedown NB, 5v, 8r). The right panel, Margaret's, hammers home the themes of victimization and the ruination of the virtuous poor. The whole poem renders quite poignantly the cottage weavers' vulnerability to economic disorders and the way the military's opportunistic purchase of manpower destroys the very basis of a healthy community. The most telling details of all, however, concern the way the couple internalizes political corruption. Their economic catastrophe poisons their love for one another, not by destroying it, but by transforming its very persistence into a "reckless" abandonment of home and children.

The point of this poem is the violation of the *material basis* of Robert's and Margaret's virtue. It says that in contemporary England poverty is an excuse for theft: the thief is the government, and the stolen goods are the souls of the poor. The poem argues, not didactically, but by powerful mimetic representation of the problem, that poverty produces indolence and vice rather than being the deserved fate of the indolent and the vicious. Even in this truncated version, the tale of Margaret is already one of Wordsworth's most powerful exercises of sympathetic understanding for the victims of England's decaying cottage industry.

In the Fenwick note to *The Excursion* Wordsworth says that the first passage he composed was the account of Margaret's decline that comes after the pedlar's last visit to her in later versions of the poem. The lines Coleridge copied into a letter to John Estlin on 10 June 1797 comprise the last three-fourths of this passage. These lines deserve special attention because they are the earliest finished lines of the poem available to us and because we have Wordsworth's testimony that they are, in fact, the kernel from which the rest of the poem grew. What is most impressive about the Estlin text is its remarkable degree of uniformity with all later versions of the passage, which tends to corroborate the status of this vignette as the core of *The Ruined Cottage*. The closing lines about Margaret, "reckless and alone," buffeted by winter storms in her ruined cottage, are a perhaps not very unusual example of the commonplace figure of the abandoned female.[21] The more impressive and original moment comes earlier and leads directly into the conflicts Wordsworth would concentrate upon later:

> her eye
> Was busy in the distance, shaping things
> That made her heart beat quick. See'st thou that path?

(The green-sward now has broken its grey line;)
There, to and fro she paced, through many a day
Of the warm summer: from a belt of flax
That girt her waist, spinning the long-drawn thread
With backward steps.

The contrast between foreground and distance articulates the pathetic incompatibility between Margaret's indomitable hope and her economic servitude. The foreground image of Margaret literally bound to her place suggests the restriction of perspective that, in Ms. A, leads the narrator to conflate economic hardship and political injustice under the category of what "pleased Heaven" (83). But the imaginary fulfillment that Margaret sees everywhere in the distance cuts against such resignation, implying instead that a bitter authorial irony might be asking what sort of "Heaven" could take pleasure in these events.

The quality of Margaret's hope cannot be disentangled from the narrator's questionable reliability. The narrator's eyes, like Margaret's, are "busy . . . shaping things"; and Margaret's labor is likewise matched by the narrator's "spinning the long-drawn thread" of the tale itself.[22] Margaret's repetitious pacing to and fro, under a compulsion both economic and psychological, inscribes her history on the landscape. The narrator's peculiar gift is his capacity to read her writing ("See'st thou that path?"); but the story may also express his own psychological and economic necessities. This entwinement of compulsion, repetition, writing, vision, and narration will be magnified in 1798.

The fragment's last lines signal that such concerns have already achieved a self-reflexive status at this stage of composition, however: "And, Stranger, here / In sickness she remained, and here she died, / —Last human tenant of these ruined walls." Here the poem mimics an inscription, and the narrator becomes momentarily transparent, as if the ruined walls themselves bore the writing that addresses the passing stranger. Although *The Ruined Cottage* could not have been simply an inscription in June of 1797 (it makes no sense for a wall to ask the "stranger," "See'st thou that path?"), the description of Margaret certainly bears sustained comparison to that of the solitary man in Wordsworth's contemporaneous inscription, "Lines Left upon a Seat in a Yew-tree, Which Stands near the Lake of Esthwaite, on a Desolate Part of the Shore, Commanding a Beautiful Prospect" (LB 47–50):

Stranger! these gloomy boughs
Had charms for him; and here he loved to sit,
. . . .

> Fixing his downcast eye, he many an hour
> A morbid pleasure nourished, tracing here
> An emblem of his own unfruitful life:
> And lifting up his head, he then would gaze
> On the more distant scene;
>
> . . . .
>
>   and so, lost man!
> On visionary views would fancy feed,
> Till his eyes streamed with tears. In this deep vale
> He died, this seat his only monument.
>
>   (21–22, 27–31, 40–43)[23]

Although Margaret is pathetic and persevering while the yew-tree solitary is indulgent and self-pitying, both are afflicted by "visionary views," and the pathos of both their situations arises from a sharply drawn contrast between the sympathetic community they shape in the distance and the actual abandonment and isolation closer at hand. (The solitary egotistically reads his own situation as the world's abandonment of him.) This contrast is echoed formally in the two poems by a self-conscious distance between telling stories about isolated people and the solitary act of reading their traces on things.

This formal dichotomy appears in an exaggerated way in the two fragments usually associated with the early composition of *The Ruined Cottage,* titled "The Baker's Cart" (RC&P 463–67) and "Incipient Madness" (RC&P 468–75). "The Baker's Cart" is a sketch of a poor family whom the baker's cart passes by "as if / [They] were not born to live." Wordsworth, as usual, emphasizes the psychological effect this neglect has on the family's mother, whose "look and voice":

>   bespoke a mind
> Which being long neglected and denied
> The common food of hope was now become
> Sick and extravagant—by strong access
> Of momentary pangs driv'n to that state
> In which all past experience melts away
> And the rebellious heart to its own will
> Fashions the laws of nature.

This close-up portrait of a member of the potentially revolutionary crowd is clearly sympathetic, because the poem firmly assigns responsibility for her "sick and extravagant" desire to dereliction of duty by the economically privileged rather than to her own ingratitude, thoughtlessness, or overweaning ambition. Yet, as is so often the case in the poetry of Racedown, a diagnosis of the social body's disease lies beyond the capabilities of the poem's narrator, who speaks directly to the suffering woman as an equal and attentively reads the story written on her face: "The words were simple, but her look and voice / Made up their meaning."

"The Baker's Cart" is most likely an immediate predecessor of *The Ruined Cottage,* while "Incipient Madness" may well be generated out of a failed attempt to characterize the narrator of Ms. A.[24] "Incipient Madness," by focusing on the mental state of the narrator viewing the ruined cottage rather than on the plight of its former inhabitants, certainly points toward most of the later development of *The Ruined Cottage.* Both fragments concern "sick and extravagant" desire, but, where "The Baker's Cart" is about hunger and hope, "Incipient Madness" is about grief. Yet Wordsworth portrays grief as a form of hunger as well. The narrator of "Incipient Madness" fetishizes a "broken pane of glass which glitter'd in the moon," explicitly calling it a substitute for the mother's breast:

> There is a mood,
> A settled temper of the heart, when grief,
> Become an instinct, fastening on all things
> That promise food, doth like a sucking babe
> Create it where it is not. From this time
> I found my sickly heart had tied itself
> Even to this speck of glass.

The point is not just that, like a baby putting a toy in its mouth, he uses the glass to satisfy a displaced desire, but also that he really does draw consolation from an object where it exists only because of his demand, just as the suckling babe's demand produces the mother's milk.

A psychoanalytic reading of these lines is inescapable for modern readers. The danger of grief is its severely regressive power, since the desire (libido) one has detached from the beloved dead person may bring about a return of the primary desire to be at one with the mother and therefore to identify with the beloved, to lose one's individuality in death. The "speck of glass" here performs an anaclitic function, then; the griever needs something (anything!) to attach libido to. The metaphoric exchange of "glass" for "breast" defers a drive toward death.[25] The narrator's compulsion to repeat his visits to the ruin is morbid, again indicating the strength of primary desire or death instinct, but it is also the first indication in the manuscript history of *The Ruined Cottage* of the poem's most remarkable technical achievement—the device of the pedlar's visits—which produces the slow-motion description of Margaret's decline. "Incipient Madness" is crucial to the history of *The Ruined Cottage,* then, because it seems to open the way to Wordsworth's extremely canny submission of tragic narrative to an essentially lyrical, elegiac impulse. "Incipient Madness" implies (if only as deviance implies a norm) that the act of *reading* the traces of lost community can become a form of therapy for the survivor.

Wordsworth's lifelong interest in inscriptions and epitaphs is obvious, and Geoffrey Hartman makes an important connection between inscriptions and Romantic lyric poetry, especially Wordsworth's, in one of his finest essays, "Wordsworth, Inscriptions, and Romantic Nature Poetry." According to Hartman, the oddly elegiac tone that haunts so many of Wordsworth's lyrics has to do with its emergence from and purification of the inscription: "[Wordsworth] frees the inscription from its dependence, he gives it weight and power of its own, by incorporating in addition to a particular scene the very process of inscribing or interpreting it. . . . A secondary consciousness of death and change associates itself with the very act of writing."[26] The manuscript history of *The Ruined Cottage* implies that this "secondary consciousness of death and change" is fundamentally political and social rather than metaphysical or psychological. That is, it is more accurate to say that, in the poems we have been considering, a primary consciousness of personal isolation and a wounded sense of community—a pathos closely associated with and to some extent conflating the situations of Rivers and Mortimer—overflows onto the acts of reading, writing, and narrating. Wordsworth's lyricism would then appear not as a purification of the inscription, but as the result of a difficult transference of his emotional investment in interpersonal narrative to a visionary encounter between person and thing: the "face" of kinship exchanged for prosopopoeia.

This lyrical transference is crucial to *The Ruined Cottage* in all its versions. The project of representing a lost relation between persons as a consolatory relation between persons and things dominates the framing of Margaret's tragedy. The transformation of anger into sympathy that McGann describes in *The Ruined Cottage* resembles closely, and not coincidentally, the early stages of grief and its displacement into conventionalized expression. Both Liu and Levinson describe how the "riches" associated with the Pedlar's vision and the consolatory powers of vegetation substitute a symbolic economy for the monetary one that has failed Margaret.[27] Such highly conventional elegiac images derive their emotional value from the grief they transmute, which is to say that they are valorized precisely by the *work* of mourning. This is the work of turning away, of troping one's loss and one's anger by giving it a representation that covers over the loss. The objects of the elegist's vision are not so much substitutes or surrogates for the dead as they are palimpsests, and the landscape of *The Ruined Cottage* is one of the great examples of this generic property of elegiac imagery. The change in tone McGann describes can be restated, then, as the process by which Wordsworth assimilates the poem of protest to a highly original form of the pastoral elegy. If the later poem apparently hopes to frame the earlier version's stunning representation of the material contingency of sanity and virtue with a network of lyrical imagery, the function of the frame is essentially elegiac.

Some lines written in the margin of "The Baker's Cart" recapitulate the developing tension between protest and elegy. The lines describe the poor woman's manner as she speaks in "a low and fearful voice":

> by misery and rumination deep
> Tied to dead things and seeking sympathy
> In stocks and stones.

> (467)

On the one hand, these lines capture the emotional desperation that accompanies the woman's poverty. Considered as protest poetry, their strategy is directly descended from, but considerably more powerful than, a similar passage in the *Letter to Llandaff*: "Mr Burke rouzed the indignation of all ranks of men, when by a refinement in cruelty superiour to that which in the East yokes the living to the dead he strove to persuade us that we and our posterity to the end of time were riveted to a constitution by the indissoluble compact of a dead parchment, and were bound to cherish a corse at the bosom, when reason might call aloud that it should be entombed" (PrW1 48). The ridicule of Burkean folly has disappeared in 1797, and the barely suppressed comparison of the oppressed to a mother (whom the oratorical Wordsworth rationally corrects) attempting to nurse a dead child yields to closer, more sensitive observation. On the other hand, however, the woman "seeking sympathy / In stocks and stones" anticipates the pedlar's speech on elegy in Ms. B: "The Poets in their elegies and songs / Lamenting the departed call the groves / They call upon hills and streams to mourn / And senseless rocks, nor idly" (19v, 195). In Ms. B Wordsworth asserts that poets' invocation of dead things to compensate for the absence of dead persons bespeaks a "strong creative power" (19v, 195), but the problematic status of poetic sympathy emerges when he anxiously deflects the unstated accusation that the poets' labors are mere idleness.

TALE AND FRAME, 1798–1814

The two-part structure of the 528-line *Ruined Cottage* composed in early 1798 reflects the earlier balance of Robert's and Margaret's stories, but the diptych has been replaced by something different. Now the most important formal structure of the poem involves the relation between the tale and its frame. Instead of two parallel character studies, the poem now offers a contrast between Community Lost in the tales of Robert and Margaret, and Community Regained in the act of telling their story. In other words, the new poem dissolves the inscription into its elements—the inscribed events and the place of the beholder (the "stranger") whom the inscription summons—refashioning the structural balance between the portraits of Robert and Margaret into an opposition between the decaying relationship of Robert and Margaret and the bond the story itself forms between the narrator and the pedlar. As a result, on the one hand, the elegiac mode of the frame is motivated by the priority of the cottagers' deaths to the narrative situation, but, on the other hand, the tale of loss is embedded within a much more self-consciously antithetical account of recovering, memorializing, and sharing it.

An obvious implication of this model is that the theme of community regained offers a broader perspective than the theme of loss. Storytelling itself becomes a mode of healing in version 2a, as it is in *Adventures on Salisbury Plain;* and the progress of the narrator in "The Discharged Soldier" from spectator to interlocutor offers an exactly contemporaneous, comparably complex example of the beneficial effects of an embedded story on the listener. 2a, "The Discharged Soldier," and "The Old Cumberland Beggar" cohere in that all three show how an authentic community recognizes itself precisely by converting the appearance of unintelligibility or uselessness into a "bond of brotherhood" (Ms. B 20r, 197). But, as Johnston says of these 1798 *Recluse* poems, "each . . . is a scene of tragic recognition *for the narrators rather than the sufferers.*"[28] The philosophical consolation speech given to the pedlar in 3a begins, "Not useless do I deem / These quiet sympathies with things that hold / An inarticulate language" (Ms. B 46r, 261): the soothing power of such sympathies is not shared by the inarticulate Cumberland beggar or the dead weavers, Robert and Margaret. The dissolution of the inscription into story and meditation seems to create a new, perhaps unintentional, gulf between the storytellers and the characters. This gulf renders silent the whole problem explored in *The Borderers,* where narrative can actively *destroy* community. That is, privileging the healing powers of the pedlar's narrative over its distressing contents ends up emphasizing the distance between social responsibility and aesthetic response, substituting catharsis for responsibility.[29] Thus, the theme of community regained ends up nonetheless rehearsing a variety of alienation, which can be measured in the difference between the community that is restored and the one that was lost.

The differences between these communities have to do with the anxieties of poetic vocation and with the problematic articulation of sympathy across class boundaries. Wordsworth's sense of belonging to a poetic community was greatly enhanced by the close friendship he enjoyed with Coleridge after his move to Alfoxden in July 1797. Coleridge's impact on Wordsworth is obvious in the direction Wordsworth's philosophic ambitions take in the 1798 poem, for instance, in the pantheistic passages about the pedlar's youth.[30] Wordsworth's use of Robert Burns's "Epistle to J. L*****k" as an epigraph to 2a signals a strong sense of membership in a northern poetic tradition allied to nature and the common man:

> Give me a spark of nature's fire,
> Tis the best learning I desire.
> .   .   .   .
> My Muse though homely in attire
> May touch the heart.

Invoking Burns's "homely attire" in this context seems to link poets and weavers.[31] Burns's emphasis on feeling and on "nature's fire," and his disdain for "learning," all indicate attitudes similar to ones later announced in the "Preface to *Lyrical Ballads.*" Wordsworth invokes Burns as a kind of metaphor for his own persona ("You wha ken hardly *verse* frae *prose*") and, by analogy, assimilates the pedlar to John Lapraik, whose songs "thirled the heartstrings through the breast."[32]

Wordsworth's poem, however, is far more heavily fraught with anxieties about the efficacy of the poetic vocation than with the boisterous and gregarious goodwill of Burns's epistle. The pedlar interrupts his tale with a question about the ethics of narrative, and his self-confident assertion that there is "A power to virtue friendly" (Ms. B 29r, 223) in recounting tales of suffering by no means clearly overcomes the hints of voyeurism and indolence implied by his similarity to the "dreaming man" in the opening scenario (Ms. B 2r–3r, 137–39). Indeed, these hints are highlighted in the continuation of his speech: ". . . were't not so / I am a dreamer among men—indeed / An idle dreamer" (Ms. B 29r, 223). Such anxieties no doubt express an ambivalent disaffection from the political world similar to Coleridge's in his letter of 10 March 1798 to his brother George. They are also economic, expressing doubts about the kind of work a poet does as opposed to a weaver. Perhaps the act of storytelling seems too much like an abdication of the moral responsibility to *do* something about the suffering caused by economic inequality and political injustice.[33]

Anxieties about indolence and voyeurism are the anxieties of spectators. Much of what is problematic about *The Ruined Cottage* arises from the way the narrator-pedlar community seems to constitute itself by appropriating the suffering of Robert and Margaret and above all by taking possession of Margaret's visual image and reproducing or regenerating its passionate power. This appropriation abstracts and sublimates Margaret's domesticity into "Colours & forms of a strange discipline" (Ms. B 43v, 257). The problem with Wordsworth's sympathy for the suffering poor is that it seems too much like a kind of poetic "discipline" focused on a limited range of "simple" objects: abandoned women, old beggars, war veterans, cast-out servants, children. His poetic appropriation of these objects seems to depend less on his ability to remove himself from the harsh emotions attendant upon their sufferings than on the considerable social distance that already separates him from them. The ideology that represents this movement as transcendence, purification, elevation of the contingent to the profound and universal is actually a way of explaining away the socioeconomic distance that makes possible this form of sympathetic meditation. The ideology assimilates the spectacle of lower-class suffering to the gentlemanly skill of apprehending landscape views, but at the same time it turns that cultural skill into something apparently natural, perceptual, prelinguistic.

It is no accident, then, that the narrative situation of 2a should generate the first myth of "love of nature leading to love of man" in the pedlar's biography in 3a:

The Ocean and the earth beneath him lay
In gladness and deep joy. The clouds were touched
And in their silent faces did he read
Unutterable joy.

(Ms. B 9r, 157)

Peter Manning, who reads "Incipient Madness" as the "germ" of *The Ruined Cottage* and lays heavy emphasis on images of orality and nursing, interprets this passage as a screen for a repressed nursing image and argues that the "Blessed the infant Babe" lines in the 1799 *Prelude* uncover the "real" meaning of such passages.[34] Rather than reducing the Ms. B lines to a distorted version of a real meaning found elsewhere, the reading offered here connects the images of nursing in "Incipient Madness" or of the "silent faces" of the clouds in Ms. B to an explicit thematics of community worked out most fully in *The Borderers* and refashioned in the pedlar's visionary relationship with nature in early 1798. Here the elegiac substitution of things for persons is actually celebrated as nature's gift to the pedlar. The ideological character of this gift is apparent above all in its presentation as virtual common sense: ". . . nor did he *believe*—he saw" (Ms. B 10r, 159). Nowhere is the chasm separating *The Borderers* from the pedlar's biography more clear. Yet both inhabit a sequence of related moments that all concern the theme of community: beginning with the oppositions between private and public perspectives in the *Salisbury Plain* poems; developed into the tension between commercial interaction and familial or popular bonding and between theatricality and spontaneity in *The Borderers;* then reworked into an attempt to ground community in the pedlar's rural sensorium, thereby making the private and familial world into a prelinguistic but universal one; and finally, as we will see below, turning in the "Blessed the infant Babe" lines to the child's bond with the nursing mother as a scene of primary self-recognition.

This context makes it even more remarkable that the revisionary work of early 1798 also makes Margaret a much more powerful character. The pedlar's appropriation of her image in the ideological frame of his vision is only half of what happens; at the same time, Margaret's voice comes through his narrative far more directly. This adds greatly to her stature and virtually makes her into another narrator. In Ms. A, Margaret's speech is reported twice, once directly and once indirectly. In both cases, it is almost as if her speech were inscribed in the locale: "Margaret told me on this very bench"; "Said Margaret to me beneath these trees" (87, 83).

As a narrative source, she is not very clearly differentiated from the ruin and its surroundings. Nothing in Ms. A anticipates the power of her direct speech in 2a:

> "I am changed,
> And to myself," said she, "have done much wrong,
> And to this helpless infant. I have slept
> Weeping, and weeping I have waked; my tears
> Have flowed as if my body were not such
> As others are, and I could never die."
>
> (64)

The combination of her self-recognition and its utter futility in the face of her suffering places Margaret's hope in the realm of *hamartia,* the flaw of a tragic heroine. This elevation of Margaret's character alters everything else in the poem. Thus the original diptych structure of *The Ruined Cottage* is not only displaced by the new importance of the frame in 1798; it is also unbalanced by the drastic increase, in both length and quality, of Margaret's story. Now Robert's decay and desertion are merely preliminaries to the almost superhuman longing which wracks the abandoned Margaret. The intensity of Margaret's speeches changes even the pedlar's sentimental commonplaces—"it moved my very heart"—into appropriately understated responses to a character who speaks so eloquently for herself.

Therefore it is not enough to observe that the expansion of the frame tends to muffle the political themes of virtue and corruption or, more precisely, to twist them toward the apologetic theme of resignation to mortality. For if the expansion of the role of Margaret rather than of Robert testifies to her status as one of those simple objects of compassion commonly appropriated by the voyeuristic sympathy of sentimental meditation, then it becomes all the more striking that Wordsworth gives this pathetic character an extremely convincing tragic dimension. From the point of view of the framing devices, the 1798 poem struggles to reduce the tension between protest and elegy into the unequal partnership of the pathetic object and the sympathetic observer. But if one focuses instead on the strength of Margaret's voice, the frame becomes antiphonal, an elegiac, choral formalization of the raw emotions in the central episodes.

There are thus two quite distinct alternatives present in 2a, each of which Wordsworth tried out in later versions of *The Ruined Cottage.* On the one hand, he could attempt to make the pedlar's sympathy more authoritative, thus making the basis, extent, and quality of his response to suffering into the poem's major theme; or, on the other hand, he could emphasize the antiphonal character of the frame, limiting it to a representation of the very activity of responding. The second alternative is the one chosen in Ms. D, the 1799 text that has been canonized in the last two decades. The first response produces the embellishments that distinguish 3a from 2a and is the one Wordsworth finally pursued in *The Pedlar* and "The Wanderer."

The Ms. D version of *The Ruined Cottage* makes a few very telling changes in 2a. The most important are Wordsworth's excision of the pedlar's biography and his addition of the closing sequence (493–538, adapted partly from Ms. B 21v). The most obvious effect of these changes is to restore the formal symmetry of the original diptych structure. In Ms. D the closing sequence balances the opening encounter between Armytage (as the pedlar is now called) and the narrator, and Armytage's interruption of his tale provides an effective hinge between the two halves of the poem. The other effect of the changes is to make Armytage's character emerge directly from his responses to the scene and his grief over Margaret, rather than from the description of his youth and his profession. Ms. D is altogether more focused than previous versions upon the act of narrative as such, and the one other fairly substantial addition to the poem bears this out. This is the passage on elegy (73–84, from Ms. B 19v–20v).[35] Ms. D is as much a poem about poets and poetry as one about suffering and grief.

The removal of the pedlar's biography from Ms. D no doubt reflects Wordsworth's decision to use some of its best lines in a newer composition, the two-part *Prelude*. Ms. D is very much of a piece with the other great projects of 1798–99. As a crisis-poem on poetic vocation, it is comparable to the two-part *Prelude;* as a poem very firmly focused on grief, it recalls the Lucy and Matthew poems. Its self-conscious meditation on the ethics of narrative also anticipates the "Preface" to *Lyrical Ballads* and poems like "Hart-Leap Well." Its congruence with this dazzling context of poetic achievement surely has much to do with its present canonical status.

If we pursue the metaphor of the diptych with regard to *The Pedlar* of 1803–4 (Ms. E), we must now say that both the Robert-Margaret and the frame-tale pairs have finally been superseded by the opposition of Margaret and the pedlar. Wordsworth achieves this opposition not just by devoting a large portion of the poem to the pedlar's biography, but by making this biography into an *authorization* of the pedlar, an elaborate guarantee of his trustworthiness and wisdom. The unfortunate side effect of this strategy is that it reduces Margaret's downfall into a cautionary tale. Her delusive hope becomes the weakness that allows the pedlar's visionary strength to display itself. The tension between tragedy and elegy weakens into the slack codependence of *exemplum* and hagiography. The later development of the poem into book 1 of *The Excursion* expands this pattern into the full-blown homiletic didacticism of "Despondency Corrected," book 4 of *The Excursion*.

The Excursion also provides an added political context for the scene of narration, however, by echoing the domestic tragedy of Robert and Margaret in the story of the Solitary, who compensates for his own domestic tragedy by throwing himself enthusiastically into the French Revolution. Yet this compensatory relation between political and domestic desire is quite far from the fiercer thematics of 1797. In 1797 domestic virtue is the site of a powerful critique; the deteriorating cottage literally brings home Wordsworth's theme that militarism exploits economic inequality and corrupts the commonwealth. In *The Excursion* politics has retreated to the far side of domesticity. Rather than political corruption penetrating even to the family, now Wordsworth portrays political desire as the afterimage of domestic discontent. Instead of politicizing psychology he psychologizes politics. The 1802 sonnets, in which Wordsworth's turn to public oratory on political themes may well provide an outlet for domestic and psychological crisis, perhaps stand as the transitional moment in this reversal of perspective. It is more clear, however, that *The Excursion* represents a doctrinal hardening of the position accorded to the French Revolution in *The Prelude* of 1805, that is, as a counterexample, or the veritable counterplot, of the story of the poet's maturation.

Nonetheless, *The Excursion* is hardly a univocal text, and there is room for considerable argument over the way its dialogic form synthesizes or ironizes any one of the characters' political or moral opinions. Those who have argued for the superiority of "The Wanderer" or *The Pedlar* to the shorter *Ruined Cottage* of Ms. D have done so most plausibly on the basis of the later poems' added complexity; and yet in these arguments it always seems to happen that the tale of Margaret is subsumed into a kind of psychomachia, a war of competing Wordsworths.[36] But the fact that Margaret's speech remains more autonomous in Ms. D does not in itself make that poem superior, either. The important critical and historical question is not which poem is better but rather what values are at stake in the choice, beginning with Wordsworth's own choices in the process of revision, between the different versions of the poem. The basic value is not complexity for its own sake, nor is it correctness of any ideological kind. If we are to take Wordsworth's own pronouncements on the topic seriously, the fundamental value must be pleasure. What, then, is the difference between Ms. D and *The Pedlar* in terms of the pleasure each poem offers to the reader?

Shelley's response is again instructive, for the impact of *The Excursion* on his career was to direct him away from its didacticism and to reject his own earlier didacticism in *Queen Mab* in favor of a more ironic exploration of the economy of desire.[37] It seems that *The Excursion* offers a form of literary pleasure crucially different from the mode we now recognize as High Romanticism. The distinction has something to do with didacticism, even though the High Romantic mode of Ms. D, as well as Shelley's *Alastor,* is remarkably well focused on a central scene of instruction. The difference has to do with the institutional affiliations or alliances the scene of instruction seeks to invent or reinforce. *The Pedlar* and "The Wanderer," with all their detailed attention to authorizing the pedlar by granting him a special form of visionary experience, tend to corroborate the authority of metaphysically grounded institutions over individuals. Specifically, these poems seem to ask readers to enjoy recognizing their inclusion in a social body that reproduces its essential relationships in religion (here the wanderer's dissertation on paganism in book 4 would no doubt provide the most interesting text) and, in a more forward-looking move near the end of *The Excursion,* in public education. But the trend of Wordsworth's later career toward an increasing affiliation with Church, State, and Nation is clear enough. What paved the way for this development in Ms. B is the role of "nature" in the pedlar's biography. Wordsworth grants nature the same kind of priority given to the "face" in *The Borderers,* but, by making the face of spontaneous community into a quality of things rather than persons, Wordsworth also strips it of its radical social and political implications. It loses its subversiveness and allows visionary experience to become instead a form of access to metaphysical, almost theophanic authority. Nature, in the pedlar's biography, is Wordsworth's mythic solution to the problems of theatricality and community. It gives Wordsworth a differently authorized spectator, and he eventually assumes that spectator's authority in a movement that constitutes the plot of his autobiography.

But at the same time nature was becoming essentially *pleasurable* rather than authoritative:

> The birds around me hopp'd and play'd:
> Their thoughts I cannot measure,
> But the least motion which they made,
> It seem'd a thrill of pleasure.

(LB 76)

The scene of instruction in Ms. D turns on the theme of pleasure rather than authority. Like the "Lines Written in Early Spring," it has to do with the difficult integration of receptiveness to nature with a narrative meditation on "what man has made of man" (LB 76). At stake in Ms. D is not so much the pedlar's authority as the charge of voyeurism that can be leveled against those who trade in tales of suffering. Rather than appearing to solve political, moral, and philosophical questions, the poem articulates a sense of community based upon the fruitful, that is, pleasurable relationship between poet and reader. This alternative is the High Romantic one, and it is of far more historical importance because it comprises Wordsworth's contribution to an emergent discipline of literary pleasure.

PLEASURE IN MS. D

When I write the strange phrase, "the discipline of literary pleasure," I mean to emphasize that taking pleasure in literature is a social practice with certain rules and limitations, a protocol all the more important for its usually not being made explicit.[38] In fact, to be able to read literature properly means being a proper kind of person. Raymond Williams has argued that the practice of reading literarily is a class discipline, invented in the eighteenth century and elaborated into the nineteenth century ideology of humanism (see Arnold) and the twentieth century academic discipline of literary study.[39] If literature is a class practice, this repositions the classical association of literary pleasures with the pleasures of recognition. The proper reader must learn to recognize literature as distinguished from its inferiors—for instance, from "frantic novels, sickly and stupid German Tragedies, and deluges of idle and extravagant stories in verse" (PrW1 128). But perhaps more importantly, reading becomes a form of self-recognition based on possessing a certain practical capability—hence Wordsworth's emphasis in the "Preface to *Lyrical Ballads*" on cultivating "habits of mind" that distinguish serious reading from a "degrading thirst after outrageous stimulation" (PrW1 126, 128–30). What is at stake is, in fact, a *technique* of spontaneity: "For all good poetry is the spontaneous overflow of powerful feelings; but though this be true" such spontaneity is the result of a long-continued mental discipline, so that "by the repetition and continuation of this act feelings con-nected with important subjects will be nourished, till at length . . . such habits of mind will be produced that by obeying blindly and mechanically the impulses of those habits" the poet will utter proper, salutary sentiments to a listener "in a healthful state of association" (PrW1 126). The poet's discipline is a moral training, an "art of sympathy";[40] but Wordsworth adds that "we have no sympathy but what is propagated by pleasure; . . . wherever we sympathise with pain, it will be found that the sympathy is pro-duced and carried on by subtle combinations with pleasure" (PrW1 140).[41] To read the scene of instruction in Ms. D as a lesson in the discipline of literary pleasure, then, means taking note of the way Armytage coaches the younger man in a technique of meditative response and being alert to the "subtle combinations with plea-sure" he weaves between Margaret's tale and the act of telling it. *The Ruined Cottage* of Ms. D conflates one of the most inevitable of social rituals, mourning, with a problem in the ethics of narra-tive. The result is to ritualize narrative itself, to highlight its func-tion not so much as a way of communicating knowledge about events, but rather as a way of responding to them.

The quality of response peculiar to version 2 of *The Ruined Cottage,* and especially Ms. D, involves an intensification of the pedlar's/Armytage's involvement with Margaret. In the 1797 poem, the speaker says of Margaret:

> She is dead
> And nettles rot and adders sun themselves
> Upon the floor where I have seen [her] sit
> And rock her baby in its cradle.
>
> (81)

In Mss. B and D this passage undergoes small but crucial changes:

> She is dead
> And nettles rot & adders sun themselves
> Where we have sat together while she nursed
> Her infant at her bosom
>
> (Ms. B 21r, 201)

> She is dead
> And nettles rot & adders sun themselves
> Where we have sate together while she nurs'd
> Her infant at her breast.
>
> (Ms. D 47v–48r, 291–93)

The image of Margaret rocking her baby in its cradle becomes the more intimate one of her nursing the baby at her bosom and finally at her breast.[42] Strangely enough, the image disappears in *The Pedlar:*

> She is dead,
> Forgotten in the quiet of the grave.
>
> (418)

The image of the nursing mother signals a heightened danger and a concomitant chastening of voyeurism, as well as an increased valuation of the prefallen Margaret's symbolic importance, that is peculiar to the 1798–99 versions of *The Ruined Cottage.* What draws this image into the same movement that makes politically articulate anger more distant and brings the anxieties of poetic vocation into the foreground?

Nursing itself attains the status of a kind of primal scene of recognition in Wordsworth's poetry in the "Bless'd the infant Babe" passage composed in spring of 1799, about the same time Ms. D was assembled. There is no stronger or more explicit formulation of the "face" of spontaneous, authentic community in Wordsworth's poetry. The nursing infant is the thematic antithesis of the many figures of abandonment that haunt the poetry of the 1790s:

> No outcast He bewilder'd & depress'd
> Along his infant veins are interfused
> The gravitation & the filial bond
> Of Nature that connect him with the world.
>
> (P1799 189)

Two features of this passage are particularly interesting in connection with *The Ruined Cottage:* first, the fact that this archetypal baby is male; and second, that the gift his mother (and Nature) gives him is literary. This is not just because he manifests the "first / Poetic Spirit of our human life" (191), although this attempt to connect maternal passion to the poet's activity is certainly important. Wordsworth also attributes to the child an innate capacity for a certain kind of *reading.* He "Doth gather passion from his Mothers eye" (189); he exercises a "discipline of love" that makes his mind "prompt and eager to combine / In one appearance all the elements / And parts of the same object else detach'd / And loath to coalesce" (189). This adaptive fantasy of coherence is quite similar to the discipline Armytage teaches the younger man in *The Ruined Cottage.*

Armytage's lesson, the substance of the symmetrical frame constructed around the tales of Margaret and Robert in Ms. D, has to do with grieving and reading. It hinges upon the question posed in the central interruption, at the break between parts one and two, of what kind of moral ground the two men occupy if they "hold vain dalliance with [Margaret's] misery" (59). The image of the nursing mother enters into this pattern as the absence that is the necessary condition of Armytage's narrative practice; it symbolizes both the bond that has been broken and the fundamental possibility of healing the wound.

The image appears in a longer, quite remarkable passage of lamentation:

> She is dead,
> The worm is on her cheek, and this poor hut,
> Stripp'd of its outward garb of houshold flowers,
> Of rose and sweet-briar, offers to the wind
> A cold bare wall whose earthy top is tricked
> With weeds and the rank spear-grass. She is dead,
> And nettles rot and adders sun themselves
> Where we have sate together while she nurs'd
> Her infant at her breast. The unshod Colt,
> The wandering heifer and the Potter's ass,
> Find shelter now within the chimney-wall
> Where I have seen her evening hearth-stone blaze
> And through the window spread upon the road
> Its chearful light.
>
> (51)

The twice-repeated phrase, "she is dead," and the thrice-repeated comparisons of the present, degenerated scene with a fuller, brighter past are typical elegiac strategies. The repetitions struggle both to assert the reality of Margaret's death and to retain a sense of the reality of things in her absence. At the same time, the angry, vengeful emotions of grief are vented upon the scene itself. There is a strong sense as well that, if Armytage's bitterness over Margaret's death has momentarily returned upon him, his lament repeats, almost ritualistically, an earlier, more defiant stage of mourning.[43] Thus, while his naming the vegetation and the animals that here insinuate themselves into Margaret's place seems almost to constitute a curse against nature, some of these very images will later be called upon to restore continuity and to reintegrate death and grief into the healing processes of time.[44]

The image of the nursing mother plays a more original and idiosyncratic role, that of positioning Armytage in both the lost and the present scenes. Its function emerges from the eroticism and violence that pervade Armytage's lament. The nettles, worms, and adders reverse his unstated, but clear sexual desire into images of hostile penetration and disgust. The hut, "stripp'd of its outward garb," and the "cold bare wall . . . tricked with weeds" represent Margaret's sexual appeal as a provocation, as if the descent from the domestic warmth of her hearth to the visitations of colt, heifer, and ass merely fulfilled an animalistic, brutal potential in her attractiveness.[45] All of these images seem to duplicate an unacted, guilt-ridden set of desires. Armytage's proximity to the baby at Margaret's breast rehearses a starkly different possibility, one that will make the pattern of loss and decay coherent and benevolent. An implicit identification of Armytage with the nursing child places Margaret at the center of the narrative both as visual object and as a source of nourishment; but the nourishment and passion the baby "gathers" from Margaret are transmuted by Armytage into a "power" attached to narrative: "A power to virtue friendly" (59). The teleology of this power is the opposite of violence, "repose." Thus the image of the nursing mother is at the nexus of the crucial elegiac exchange, allowing violent sexuality to be transformed into calmness and tranquility by way of their synthesis in the archetypal moment of domestic passion and spectatorial self-recognition.

The frame places different versions of repose at the beginning, middle, and end of the poem. The first comes during the opening landscape description, with its muted hints of an allegory of Fortune—"surfaces with shadows dappled o'er / Of deep embattled clouds"—or perhaps of the cosmic balance of *concordia discors:* ". . . those many shadows lay in spots / Determined and unmoved, with steady beams / Of clear and pleasant sunshine interposed" (43). Whether such a landscape is "pleasant" depends largely upon one's perspective, apparently, since the narrator's pedestrian lot is presented in sharp contrast to that of a more detached spectator. The view is

> Pleasant to him who on the soft cool moss
> Extends his careless limbs beside the root
> Of some huge oak whose aged branches make
> A twilight of their own, a dewy shade
> Where the wren warbles while the dreaming man,
> Half-conscious of that soothing melody,
> With side-long eye looks out upon the scene,
> By those impending branches made more soft,
> More soft and distant.

(43)

The significance of the dreaming man is not just his difference from the narrator, of course, but, more importantly, his similarity to the recumbent Armytage, who lies in the shade of the elms by the ruined cottage with "no thought / Of his way-wandering life" (49). The dreaming man's half-conscious, sidelong glance at things stands as a veritable accusation against Armytage, and the task of the narrative and the consolation sequence becomes that of refuting the charge of langorous detachment implied by the initial, apparent similarity between the two spectators in the shade. The scene itself alludes to a traditional site of lofty instruction, perhaps most strongly those in Milton's "Il Penseroso," Thomson's "Summer," and the interview of Adam and Gabriel in *Paradise Lost*.[46] But Thomson's wizard Indolence, singing in the checkered shade at the gate of his castle, suggests a different set of associations; and John Barrell has analyzed the shady noontime scene in eighteenth-century landscape art as a symbolic resolution of the conflicting demands of industry and indolence into a gentlemanly representation of the harmonious nature of rural life, which reconciles the upper-class spectator's idleness with the workers' industry.[47]

The problems emerge more clearly in the middle of the poem, when Armytage breaks off his story and the narrator convinces him to resume it. Armytage replies:

> "It were a wantonness and would demand
> Severe reproof, if we were men whose hearts
> Could hold vain dalliance with the misery
> Even of the dead, contented thence to draw
> A momentary pleasure never marked
> By reason, barren of all future good.
> But we have known that there is often found
> In mournful thoughts, and always might be found,
> A power to virtue friendly; were't not so,
> I am a dreamer among men, indeed
> An idle dreamer."

(59)

In the background is a century-long debate over tragedy, based upon a logically prior inquiry whether pity is a natural, benevolent affection or merely a form of self-love. The uncompromising views of Mandeville, who condemned the pleasures of tragedy as "intellectual indolence,"[48] and of Hutcheson, for whom pity and sympathy were the automatic and instinctive bases of moral judgment, were modified in the course of debate so that by the end of the century it was not uncommon to speak of tragedy, and art in gen-

eral, as contributing to an "art of sympathy," a consciously developed capacity for compassion and hence for making correct moral
decisions.[49] Shelley's famous apothegms on imagination as the instrument of moral good in his "Defence of Poetry" grow directly
out of this discourse, as well as representing a climactic theorization of the High Romantic mode of understanding literary pleasure
that he embarked upon in reaction to *The Excursion*. The power
Armytage hopes to impart to the narrator is a technique of sympathetic response with widespread analogues in contemporary moral
philosophy.[50]

The ethical function of narrative as a way of exercizing the
reader's capacity for sympathetic imagination underlies Armytage's famous description of Margaret's tale in the continuation of
his speech:

> " 'Tis a common tale,
> By moving accidents uncharactered,
> A tale of silent suffering, hardly clothed
> In bodily form, and to the grosser sense
> But ill adapted, scarcely palpable
> To him who does not think."
>
> (59)

The ghostliness of the tale, its near escape from "bodily form,"
defends against the charge of "vain dalliance." We are developing
our powers of compassion, says Armytage, not titillating ourselves
by contemplating the sufferings of the ("hardly clothed") object of
our (displaced) desire. The charge that Armytage is indulging in
self-delusion has been spelled out before:

> As has often been noted, one of the things that happened to the man
> of feeling in the romantic period is that the enjoyment of the emotion
> of pity, the sympathetic identification with the sufferer, became an end
> in itself and the compulsion to relieve the suffering proportionately
> less urgent. This is the same as saying that compassion became more
> literary and less a matter of practical morals.[51]

Or as DeQuincey would put it,

> It might be allowable to ask the philosophic wanderer who washes the
> case of Margaret with so many coats of metaphysical varnish, but ends
> with finding all unavailing, "Pray, amongst your other experiments, did
> you ever try the effect of a guinea?"[52]

The whole problem of the ethics of narrative and the technique of sympathetic response arises because of Armytage's odd, abrupt interruption of the tale. This is the frame's second version of repose:

> At this the old Man paus'd
> And looking up to those enormous elms
> He said, "'Tis now the hour of deepest noon.
> At this still season of repose and peace,
> This hour when all things which are not at rest
> Are chearful, while this multitude of flies
> Fills all the air with happy melody,
> Why should a tear be in an old man's eye?
> Why should we thus with an untoward mind
> And in the weakness of humanity
> From natural wisdom turn our hearts away,
> To natural comfort shut our eyes and ears,
> And feeding on disquiet thus disturb
> The calm of Nature with our restless thoughts?"
>
> (57)

Armytage unobtrusively offers a far more radical objection to narrative than the charge of vain dalliance. For here "humanity," that is, the compassion that leads him on to repeating the stories of the dead, turns into "weakness." The "natural wisdom" and "natural comfort" he appeals to here are identical with "repose and peace" and are achievable precisely by *not* telling the story. It is as if the wizard Indolence's shadowy presence were suddenly transformed into that of his more sinister Spenserean forebear:

> "Then doe no further goe, no further stray,
> But here ly downe, and to thy rest betake,
> Th' ill to prevent, that life ensewen may;
> For what hath life that may it loved make,
> And gives not rather cause it to forsake?"[53]

Armytage's calm is uncannily close to despair, and the pleasure of repose puts an end to narrative with the risk of identifying natural pleasure as death. Thus Armytage's case for tragedy can dismiss the moral dangers of voyeurism partly because they have already been pre-empted by a stronger threat. Perhaps a clue to the situation comes from the placement of the interruption: not just at the end of Robert's story (the obvious place for dividing the diptych), but immediately after *the first instance of Margaret's direct speech*. Is it really when Margaret's presence becomes too powerful that the "power to virtue friendly" must be invoked in order to continue the story? If so, then the technique of sympathetic response will be more accurately interpreted as a discipline of detachment not from voyeurism (which it actually revives), but from mother Margaret and mother earth. Narrative exchanges a severely regressive fantasy of community for a partnership in crime or at least in a community of spectatorial pleasures. That is, narrative fends off, for the moment, a lyric pleasure represented as aesthetic delight in things (the flies and their melody) but flirting with a deeper, deathly attraction.

The third instance of repose rounds the poem toward elegiac consolation and closure. The closing passage of Ms. D has three distinct phases: the young man's reception of the story, Armytage's final speech, and the closing turn in which the two men depart the scene. In the first phase everything is repetition, and this serves to bring out the ritualistic function being attributed to narrative. The repetitions begin with the young man's response to the bleak closing passage of Margaret's tale:

> The Old Man ceased: he saw that I was mov'd;
> From that low Bench, rising instinctively,
> I turned aside in weakness, nor had power
> To thank him for the tale which he had told.
>
> (73)

"Rising instinctively," the young man moves because the story moves him. He turns aside because the powerful tale of fixation and entrapment makes him want to escape it. He dissipates an intolerable emotion in sheer physical gesture. Yet his aimless motion (even the minor breach in manners, his failure to thank Armytage) also clearly repeats, at the level of an instinctive, sympathetic imitation, Margaret's own defensive wandering.

Once this initial sympathetic gesture is done, the young man repeats the story to himself:

> I stood, and leaning o'er the garden gate
> Reviewed that Woman's suff'rings, and it seemed
> To comfort me while with a brother's love
> I blessed her in the impotence of grief.
>
> (73)

He moves from repeating Margaret's restlessness to repeating Armytage's storytelling, and he assumes the emotional attitudes Armytage expressed at the outset: "I loved her / As my own child";

"my wiser mind / Sinks, yielding to the foolishness of grief" (51). His blessing is antiphonal and proceeds from narrative as the synthesis of sympathy ("brother's love") and unbridgeable distance ("impotence").

Finally the young man finds himself where Armytage began, and so he manages to repeat Armytage's initial act of reading the text, or palimpsest, of the ruined cottage and garden themselves:

> At length [upon] the [hut I fix'd my eyes]
> Fondly, and traced with milder interest
> That secret spirit of humanity
> Which, 'mid the calm oblivious tendencies
> Of nature, 'mid her plants, her weeds, and flowers,
> And silent overgrowings, still survived.
>
> (73)[54]

He knows now that "we die, my friend" (49) and that these environs proclaim "a bond of brotherhood is broken" (51). This last act of reading revives an abstract Margaret, a "secret spirit of humanity"; the revival is identical with the way reading and narrating themselves trope and transform Margaret's death.

All of this sets the stage for the second and climactic phase of the consolation sequence. Armytage now makes the most famous and controversial speech in the poem:

> "My friend, enough to sorrow have you given,
> The purposes of wisdom ask no more;
> Be wise and chearful, and no longer read
> The forms of things with an unworthy eye.
> She sleeps in the calm earth, and peace is here.
> I well remember that those very plumes,
> Those weeds, and the high spear-grass on that wall,
> By mist and silent rain-drops silver'd o'er,
> As once I passed did to my heart convey
> So still an image of tranquillity,
> So calm and still, and looked so beautiful
> Amid the uneasy thoughts which filled my mind,
> That what we feel of sorrow and despair
> From ruin and from change, and all the grief
> The passing shews of being leave behind,
> Appeared an idle dream that could not live
> Where meditation was."
>
> (73–75)

In this speech Armytage emerges as the true economist of pleasure, who knows where grief ends and literature goes on. Armytage transforms the "rank spear-grass" (53) of an earlier speech into a countermemory, an image that asserts an independent power against the inscriptive or referential character of the scene as it has been treated up to this point. The conventional elegiac assurance, "She sleeps in the calm earth, and peace is here," introduces an image that *disrupts* the coherence the landscape has just been given in order to enact a turn from narrative response to lyric pleasure. Just as the lyric image disrupts the coherent text of the narrative, lyric pleasure vacates and disperses the "uneasy thoughts that filled [Armytage's] mind." The images that before ironically signified Margaret's absence now turn into the purest of metaphors, a play of light that silvers over decay and makes time the signifier of timelessness. Armytage's speech concerns desire and aesthetic detachment; and its strong religious overtones, rather than serving a doctrinal purpose, instead corroborate its status as one of the great secularizing moments in Wordsworth's poetry. Lyric pleasure is itself a secularized conversion narrative: the story of attaining worthy vision, of metaphorically *conveying* the image's stillness, calm, and beauty to the heart. Thus Armytage's pleasure is not only aesthetic but also aestheticizing, turning "ruin and change" into "passing shews." Armytage translates the story of Margaret into the story of his own nourishment and self-recognition. The final lines of his speech, which might appear almost an afterthought, are thus actually essential and climactic: "I turned away / And walked along my road in happiness." Lyric pleasure, at last fulfilling Armytage's identification with the nursing child and satisfying the teleology of repose, also paradoxically weans Armytage from his grievous attachment. The now transcendental fantasy of coherence, subsuming Margaret into the vanity of vanities, specularly integrates Armytage himself as capable reader. The final moments of the poem then unfold the social character of Armytage's self-recognition, as Armytage and the young man share their pleasurable awareness of the "sweet hour" and depart the text as an independent, reunited community.

Like the other two moments of repose, Armytage's consolation turns upon issues of reality and illusion that in turn problematize the value of his activity. As in both earlier instances, idle dreaming represents the negative evaluation of his visionary calm. His consolation has proved remarkably disturbing to many readers because it relegates sympathy itself—that is, precisely the "power" one would have thought friendly to virtue—to the status of wasteful illusion: ". . . what we feel of sorrow and despair / From ruin and from change, and all the grief / The passing shews of being leave behind, / Appeared an idle dream." Armytage represents his spear-grass vision as the full illumination of natural light, the most inevitable of metaphoric constructions for truth.[55] But the dynamics of sympathy here take a decidedly "side-long" movement, substituting an aesthetic pleasure in the *text* of Margaret for his doomed desire for the woman. He triumphs over his regressive desire for reunion and obliteration by allying it to a mystified voyeurism, a voyeurism purged of violence by the alliance, but all the more appropriative as a consequence. It is a classic example of sublimation, the process Derrida calls the *usure* of metaphor (of Margaret): "White mythology—metaphysics has erased within itself the fabulous scene that has produced it, the scene that nevertheless remains active and stirring, an invisible design covered over in the palimpsest."[56] But the relation between the climactic accomplishment of usury, when Armytage and the young man forge their community in the light of truth and over Margaret's dead body, and "the fabulous scene that has produced it" is precisely what the poem ultimately offers. In a process uncomfortably similar to that by which abandonment produces community in *The Borderers,* the narrator and Armytage remember Margaret in order to be able to forget her. Lyric pleasure is the recessional hymn that closes the ritual of mourning; but the moment of transcendence is not so much secular scripture as the hard-earned scripting of the roles Armytage and the young man have learned to act.

The Tale of Margaret, January-March 1798

We are finally in a position to return to January–March 1798 and to measure the distance between the community lost in the tales of Robert and Margaret and the community regained in the framing scene of instruction. Labor holds together the first community: the "touch of human hand" forges the "bond of brotherhood" (Ms. B 20r, 197), and both Margaret's and Robert's ministry of the cottage and garden receive detailed descriptions. The most memorable ones, of course, are those recounting the decay of this laborious bond: Robert's restlessness after he is thrown out of employment (Ms. B 24r-26r, 211–15) and the mounting evidence of Margaret's neglect during the pedlar's second and third visits (Ms. B 33r-39r, 231–47). These passages deliver the fierce theme of the contingency of the cottagers' virtue upon their economic competence, as their energies, deprived of fruitful and productive expression, consume them.

In the second community, virtue has mellowed, no doubt because it has at the same time acquired the force and necessity of a natural process. The transformation, or troping, of the virtue of labor is no simple operation. At its endpoint (fully realized in Ms. D) we find lyric pleasure, a communicable passion, that (to use the appropriate Wordsworthian phrase) usurps upon compassionate narrative. The energies invested in the narrative itself are tightly focused on Margaret, but not entirely on her labor. On the contrary, she becomes the virtual embodiment of the now-deserted well:

> Many a passenger
> Has blessed poor Margaret for her gentle looks
> When she upheld the cool refreshment drawn
> From that forsaken spring, & no one came
> But he was welcome, no one went away
> But that it seemed she loved him.
>
> (Ms. B 21r, 201)

It is Margaret's love, not her labor, that provides the center of the regained community; Margaret, drawer from the well, becomes herself the wellspring of passion. Thus her role in the economy of labor she shares with Robert differs radically from her status as image and actor in the pedlar's narrative. His narrative constructs an economy of vision in which her "gentle looks" are stored, accumulated, and deployed in his powerful sympathetic response:

> As I stooped to drink
> Few minutes gone, at that deserted well
> What feelings came to me! A spider's web
> Across its mouth hung to the water's edge
> And on the wet & slimy footstones lay
> The useless fragment of a wooden bowl
> It moved my very heart.
>
> (20r, 197)

An unobtrusive allusion to Ecclesiastes 12:6[57] prepares the ground for the pedlar's conversion narrative, but what makes the moment effective is the incommensurability between the mundane object and the pedlar's emotion. This sublime effect also derives from an act of re-evaluation. Margaret's passions are familial, maternal, sexual; the pedlar's vision transforms familial passion into a secularized form of grace.

The tension between the family and the community of faith is a typical and crucial feature of religious conversion,[58] but here it takes the form of an intersection between a subsistence economy and an economy of accumulation that exploits it. What finally allows the two men to come together in a newfound social body is precisely the transubstantiation of the body of Margaret from laborious, contingent producer to essential, timeless source and repository. The way that Margaret, family, labor, and subsistence turn into the metaphysical reserve fund for lyrical pleasure indicates the ideological and class function of Wordsworth's literary transaction. This transformation itself is the work of the frame, and the parasitical relation of the pedlar's vision to Margaret's passion and suffering accounts, at least in part, for the drive to revise the pedlar's character while leaving Margaret's story nearly untouched. But what still needs to be accounted for is the power of the narrative itself.

The major portion of the January–March revision comprises the pedlar's first three visits in the four-visit sequence that now precedes the oldest, concluding passage.[59] The new material, Ms. B 30r–39r, incorporates the older Racedown NB lines in the first visit and dovetails in the third visit with the Christabel NB text. Two features predominate. First, the pedlar's narrative strategy becomes strikingly pictorial. The sequence of visits expands the older diptych structure into something like a series of allegorical etchings, a rake's progress, or, in its fascination with the ruin and the encroaching vegetation, even more like the many eighteenth-century series depicting the progress and decline of empire. This pictorial strategy strengthens the comparison, which now amounts almost to an identification, of Margaret with the cottage and garden. The second feature works directly against this identification. The revised narrative imparts remarkable power to Margaret's voice, her gestures, and her sheer physical presence. This passionate energy resists being subsumed in the grinding process of her economic and domestic catastrophes, and in all versions of the poem, from Ms. B to "The Wanderer," it remains troubling to both the authority of nature and the lyrical teleology of repose with which Wordsworth strives to frame and contain it.

The pictorial strategy has the function of telescoping the pedlar's disconcerting wisdom—"I see around me / Things which you cannot see. We die my Friend" (19r, 193)—into a process (indeed a procession) that the young man can repeat or work through; and at the same time it eerily retains the stillness, whether of death or of tranquility, that characterizes the pedlar's vision and pervades the elegiac substitution of things for persons. There is a tendency toward emblem and allegory that seems to be allied with elegiac distancing and displacement. Consider the crucial second visit, when Margaret's neglect of home and child first comes into view. A verbal echo reinforces the implicit comparison of Margaret to the garden: "I turned aside / And strolled into her garden. It was changed" (33r, 231); "I turn'd and saw her distant a few steps / Her face was pale & thin, her figure too / Was changed" (35r, 235). Allegorical possibilities emerge when the cottage's blood-stained threshold shows that it has become a "couching-place" for sheep (35r, 235), hinting perhaps at the imminence of an Old Testament day of judgment, or at the possibility that the progress of civilization has here been halted.[60] But Wordsworth's fidelity to natural detail prevents such allusions from becoming explicit or from constituting anything like a didactic or polemical utterance. It is as if the pedlar's attention to the scene, even while it encodes certain politically charged messages, also subdues them to a whisper because the force of the images simultaneously carries the pedlar through and away from the scene's grievous impact. Thus the description of the garden also attains a more conventional elegiac moment when the pedlar catalogues the flowers growing over the paths: "Daisy, & thrift & lowly camomile / And thyme" (34r, 233).

The most disturbing sign during this description that the laborious bond between cottage and cottagers has dissolved is, however, an image of voice: "From within / Her solitary infant cried aloud" (34r, 233). The image of voice refers the pictorial scene forcefully back to the realm of immediate human suffering. The infant, as elsewhere in the poem, metaphorically signifies the pedlar's emotional perspective, and metonymically signals Margaret's own power to give coherence to her family and her world. This raises her status from an allegorical or typical figure to that of the symbolic or theoretical centerpiece in the pedlar's construction of a sense of community. The whole force of the "power to virtue friendly" in the pedlar's narrative depends upon Margaret's symbolic value, since the moment of insight itself must cross the distance between grieving the community she held together and affirming the one the pedlar's narrative produces. Therefore Margaret's symbolic value, even as it elevates her, also consigns her to figuration and abstraction, that is, to modes of literary nourishment that instrumentalize the nursing mother in the interest of producing ideological closure. What finally resists such closure, making the revision of the *Ruined Cottage* into the ongoing, obsessive task it became, is the way Margaret's own person, her voice, and her gestures overpower such figural schemes.

The pedlar's pictorial strategy carries throughout the implicit function of defining and maintaining the pedlar's distance from Margaret. When he encounters her face to face, the tone of his narrative changes from mourning to something more complicated, closer to fear, because his response to Margaret threatens to overwhelm his elegiac capability of moving on. Margaret's power of *interrupting* the pedlar emerges at the beginning of the first visit. "When I entered with the hope / Of usual greeting," he says,

> Margaret looked at me
> A little while, then turned her head away
> Speechless, & sitting down upon a chair
> Wept bitterly. I wist not what to do
> Or how to speak to her.
>
> (29r–30r, 223–25)

Margaret's tears contribute to the dumbfounding effect she has on the pedlar here and at the end of the visit: "This tale did Margaret tell with many tears / And when she ended I had little power / To give her comfort" (31r, 227). But the sentimental convention of weeping serves mainly as a foil to the greater, more characteristically Wordsworthian, power of Margaret's "look":

> She rose from off her seat—and then—Oh Sir
> I cannot *tell* how she pronounced my name
> With fervent love & with a face of grief
> Unutterably helpless & a look
> That seemed to cling upon me she inquired
> If I had seen her husband.
>
> (30r, 225)

Using the inexpressibility topos to describe Margaret's pronunciation of the pedlar's name craftily elevates her dramatic presence above his narrative role, and it points toward the central and unutterable value of her face. As in *The Borderers,* the face speaks a language beyond language. Here Margaret's face conveys a language of pure performance that supplements and vitalizes the verbal communication that accompanies it. Her look *clings* upon the pedlar, more like an aggressive embrace than "a gravitation and a filial bond." The way all of this disrupts the pedlar's expectations helps to render it sublime: "A strange surprize and fear came o'er my heart" (30r, 225); but her power over him is also uncanny in Freud's sense of the term, because Margaret, helpless as she is, exercises the most "familiar power" conceivable in the pedlar's "homely tale" (27r, 219).

The quality of Margaret's sublimity changes in the second visit. At this point, her longing for her husband has become morbid, and her bonds with her children are dissolving as a consequence. Her elder child is apprenticed to the parish, and her youngest one cries helplessly while she wanders the fields. Her speeches in this scene represent the climax of her tragedy in their full and utterly futile recognition of her self-destructive obsession. At the same time her speech becomes strangely disembodied:

> still she sighed
> But yet no motion of the breast was seen
> No heaving of the heart. While by the fire
> We sate together, sighs came on my ear
> I knew not how and hardly whence they came.
>
> (37r, 243)

The false optimism that pathetically concludes the first visit yields to an equally pernicious form of resignation. Her hope "that heaven / Will give me patience" ironically apologizes for the devastation of her real power:

> She did not look at me. her voice was low
> Her body was subdued. In every act
> Pertaining to her house affairs appeared
> The careless stillness which a thinking soul
> Gives to an idle matter.
>
> (36r–37r, 239–43)

Margaret's "careless stillness" is antithetical to the pedlar's achievement of tranquility, but also to the idle "dreaming man" of the opening scenario. Thus her resignation and detachment point up the similarity between pedlar and dreamer, which is their practical noninvolvement in the scenes they behold and, therefore, their common ability to move "side-long" away from them and to profit from them.

Nonetheless Margaret's stillness bears a disturbing similarity to the pedlar's credo of sublimation and particularly to the ghostliness or incorporeality of his "tale of silent suffering, hardly clothed / In bodily form" (29r, 223). Margaret's subdued manner directly links the deterioration of her practical virtue (her labor) to the increasing alienation of her body from her "thinking soul," that is to say, her indomitable love, desire, and hope. That alienation is most memorably expressed by Margaret herself earlier in the scene:

>   I have slept
> Weeping & weeping I have waked my tears
> Have flowed as if my body were not such
> As others are, & I could never die.

(36r, 239)

But where the ultimate identification of Margaret's sleeping, that is, dead body with the calm earth opens the way to the pedlar's metaphor of timelessness, Margaret's own complaint is that her body cannot be used up. Her body is the source of her agony and at the same time a seemingly inexhaustible source of strength; and what, after all, is the nexus of family, spontaneous passion, and authentic community if it is not Margaret's body itself in all its materiality? This speech climaxes Margaret's tragedy because in it her body is both set aside from her and made into the most intimate of prisons.

Margaret's look and speech comprise the entire substance of the first visit. In the second visit, the cottage's deterioration prepares her entrance. In the third visit, the pictorial strategy predominates because Margaret's tragedy has moved into anticlimax. What persists is the ironic relation between her body and her catastrophe: ". . . she seemed not changed / In person or appearance, but her house / Bespoke a sleepy hand of negligence" (37r–38r, 243–45). When the description thus introduced comes to an end, the third visit quickly returns to the Christabel NB scene of Robert's "idle loom / Still in its place" and his "sunday garments hung / Upon the self-same nail" and harshly juxtaposes it with Margaret's most overt expression of despair: "But for her babe / And for her little friendless Boy she said / She had no wish to live" (39r–40r, 247–49). From this point on the pedlar retreats further into the distance. In the context provided by the first three visits and the image of the nursing mother, the report of the baby's death during the fourth visit confirms that his detachment bears a terrible cost. The vehicle for his metaphor of truth is finally not just one dead body, Margaret's, but two, the second one a discarded, but still pertinent, metaphor for his own.

The power of Margaret's voice, face, and body in this narrative cannot be fully contained by Wordsworth's later attempts to authorize the pedlar's vision or to make nature the source of the pedlar's consolation rather than merely a site for transforming and relinquishing Margaret's grip upon him. Whatever status his biography affords the pedlar, the narrative leaves him in the role of infant surrogate. It is precisely by isolating and more fully exploring this dependence that Wordsworth recasts *The Ruined Cottage* in Ms. D as an exercise in the discipline of literary pleasure. Turning the nursing mother into the palimpsest of literary community enables Wordsworth to rework the sheer brutality of class into the material of High Romantic lyricism. But the nursing mother as symbolic value is already a palimpsest; Margaret's power as *image* of the mother, nourishing the literary spectator, is written over her practical virtue, her role in an economy of subsistence supporting the spectator's political, civic virtue. In both cases, the resources of public competence draw upon the supplies (nourishment, cohesiveness) of private labor. When Wordsworth's lyricism imposes the community of humanity over the community of the polis, politics are not so much erased as overwhelmed by the trope that changes the basis of competence from ownership of property to the passionate responses of the body itself. Class turns into human nature. In the process, however, the laborer turns into a woman, and the body becomes an all too alienable possession. Thus the turn from person to thing, the accomplishment of mourning, here proceeds from the prior valuation of the woman's body as the *instrument,* the source and repository, of community. Margaret's tragedy, her alienation from and entrapment in her body, writes bodily spontaneity over economic contingency. Yet at the same time the best measure of Wordsworth's achievement is that he has rendered her exploitation so intensely that no practice or ritual of literary distance and self-recognition can quite discipline it into silence.

7

"Therefore Am I Still": The Poet's Authority in "Tintern Abbey"

THE FINAL EXHIBIT IN THIS STUDY OF WORDSWORTH'S EARLY career, "Lines Written a Few Miles above Tintern Abbey, on Revisiting the Banks of the Wye during a Tour, July 13, 1798,"[1] convenes a community of recognition that, like the poet's authority, fails to settle easily on either side of the boundary between universalistic abstraction and material practice. In the process it brings to a head Wordsworth's inharmonious claims to metaphysical, political, and literary authority. Nonetheless, it represents a triumphant moment in Wordsworth's early career, for in it the autobiographical self of his greatest poems (*The Prelude*, "Resolution and Independence," "Ode: Intimations of Immortality from Recollections of Early Childhood") first achieves a precarious balance between his most characteristic posture, that of rediscovering himself, and his anxious notations of social instability or personal mortality.

THE PLOT OF REVISITATION

Wordsworth's powerful plot of rediscovery emerges from a commonplace locodescriptive and sentimental scene of revisitation, a convention of which William Lisle Bowles was the most notable practitioner.[2] The usual tone of Bowles's sonnets is nostalgic, but Wordsworth's revisitation of the Wye deepens this sentiment into something stronger and less easy to define. Part of the remarkable disparity between Wordsworth's emotional response and its apparent occasion[3] may arise from an associative intermingling of the Wye's "sweet inland murmur" with the voice of the Derwent, the stream that flowed by his childhood home. The opening lines of "Tintern Abbey" recast a fragment composed between a year and two years earlier about revisiting the Derwent:

185

> Yet once again do I behold the forms
> Of these huge mountains, and yet once again,
> Standing beneath these elms, I hear thy voice,
> Beloved Derwent, that peculiar voice
> Heard in the stillness of the evening air,
> Half-heard and half-created.
>
> (LB 274)[4]

The scene bears a palpable resemblance to that which opens "Tintern Abbey," with its steep and lofty cliffs, the murmuring voice of the stream, and the beautiful forms that impress themselves upon the returning poet. But the emotion generated by a return to the Derwent, unlike the touristic visits to the Wye, draws upon an easily understood source, the return to one's childhood home. The scene's power is "half-created," turning hearing and seeing into reading and understanding, because the plot of reviving childhood memories turns the scene's natural features into articulate language and the poet's encounter with things into something intensely personal and passionate: "I hear thy voice, / Beloved Derwent."

This prosopopoeia, as in *The Ruined Cottage,* indicates both the theme of a community lost and regained and an elegiac process of substituting natural presences for lost people. Thus the most useful similarity between the "Yet once again" fragment and the opening lines of "Tintern Abbey" may be the fragment's more obvious, but shared allusion to the opening lines of Milton's "Lycidas:" "Yet once more, O ye laurels, and once more / Ye Myrtles brown." The fragment's clear allusion to Milton ("Yet once again . . . yet once again") gives way to a mysteriously specific, more prolonged, more distant echo in "Tintern Abbey": "Five years have passed; five summers / With the length of five long winters! and again I hear . . . Once again do I behold . . . I again repose . . . Once again I see." The elegiac tone is muted, attenuated, but still hauntingly present. What is most disturbing, however, is that the subdued hint of elegiac grief leads to a tone of triumphant consolation without any loss ever having been acknowledged; before the poem has begun, the (absent) dead have already taken on "the life of things." The entire poem carries out this strategy of self-congratulatory triumph over unacknowledged grief.

In fact, Wordsworth's handling of the convention of revisitation yields the contradictory claim that he has both learned from experience and remained radically untouched by it. The elegiac process seems to be both alluded to and turned on its head in

Wordsworth's central assertion of integrity, where he characteristically transforms his aesthetic apprehension of the rural scene into a pleasurable, lyrical recognition of a quasi-familial attachment to nature:

> Therefore am I still
> A lover of the meadows and the woods,
> And mountains; and of all that we behold
> From this green earth; of all the mighty world
> Of eye and ear, both what they half create,
> And what perceive; well pleased to recognize
> In nature and the language of the sense
> The anchor of my purest thoughts, the nurse,
> The guide, the guardian of my heart, and soul
> Of all my moral being.

The crux of this famous, rounded sentence is concentrated in its first half line: "Therefore am I still." He claims, first, that his healthy state of mind can be assigned a definite cause, since "therefore" refers back to the "presence that disturbs me with the joy / Of elevated thoughts" in the previous sentence. At the same time "therefore" seems to announce a decision or a resolve on his part, so that his love of nature, his attentiveness to "the language of the sense," and his stewardship of his moral being all testify to his sense of responsibility. (One of the seductions of Wordsworth's tone is to make a statement like "Therefore am I still / A lover" take on a kind of matter-of-factness, so that what is actually a performative utterance, a kind of declaration of allegiance, presents itself as a simple declarative.[5]) The phrase "am I" simply asserts his presence, accepting and answering to the sublime presence he has felt; yet this simplicity is quite canny, since it lends the poet's sense of origins and destiny an air of inevitability. Rather than a plot, we seem to be dealing with the mere unfolding of the poet's being.

Wordsworth's most problematic and important claim comes in the final word of the half line: Wordsworth is *still* a lover, *still* pleased to recognize and respond to nature. The problem arises from an important ambiguity in the word "still" between continuity and motionlessness. This ambiguity results from a tension between poetic and grammatical form: the syntax of the sentence militates strongly for the sense of continuity, but in order to do so it must overcome or submerge the suggestion of motionlessness that is thrust into view by the enjambment. The word "still" thereby condenses in itself the poem's two potentially contradictory arguments: first, that the poet's changes have been growth, a continuous, healthy development from his somewhat reckless and overstimulated youth to his present, more sober maturity; second, that nothing has really changed, that what nature gave to him once it gives him now and always.[6] Thus it remains difficult to decide whether the poem celebrates a hard-won lesson ("I have learned to look on nature, / Not as in the hour of thoughtless youth . . .") or merely his success at remaining essentially pure, undisturbed, "still."

Far from resolving this tension, the entire poem seems to be driven forward largely by the repetition of its competing claims. This conflict between active learning and passive recognition also encapsulates the problem of assessing Wordsworth's poetic maturity as embodied in this poem. The conflict brings into play, on the one hand, Wordsworth's continuing ambition for poetry to *advocate* a moral and philosophical program and, on the other, the poet's strong accession to a desire for pure *mimesis* of the enraptured self. It is hard, perhaps impossible, to tell whether the poem is finally a discursive intervention in the dreary social world it refers to at a distance or whether it is primarily and finally an interlude from that world, concerned most of all with discovering and enjoying its autonomy. It is not at all the case that the tension between advocacy and mimesis in the Salisbury Plain poems disappears into self-referential artistry in "Tintern Abbey." On the contrary, the poet's apparent desire throughout this poem is to have things both ways, that is, to argue that the poem *as interlude* is the most essential of all interventions.

The poem's engagement or disengagement of political and social reality is a crucial aspect of whatever community of recognition it constructs. Various scholars have discerned a background of muted political allusion and marginal contact with the radical movement in "Tintern Abbey."[7] This context informs Kenneth R. Johnston's astute reading of the poem in "The Politics of 'Tintern Abbey.'" Johnston notes both Wordsworth's deliberate mellowing of such socially unpleasant details of Tintern Abbey and environs as pollution and poverty[8] and his concomitant exaggeration of the evils of day-to-day urban life. He then connects the poem to Wordsworth's decision in 1795 to leave London and, especially, to divorce himself from his involvement in *The Philanthropist* and London's radical culture. Johnston concludes that "Tintern Abbey" smooths out and makes continuous what was, for Wordsworth, a quite difficult and disruptive learning process and that it therefore may be "one of the most powerfully *de*politicized poems in the language."[9]

Laying the movement from London political life to country retirement alongside the retrospective meditation in "Tintern Abbey" brings into focus another pattern in the poem: the poet's transformation of spatial relationships into temporal ones. This strategy both marks and naturalizes the discontinuty between the social world and the individual. Where spatial distance or separation hints at a context of social conflict, the poet internalizes the distance as an anxiety about the relation between his past and present selves. The personal crisis and its resolution gesture toward their social origins, but also detach themselves from them. Thus the opposition between the idealized rural setting and the hyperbolically undervalued urban one yields not a meditation on the disparate social settings but rather Wordsworth's avowal of personal maturity and a resolve to keep on keeping faith with his natural legacy. Although Wordsworth represents this as a discovery of his inwardness, a movement from the surface into the depths (or heights), it actually covers over the prior movement out from London. Like the "spear grass" passage in *The Ruined Cottage,* retrospection in "Tintern Abbey" serves the purposes of countermemory; Wordsworth's recovery of his past is actually a progressive movement into a reorganized future.

Another and more complicated transposition also takes place in the course of the poem. The troubling juxtaposition of "pastoral farms" with "vagrant dwellers in the houseless woods" in the opening scene at first yields the image of the isolated and meditative hermit in his cave, which serves as a plausible metaphor for the poet and the imaginary place he proceeds to stake out for himself. By the poem's final movement, however, the metaphor of the hermit's cave seems to be synthesized both with the pastoral farms and with anxiety about homelessness in Wordsworth's wish that his sister's "mind / Shall be a mansion for all lovely forms, / Thy memory be as a dwelling-place / For all sweet sounds and harmonies." The place Wordsworth hopes to establish for the imagination is now shared rather than isolated; but as his hopes migrate they also become more tentative, more deferred, and even more abstract. The economic anxiety hinted at in the opening scene seems in every sense closer to home in the later image. If the hermit in his cave intimates the asceticism and monasticism Wordsworth sometimes invoked in *The Recluse,* most strongly in "The Tuft of Primroses," then the turn to Dorothy and the "mansion" of her mind points to *The Recluse* project's consistent, but never entirely successful desire to move from the apocalyptic marriage of nature and the mind of man to a place where imagination finds a truly *social* "dwelling-place."[10]

The way social conflict comes home to Wordsworth can also be aligned with the way the image of the mansion in "Tintern Abbey" alludes to the literary tradition Wordsworth is engaging and revising: the broad expanse of poems on retirement and on the country estate as an ideal social formation. Problems of economy and social class are pervasive concerns in this tradition, and it can be shown that the plot of "Tintern Abbey" finally rests upon the way Wordsworth's turn from a metaphysical to a literary form of authority emerges from this tradition and these concerns. The same problems also determine the place finally given to politics itself in the poem. When Wordsworth recasts retirement and the estate as psychological moments in "Tintern Abbey," these internalized classical ideals still allude in crucial ways to the central political thematics of this tradition.

RETIREMENT, POLITICS, AND DOMESTICITY

The most important aspects of the classical theme of retirement as it bears upon "Tintern Abbey" are embodied in the two most influential sources of the theme in English poetry: the concluding passage of the second book of Virgil's *Georgics* (2.458–540, beginning "*O fortunatos nimium, sua si bona norint*"), and Horace's second *Epode* ("*Beatus ille qui procul negotiis*"). In the "*O fortunatos nimium*" passage, Virgil sees the country life as an opportunity for elevating his poetic ambitions:

> 'Tis true, the first desire which does controul
> All the inferior wheels that move my Soul,
> Is, that the Muse me her high Priest would make;
> Into her holyest Scenes of Myst'ry take,
> And open there to my mind's purged eye
> Those wonders which to Sense the Gods deny.
>
> (Cowley 155)[11]

But he also anticipates more mundane pleasures:

> But if my dull and frozen Blood deny,
> To send forth Sp'rits that raise a Soul so high;
> In the next place, let Woods and Rivers be
> My quiet, though inglorious destiny.
> . . . .

Happy the Man, I grant, thrice happy he
Who can through gross effects their causes see:
Whose courage from the deeps of knowledge springs,
Nor vainly fears inevitable things;
But does his walk of virtue calmly go,
Through all th'allarms of Death and Hell below.
Happy! but next such Conquerours, happy they,
Whose humble Life lies not in fortunes way.
They unconcern'd from their safe distant seat,
Behold the Rods and Scepters of the great.

(Cowley 155)

Abraham Cowley, whose translation I have quoted, comments: "To be a Husbandman, is but a retreat from the City; to be a Philosopher, from the world, or rather, a Retreat from the world, as it is mans; into the world, as it is Gods" (141).[12] The contrast between the philosopher-poet's elevated detachment and the husbandman's safe distance from it recalls a persistent concern in Wordsworth's poetry during the late 1790s. What is a straightforward hierarchy for Virgil and Cowley often becomes a focus for anxieties about the poetic vocation in Wordsworth: from the difference between the dreaming man's "side-long" glance and the pedlar's tragic vision in *The Ruined Cottage,* to the colloquy of the shepherd and the poet in "Hart-Leap Well," to the oscillation between epic planning and indolent wandering in the opening of *The Prelude,* to the attempt to elevate the "Perfect Contentment, Unity entire" of his domestic establishment in the vale of Grasmere over visions of "Jehovah, with his thunder, and the quire / Of shouting angels" in *Home at Grasmere* (HAG 48, 102). "Tintern Abbey" offers one of the earliest and most crucial examples of the poet's struggle to synthesize Virgil's "holyest scenes of Mystery" with a version of the "humble Life" and to reconcile the philosopher-poet and the husbandman in himself.

Wordsworth's representation of his vocational anxieties also takes into account the final political thrust of the "*O fortunatos nimium*" passage. Virgil concludes that the farmer's life of wholesome labor, religious piety, and familial obligation ("He meets at door the softest humane blisses, / His chast wives welcom, and dear children's kisses" [Cowley 157]) is the true basis of Rome's greatness:

Such was the life the prudent *Sabins* chose,
From such the old Hetrurian virtue rose.
Such, *Remus* and the God his Brother led,
From such firm footing *Rome* grew the World's head.

(Cowley 157)

This political motif lends another kind of possible justification to detachment from the urban or courtly world. It is not unusual in the English poetry of retirement to attribute political virtue to the owner and manager of the landed estate because of his detachment and self-sufficiency. Wordsworth's location of the same type of virtue in the cottage weavers Robert and Margaret is one of the marks of radical republican sentiments in *The Ruined Cottage,* and his glorification of the Lake District's "Statesmen" in his letter to Fox makes a similar claim. In "Tintern Abbey," however, Wordsworth lays claim to this sort of Harringtonian virtue in a quite different and more subtle way.

Wordsworth's use of the figure of the mansion in "Tintern Abbey" ultimately turns upon the economic dimension Horace's second *Epode* adds to the political and philosophic values associated with country life and retirement in Virgil. Horace puts his praise of country life in the mouth of Alfius, a usurer, who envisions it as an escape from everything that characterizes his own existence:

> Happy the Man whom bounteous Gods allow
> With his own Hands Paternal Grounds to plough!
> Like the first golden Mortals Happy he
> From Business and the cares of Money free!
>
> (Cowley, 158)

In pointed contrast to the moneylender's occupation and his urban milieu, the farmer's life is not care-ridden or profit-driven, not malicious or litigious, not predatory or gluttonous. The country estate naturalizes and chastens human desires, both sexual ("Sometimes the beauteous Marriagable Vine / He to the lusty Bridegroom Elm does join"; "The Birds above rejoyce with various strains / And in the solemn scene their *Orgies* keep" [Cowley, 158–59]) and aggressive ("And all his malice, all his craft is shown / In innocent wars, on beasts and birds alone" [Cowley, 159]). Profit, too, is naturalized as fruition, and exchange turns into gift-giving and piety:

> How is he pleas'd th' encreasing Use to see,
> Of his well trusted Labours bend the tree?
> Of which large shares, on the glad sacred daies
> He gives to Friends, and to the Gods repays.
>
> (Cowley, 158)

The most pointed and comic of these reversals is Alfius's extended portrait of the "chaste and clean, though homely wife" who faithfully and cheerfully waits at the door for her husband's return from "rural duties."

It seems strange, but is quite typical, that Cowley omits from his translation the final lines that identify the speaker, so that the whole poem loses its satiric edge and becomes instead a straight-forward panegyric to country life. In his essay, Cowley also draws the opposition between country and city along Horatian lines but in perfect seriousness:

> We are here among the vast and noble Scenes of Nature; we are there among the pitiful shifts of Policy: We walk here in the light and open wayes of the Divine Bounty; we grope there in the dark and confused Labyrinths of Human Malice: Our Senses are here feasted with the clear and genuine taste of their Objects, which are all Sophisticated there, and for the most part overwhelmed with their contraries. Here Pleasure looks (methinks) like a beautiful, constant, and modest wife; it is there an impudent, fickle, and painted Harlot. (Cowley, 144–45)

By comparison, Wordsworth's contrast between the "harsh and violent stimulants" of the city and the voice of authentic human passion based in rural life in his "Preface to *Lyrical Ballads*" seems almost muted. The important point in regard to "Tintern Abbey," however, is the association of the comparison of country and city with issues of sexuality, domesticity, and appetite—that is, with the economy of the passions. When Wordsworth turns to his sister in the final verse paragraph of "Tintern Abbey," this is the economy that is put into play.

The best scholarly account of the *beatus ille* tradition in English poetry draws a sharp distinction between the classically inspired poetry of retirement and Romanticism, and it mentions Words-worth only in order to exclude "Tintern Abbey" from the study.[13] However, the development that led to a break between English locodescriptive poetry and the *beatus ille* tradition took place in the mid-eighteenth century in a group of poems that are clearly of direct relevance to "Tintern Abbey"—particularly James Thom-son's *The Seasons* and Mark Akenside's *The Pleasures of Imagina-tion*.[14] According to Røstvig, the break was instigated by Thomson in *The Seasons,* when he used the *topoi* of retirement not to justify the Stoic freedom of self-determination but rather to vindicate the *public* virtues. Akenside's *The Pleasures of Imagination* takes the process a step further by turning the philosophic man of retirement into a kind of passive receptor of the moral sense intrinsic in na-ture's harmonious order. Stoicism gives way to benevolence, the happy man to the good man.[15]

Retirement thenceforward turns into a kind of refreshment rather than a true alternative to the public life: ". . . the importance attached to active benevolence gradually led to a decisive break with the most crucial aspect of the retirement-tradition—its insistence on a self-contained, independent existence on a farm or estate."[16] Røstvig finally ascribes this break to a real socioeconomic change in the English countryside, as the older, paternalistic order of landowners was increasingly displaced by the larger estates of an aristocracy drawing its power more from money than from land. There can be little doubt that when the well-managed estate fades into the moral harmony of nature the class affiliation of this poetic mode has changed.

There are at least two ways in which "Tintern Abbey" receives and consolidates a markedly bourgeois version of the poetry of retirement. First, the classical and aristocratic opposition between the rural estate and the court, still very much alive in the poetry of Pope, has been simplified by the end of the century into the opposition of the country and the city. Along with this development comes a certain transfer of nobility to the rural dweller as such, as happens in Gray's "Elegy"[17] and, of course, in Wordsworth's "Preface to *Lyrical Ballads.*" The second feature is that Wordsworth thoroughly internalizes all of the economic and, so to speak, managerial features of the estate. Rather than finding peace through the activities of rural life, Wordsworth rediscovers his authentic self under the inspiration of a beautiful landscape—a landscape he does not own. The Horatian "paternal acres" are replaced by an act of visual appropriation; cultivation turns into meditative memory.

Certainly Wordsworth's version of retirement does not politicize his inner economy in anything like the way *The Borderers* seizes on psychology as a social issue. Nonetheless, reading "Tintern Abbey" as a version of the poetry of retirement must stir the issue of politics. An initial way of bringing politics to bear on "Tintern Abbey" would be to note that the transformation of the country estate into a version of Nature is in some ways not so drastic a change as Røstvig appears to think. Representations of the estate from "To Penshurst" to *The Task* tend to grant the stability and inevitability of nature to the social order that allots owners, tenants, and workers their respective stations. Much of the power of English landscape poetry, as James Turner observes in *The Politics of Landscape,* derives from the way it allows social prescription and political theory the appearance of mere description.[18] When Denham describes the Thames valley from the perspective of

Cooper's Hill, the nature he sees is the king's estate—that is, the state itself—and his theme is its proper management. It helps to recognize that "Tintern Abbey" emerges from a tradition in which careful description of a particularized locality serves as a catalyst for political and metaphysical speculation, as Abrams does in his famous derivation of the "greater Romantic lyric" from the tradition of "Cooper's Hill."[19] But the root motive for local description lies in the symbolic and real status of the estate. It is literally the ground of the social order that affords poetic spectators like Jonson, Denham, Thomson, and Cowper their panoramic perspective and the wherewithal to make abstractions and moralize upon it. Thus the poetry of retirement is often—it is tempting to say always—implicitly political, because it carries such a strong generic impulse either to identify a particular locale with the king's estate or to strongly differentiate oneself and one's surroundings from those of the political center.

Wordsworth engages the retirement tradition in a number of unmistakable ways in "Tintern Abbey": his salutary seclusion in a beautiful spot, his denigration of urban life and of "the world," his aspiration to a visionary experience dependent upon his seclusion, his concern to discover the radical source of his moral strength, and his desire to establish a "mansion" as the legacy of that strength. Nonetheless his revisitation remains a pedestrian tour, and his "mansion" remains a metaphor. All of this may therefore seem too distant from the *beatus ille* tradition for some readers to assign any credible political or ideological significance to it. But the vitality of the classical model of retirement lies closer to hand for Wordsworth as well. In addition to the mediated form in which it reaches him through Thomson and Akenside, two contemporary examples need to be emphasized: first, the disarmingly pure version of retirement aspired to by John Thelwall; and second, what can be called the topography of solitude and community in the recent poetry of Coleridge.

Thelwall, probably the most notorious political activist of Wordsworth's generation, was so worn down by government persecution and harassment in the later 1790s that he decided to give up political life entirely, retire to the country, and pursue a literary career. As he explains in the "Prefatory Memoir" to his *Poems, Chiefly Written in Retirement* of 1801, he decided "to lock up his sentiments in the silence of his own bosom; to concentrate his feelings in the private duties of life; and turn his attention towards making . . . a quiet establishment, for his encreasing family" (JTP xxxv). For this purpose he settled on a small farm at Llyswen, in the

Wye valley, having been "principally influenced by the wild and picturesque scenery of the neighbourhood" (JTP xxxv). There he hoped "the agitations of political feeling might be cradled to forgetfulness, and the delicious day dreams of poesy might be renewed. . . . Thelwall flattered himself that agriculture . . . and the visitations of the Muse . . . might secure to him that humble sort of subsistence to which he had determined to accommodate his desires. In the choice of this situation he was . . . influenced by its remoteness from all political connection" (JTP xxxvi).

Thelwall's "Lines, Written at Bridgewater, in Somersetshire, on the 27th of July, 1797; During a Long Excursion, in Quest of a Peaceful Retreat" is a kind of prospectus for his retirement. It is worth summarizing and quoting at some length for several reasons: the explicitness with which it rehearses some of the classical retirement motifs and modifies others; the inclusion of Coleridge and Wordsworth within the small, sympathetic community of philosopher-poets Thelwall projects; and its intertwined themes of virtue, economy, and domesticity.

The occasion of Thelwall's poem is his birthday, which he calls the "Day of my double birth" because it is also his wedding anniversary. He wonders what the next year holds for him: more woes in the "sordid World / That kindness pays with hatred"? or "hours of sweet retirement . . . studious ease . . . philosophic thought . . . poetic dreams" (JTP 126–27)? He longs to devote himself to literature, but also looks to literature as the catalyst to forming a "congenial" circle of friends around him. He invokes Homer ("Meonides"), Milton, and Shakespeare:

> O! might my soul
> Henceforth with yours hold converse, in the scenes
> Where Nature cherishes Poetic-Thought,
> Best cradled in the solitary haunts
> Where bustling Cares intrude not, nor the throng
> Of cities, or of courts. Yet not for aye
> In hermit-like seclusion would I dwell
> (My soul estranging from my brother Man)
> Forgetful and forgotten: rather oft,
> With some few minds congenial, let me stray
> Along the Muses' haunts, where converse, meet
> For intellectual beings, may arouse
> The soul's sublimer energies.
>
> (JTP 128)

His fantasy of a sympathetic community provides the major substance of the poem and also has the most direct bearing on "Tintern

Abbey." However, it is worthwhile to note the way this fantasy is couched in classical retirement motifs before looking at the community itself more closely. Thelwall's rural life, "mingling Arcadian sports / With healthful industry," will be "A Golden Age reviv'd" (JTP 131). There are many examples of Horatian economy: ". . . my soul / Is sick of public turmoil, . . . [of] sordid avarice, luxurious pomp, / And profligate intemperance" (JTP 129); he rejects "the delusive chace / Of wealth and worldly gewgaws" (JTP 131). He looks forward to healthy husbandry, to "delv[ing] our little garden plots" (JTP 130). Husbandry, however, is more important as a metaphor for the fruits he hopes to reap from this ideal future:

> The Time
> Which, tho swift-fleeting, scatters, as he flies,
> Seeds of delight, that, like the furrow'd grain,
> Strew'd by the farmer, as he onward stalks
> Over his well-ploughed acres, shall produce,
> In happy season, its abundant fruits.
>
> (JTP 128–29)

Thelwall's hopes for the company of "intellectual beings" is the least classical aspect of his poem, and it is the feature most clearly mediated by the eighteenth-century revision (or decay) of the *beatus ille* tradition. In one respect he remains quite Virgilian: the ambition to become a philosopher-poet in his retirement. However, this ambition has drifted away from the aristocratic insistence on a substantial estate to his wish merely to "Build my low cot" (JTP 129). What is more important to Thelwall than his real estate is the "philosophical amity" (JTP 129) he hopes to share with his neighbors. Chief among these will be Coleridge, "Long-lov'd ere known: for kindred sympathies / Link'd, tho far distant, our congenial souls" (JTP 129). Those kindred sympathies are as surely political in their origin as they are philosophical and literary in their ambition.

The community of sympathetic virtue was always central to Thelwall's politics and always set in sharp opposition to legal and political communities coerced into union by the state's monopoly on violence. The "philosophic amity" he hopes for in retirement was earlier a rational, cosmopolitan form of political virtue:

As we would wish to be peaceable and virtuous members of the community, it is necessary that we inform our minds by diligent cultivation. . . . [Thus employed] man feels and enjoys the noble superiority of his nature—his faculties expand, his heart dilates, his senses acquire a keener sensibility—he looks abroad on the universe, and every part of it expands and brightens; while a crowd of pleasures rush upon his imagination, to which the eye of Ignorance is for ever closed. He looks in the face of his fellow creature; and he sees indeed a brother—or a part rather of his own existence; another self—He contemplates in every individual the faculties of sufferance and enjoyment, and feels one nerve of sympathy, connecting him with the whole intellectual universe. Party distinctions and Party cavils, the offspring of ignorance and servility, vanish before him; and National Animosity itself, appears with all its native absurdity and vice.[20]

Thelwall shares some of Godwin's sublime confidence in the power of truth and reason, but his real faith is in the natural gregarious-ness of humankind. In a striking passage in *The Rights of Nature* Thelwall's sympathetic community approximates a Marxist rather than Godwinian optimism:

The fact is, that monopoly, and the hideous accumulation of capital in a few hands, like all diseases not absolutely mortal, carry, in their own enormity, the seeds of cure. Man is, by his very nature, social and communicative—proud to display the little knowledge he possesses, and eager, as opportunity presents, to encrease his store. Whatever presses men together, therefore, though it may generate some vices, is favourable to the diffusion of knowledge, and ultimately promotive of human liberty. Hence every large workshop and manufactory is a sort of political society, which no act of parliament can silence, and no magistrate disperse.[21]

What reduces these grand speculations and ambitions to the small circle of "congenial" philosopher-poet-farmers? Retirement, for Thelwall, is a way of extricating this community of virtue, and along with it a mode of virtuous action, from the web of state violence. According to Thelwall himself, he decided to leave poli-tics because "every effort he made, instead of producing the Rea-son he loved, only irritated to the Violence he abhorred. To that violence, indeed, every thing apparently tended" (JTP xxxv). The sympathetic community Thelwall envisions between himself and Coleridge is a kind of afterimage left burning on Thelwall's eye after the curse of violence turns him away from revolutionary desire.

The most highly valued mode of action that remains open to Thelwall's radical sympathies is that of literature. Thus, it is not surprising that Thelwall's ideal community extends beyond Cole-ridge to include not only their two wives and Thomas Poole but also the Wordsworths. Since Thelwall had visited them at Alfoxden during the week and a half before he wrote this poem, their presence in it is perhaps less striking than the fact that Dorothy Wordsworth appears in parallel with Thelwall's and Coleridge's wives:

> by our sides
> Thy [Coleridge's] Sara, and my Susan, and, perchance,
> Allfoxden's musing tenant, and the maid
> Of ardent eye, who, with fraternal love,
> Sweetens his solitude.
>
> (JTP 130–31)

The point is not that the Wordsworths' filial relationship need be suspected of being unduly sexualized, but rather that Dorothy Wordsworth occupies an important formal position. The final turn in Thelwall's version of retirement is to his wife and family: "To the domestic virtues, calm, and sweet, / Of husband and father" (JTP 132). This attempt at closure bears a tantalizing similarity to Wordsworth's turn to Dorothy in the final movement of "Tintern Abbey."

The strongest link between the "Lines Written at Bridgewater" and the "Lines Written a Few Miles above Tintern Abbey," however, is the intermediary presence of Coleridge (who was also responsible, of course, for Thelwall's visit to Alfoxden). Seclusion, retirement, political engagement, and domestic economy all are prominent themes in Colerdige's blank verse poems from "The Eolian Harp" to "Frost at Midnight" and "Fears in Solitude." The complex dialogue between Wordsworth and Coleridge, and their reciprocal influence upon one another, have been the subjects of a great deal of careful scholarship, and it is not my purpose here to make a detailed contribution to it.[22] But it is worth repeating that the topography of "Tintern Abbey" has strong parallels in Coleridge's recent poetry and that this similar topography in Coleridge's poems combines political and personal anxieties in a powerful way. Three moments in "Tintern Abbey" are particularly resonant: the opening scene in the secluded vale, the sublime prospect in the central passage ("I have felt a presence" and so forth), and the turn to Dorothy. The development of the themes of solitude and community in Coleridge's poetry make the last moment, especially, of paramount importance.

The secluded vale becomes a significantly less attractive spot for Coleridge during these years. "The Eolian Harp" and "Reflections on Having Left a Place of Retirement" both open in a vale that contains a cottage, and Coleridge asociates humble retirement with a blissful domestic interlude, his honeymoon. "This Lime-Tree Bower My Prison," nearly two years later, also opens in seclusion, but now it is sharpened into solitude, and this pattern is repeated the following February in "Frost at Midnight" and again in April in "Fears in Solitude." In both "This Lime-Tree Bower My Prison" and "Frost at Midnight" Coleridge's solitude modulates into a meditation on the country and the city, and in both poems the countryside becomes a kind of solution for the personal and metaphysical problems located in the city. In "Fears in Solitude" Coleridge's anxiety is political. Its immediate occasion is his fear of a French invasion, but he unfolds it fully in a lengthy diatribe against his own country's political and moral corruption. Here the secluded spot affords no solution at all except for physical protection, and the poem ends with Coleridge leaving it in search of a more social and permanent alternative to the degenerate political world.

The sublime prospects in "Reflections on Having Left a Place of Retirement" and "This Lime-Tree Bower My Prison" offer the grounds for authoritative metaphysical assertions, just as in "Tintern Abbey." The same can be said of the prospect at the end of "France: An Ode," but there Coleridge also makes his aesthetic experience into a form of liberty in sharp contrast to the political form it has taken in France. In the final verse paragraph of "Fears in Solitude" the prospect once again marks a sharp break with the context of political turmoil. Its adequacy as a counter to Coleridge's earlier solitude and fears, however, is uncertain:

> Homeward I wind my way; and lo! recalled
> From bodings that have well-nigh wearied me,
> I find myself upon the brow, and pause
> Startled! And after lonely sojourning
> In such a quiet and surrounded nook,
> This burst of prospect, here the shadowy main,
> Dim-tinted, there the mighty majesty
> Of that huge amphitheatre of rich
> And elmy fields, seems like society—
> Conversing with the mind, and giving it
> A livelier impulse and a dance of thought!

(STCPW 263)

That this prospect "seems like society" carries a certain pathos here. It is *not* society, but in two different ways. On the one hand, the force of the long meditation that comprises most of the poem is to remind the reader that the social world is more extensive and far more problematic than the scene this burst of vision takes in. On the other hand, vision can only prefigure conversation; the "dance of thought" is only another kind of solitude. Real society lies below, in Nether Stowey, and not in the poet's experience of sublimity.

Thus Coleridge, like Thelwall, seeks his final refuge from political corruption in domestic virtue. "Fears in Solitude" ends with Colerdige catching sight of

> my own lowly cottage, where my babe
> And my babe's mother dwell in peace! With light
> And quickened footsteps thitherward I tend,
> Remembering thee, O green and silent dell!
> And grateful, that by nature's quietness
> And solitary musings, all my heart
> Is softened, and made worthy to indulge
> Love, and the thoughts that yearn for human kind.
>
> (STCPW 263)

"Nature's quietness" here seems to function in much the same way as the "sympathies with things that hold / An inarticulate language" that Coleridge had seized upon in Ms. B of *The Ruined Cottage* (46r) and copied into his March 10 letter to his brother, the same letter in which he professed he had broken his "squeaking trumpet of sedition" and joined the party of humanity.[23] Just as the sympathizer with Nature "by degrees perceives / His feelings of aversion softened down" (RC&P 261) in Wordsworth's verses, so Coleridge is "softened, and made worthy" to re-enter the domestic sphere.[24] The problem is that Coleridge's negative emotions are firmly identified with his sense of political engagement and his concern for the nation's welfare. Thus the strategy of closure in "Fears in Solitude" reinforces a disturbing dichotomy between a political and a domestic sense of community. This dichotomy would seem to endanger one of the main thrusts of the poetry of retirement, particularly as it was modified by eighteenth-century notions of benevolence, because it disrupts the commonplace identification of national well-being with the good or happy man's rural virtue and the unspoiled economy of the passions in country life. When Coleridge attempts to bridge the gap between solitude and community by turning to the family, he seems with this very gesture to deepen the rift between public and private or political and domestic virtue.

The beautiful blessing Coleridge pronounces upon his infant son in the last two verse paragraphs of "Frost at Midnight", and which Wordsworth echoes in his blessing of Dorothy in "Tintern Abbey," is caught up in the same set of problems. It is strange that, when Coleridge gives his son to Nature as a teacher, the experience he projects for the boy is entirely solitary. Natural objects may speak the language of God directly to young Hartley, but in doing so they also supply the place of a remarkably absent human community. What seems like a wish for social interaction is actually a wish for an isolated aesthetic response to a secluded scene, or for what I have called lyric pleasure in *The Ruined Cottage*. One might well ask whether the recurrent turn to a familial presence in the poetry of Coleridge and Thelwall and in "Tintern Abbey" solves a crisis with its roots in political disaffection or only deepens it. This is the question that will now be put to Wordsworth's revisionary poem of retirement. To what extent do the social and political thematics of the tradition remain vital in Wordsworth's poem? And how, in particular, does the turn to Dorothy cohere with the forms of authority and vision Wordsworth claims for himself?

ECONOMY AND COMMUNITY IN "TINTERN ABBEY"

"Tintern Abbey" organizes its five verse paragraphs into three movements. The first three paragraphs make up the initial movement, and the last two paragraphs comprise the second and the third, respectively. Each of the first two movements mounts from the scene of revisitation to an extended passage of sublime intensity, but, while the first sublime passage rises to a vision of "the life of things," the second turns instead to the poet's recognition of his "anchor" in nature. In the third, crucial movement, Wordsworth turns to his sister to form an idiosyncratic but extremely influential and important version of human community. Each of the movements also engages a different aspect of the poetry of retirement. The first weaves the ideal of the philosopher-poet into a strong net of Miltonic allusions; the second grasps after the notion that chaste and diligent husbandry establishes the ground of civic virtue; and the final turn sets loose the problems of passionate and domestic economy central to the retirement poem from Horace to Coleridge.

Problems of economy are present throughout the poem, however; each segment of the poem has a distinct economic pattern. The transitions, which, as Wordsworth hoped, make this poem approximate an ode, have as much to do with these shifting economic patterns as with modulations of tone. The poem also oscillates between the esoteric and the social, on the one hand, and between assertions of cosmic order and mounting personal anxieties, on the other. A worthy reading of "Tintern Abbey" needs to keep these complexities in view as it tries to establish the coherence—or the logic of the incoherence—in the poem's collage of metaphysical transcendence, moral authority, and literary detachment.

In the poem's first movement, a strangely elegiac tone haunts the margins, while aesthetic pleasure mounts to sublime ecstasy in the foreground. The muted allusion to Milton's "Lycidas" frames this movement, since the "yet once more" motif reappears in the closing lines of the third verse paragraph: "How oft, in spirit, have I turned to thee / O sylvan Wye! Thou wanderer through the woods, / How often has my spirit turned to thee!" The odd figures of the hermit and the "blind man's eye" at the middle of the movement, which have been connected more than once with Milton's "Il Penseroso" and the narrator of *Paradise Lost*,[25] balance the elegiac and "inland" moments at either end of the movement with an antithetical version of seclusion. This pattern plays the humble, protected repose of the mere tourist against a kind of discipline aimed at producing transcendental insight. The second verse paragraph expands this discipline into an almost apocalyptic sublimation of solitude into "the deep power of joy." Along the way, this powerful Miltonic hymn to inner vision joins hands with Virgil's aspiration to the highest mode of retirement: "*Felix, qui potuit rerum cognoscere causas.*"[26]

There is, however, an important difference between Miltonic and Virgilian ambition, which has to do with the economy of the poet's authority. This tension between the classical and the Christian allusions, moreover, establishes the crucial link between the movement's sublime center and its elegiac margin. Consider the economy of the poem's first flight into the sublime. It begins with Wordsworth acknowledging his debt to the landscape:

> Though absent long,
> These forms of beauty have not been to me,
> As is a landscape to a blind man's eye:
> But oft, in lonely rooms, and mid the din
> Of towns and cities, I have owed to them,
> In hours of weariness, sensations sweet,
> Felt in the blood, and felt along the heart,
> And passing even into my purer mind
> With tranquil restoration:—feelings too
> Of unremembered pleasure; such, perhaps,
> As may have had no trivial influence
> On that best portion of a good man's life;

> His little, nameless, unremembered acts
> Of kindness and of love.

The debt Wordsworth owes to the "forms of beauty" is entirely one of gratitude to his benefactors. There is no sense of any transaction having taken place. On the contrary, Wordsworth stresses the subtlety with which they influence his "nameless, unremembered acts." The entire process is hidden, sometimes even from its recipient. At the same time, Wordsworth hints at an active, if not willed, transformation. The forms are interiorized and then sublimated in an almost alchemical refinement of blood into the "purer mind," a movement that recalls the opening paragraph's progress from the murmuring Wye to the hermit's cave.

The rest of the second paragraph mounts to the sublime by deepening the process of interiorization, hyperbolizing the poet's passivity, and passing from the hidden to the truly esoteric:

> Nor less, I trust,
> To them I may have owed another gift,
> Of aspect more sublime; that blessed mood,
> In which the burthen of the mystery,
> In which the heavy and the weary weight
> Of all this unintelligible world
> Is lighten'd:—that serene and blessed mood,
> In which the affections gently lead us on,
> Until, the breath of this corporeal frame,
> And even the motion of our human blood
> Almost suspended, we are laid asleep
> In body, and become a living soul:
> While with an eye made quiet by the power
> Of harmony, and the deep power of joy,
> We see into the life of things.

As Wordsworth passes from "tranquil restoration" to the "blessed mood," the autobiographical subject turns into a universalized one ("I" and "my" give way to "we" and "our"). Both are being liberated, but, where the one escapes from "lonely rooms" and "the din / Of towns and cities," the other receives the means to overcome "the burthen of the mystery," "the heavy and the weary weight / Of all this unintelligible world." As social locations give way to a metaphysical condition, the basis of community changes from practical interaction ("acts of kindness") to understanding or intelligibility *per se*. The community into which "we" are introduced sheds all hints of economic or political organization and is instead bound together only by shared pleasure: "the power / Of harmony, and the deep power of joy." Thus (as with Kantian aesthetics) it includes everyone and no one at the same time: everyone in our capacity for responsiveness, and no one in his or her practical situation.

The metaphysical authority by which Wordsworth assumes to speak for us has Christian and Miltonic roots. The deepening of interiority and passivity in the "blessed mood" traces a properly apocalyptic pattern of death and resurrection: "we are laid asleep / In body, and become a living soul." The climax of the "blessed mood," when the poet "see[s] into the life of things," echoes Milton's plea for inner light, "that [he] may see and tell / Of things invisible to mortal sight."[27] At the level of Christian myth, the "blessed mood" would, like Miltonic inspiration or the final judgment, be a direct experience of one's personal relationship to God, and all other kinds of relationships are clearly subordinate and ultimately inconsequential in this perspective.

In *Paradise Lost* such a perspective serves to undercut the political authority of Milton's enemies. That is, it not only transforms worldly isolation into spiritual communion; it also outflanks his political exile by identifying true freedom with one's entire submission to divine law. Wordsworth's situation is quite different, however, and it makes seclusion and community more problematic. One of the strongest tendencies in Wordsworth's poetry in the 1790s is indeed to follow Milton's apocalyptic strategy of establishing his authority at a point prior to all political organization. But for Wordsworth the ground prior to politics is still usually social, a state of nature populated by an authentic, passionately bound community. Even when "Tintern Abbey" refines those communal bonds down to the mere fact—or possibility—of intelligibility and portrays the ideal of response as deathlike passivity, the essential bond he appeals to is formed by pleasure rather than by law. Thus the assured hierarchy Milton calls upon to subordinate political catastrophe to the scheme of universal redemption gives way in Wordsworth to an attempt to overwhelm politics with "the power / Of harmony, and the deep power of joy" rather than to include it in a subordinated position.[28]

To put it another way, although Milton's influence tends to drive Wordsworth's search for metaphysical authority toward the apocalyptic moments of pure creation or final judgment, Wordsworth's modernity lies in his own tendency to revise such ultimate realities into the hyperbolic experiences of a universalized, but still human, subject. That is, the experience the Wye valley gives to the poet in "Tintern Abbey" is less like the infusion of "celestial light" into the darkness of Milton's political exile than like re-entry into Eden. In typological terms, Wordsworth seems almost to skip over Christ's suffering in order to become the new Adam.[29] His death and resurrection are not trials suffered through, and his redemption is not earned. The "blessed mood" is a gift rather than an accomplishment (or even a sign of perseverance). And as a gift, its significance falls somewhat short of the apocalyptic marriage of the mind and nature that he would project as his goal in *Home at Grasmere*. Rather than a marriage, both the "blessed mood" and the plot of revisitation point instead to his regaining a kind of prelapsarian solitude. Notice that in the initial scene every mark of cultivation or habitation—and not just the distressful evidence of "vagrant dwellers"—is ringed about with a defensive affirmation that it is not disturbing:

> These plots of cottage ground, these orchard-tufts,
> Which, at this season, with their unripe fruits,
> Among the woods and copses lose themselves,
> Nor, with their green and simple hue, disturb
> The wild green landscape.

Perhaps the "pastoral farms" are "green to the very door" because the poet's activity is a recovery of the blissful solitude celebrated by Marvell's Adamic persona in "The Garden": "Annihilating all that's made / To a green thought in a green shade" and thereby reclaiming "That happy garden state / While man there walked without a mate."

The anxiety that surfaces immediately after the poet finishes acknowledging the "more sublime" gift has to do with the poet's paradise of Adamic seclusion. The opening words of the third verse paragraph, "If this / Be but a vain belief," do not express metaphysical doubts about the source of the poet's gift, but rather fears about the usefulness, the permanence, and perhaps the communicability of the poet's pleasure. The "forms of beauty" are available to him, but his "vain belief" refers to a worry about his stewardship of his talents, that is, about the authenticity of his moods rather than their origins. The hyperbolic passivity of the "blessed mood" yields to the anxiety of indolence.

Here is where the tension between Miltonic and classical allusion exerts itself and helps to turn the poem toward its second sublime passage. The tension has to do with the relationship between economy and politics. For Virgil's philosopher-poet, the opportunity for lofty poetic achievement that retirement affords is an economic privilege rather than a divine gift. Virgil's political theme, moreover, depends upon this economic privilege rather than upon the success of the philosopher-poet. Whatever Virgil loses when he turns from the philosopher's retirement to that of the husbandman, therefore, is to a certain extent compensated for by approaching nearer to the ground of his political perspective.

With this in mind, compare Virgil's turn from sublime to country pleasures with Wordsworth's:

> sin, has ne possim naturae accedere partis,
> frigidus obstiterit circum praecordia sanguis,
> rura mihi et rigui placeant in vallibus amnes,
> flumina amem silvasque inglorius.
>
> (*Georgics*, 2.483–86)

["But if the chill blood about my heart bar me from reaching those realms of nature, let my delight be the country, and the running streams amid the dells—may I love the waters and the woods, though fame be lost."]

> If this
> Be but a vain belief, yet, oh! how oft,
> In darkness, and amid the many shapes
> Of joyless day-light; when the fretful stir
> Unprofitable, and the fever of the world,
> Have hung upon the beatings of my heart,
> How oft, in spirit, have I turned to thee,
> O sylvan Wye! Thou wanderer through the woods,
> How often has my spirit turned to thee!

In both passages, chillness or heaviness of the blood turns the poet away from sublime aspirations to a profession of love for the streams and the woods, and Wordsworth's emphasis on the "fretful stir / Unprofitable, and the fever of the world" only makes more explicit the conventional value being ascribed to rural contentment. It seems that Virgil shows Wordsworth a safe (albeit inglorious) way out of the Miltonic sublime, with its hyperbolic demands and its attendant anxieties. The way leads from one economy to another. In the Miltonic passage, the "forms of beauty" are active, quasi-divine benefactors, but in the Virgilian economy the poet's memory seems to be modelled upon the rural estate. It is there for the poet to turn to as a kind of reservoir of self-sufficiency. At the same time, perhaps the elegiac allusion re-emerges here precisely because community must once again be deciphered in nature rather than being immanent in the poet's power. However that may be, this Virgilian turn from sublime insight to the "sylvan Wye" leads the poem from the poetics of the divine gift to an economy of loss and recompense.[30]

The poem's second movement, the fourth verse paragraph, takes place within this new economy of exchange. It frames a central moment of hope in "abundant recompense" within a progressive movement between two moments of recognition: the first troubled by "sad perplexity," but the second "well pleased" with what the poet has discovered. Between the poet's initial perplexity and the central turn comes an acknowledgement of personal loss and the poet's retrospective accounting of that loss. This allows Wordsworth to revise the Miltonic gift by balancing his losses and his gains:

> Not for this
> Faint I, nor mourn nor murmur: other gifts
> Have followed, for such loss, I would believe,
> Abundant recompence.

Wordsworth discards his posture of passive receptivity for one closer to the blind Milton's unfailing perseverance: "Yet not the more / Cease I to wander where the Muses haunt" (*Paradise Lost* 3.25–26). At the same time, the Miltonic stance itself would now need to be represented as a trade off of one kind of vision for another; that is, Milton's inner light would become his "abundant recompense" for his blindness. In "Tintern Abbey," however, this means that the poet's present situation must be filled with the pathos of loss before he can claim for himself the recompense of poetic authority. Once he has this authority in view, the poet rises to a second sublime passage characterized by claims of maturity and sympathy rather than the sublimation and purification of the "blessed mood." Instead of a re-entry into Edenic solitude and beatific indolence, the second sublime resembles a theodicy. It apologizes for fallen experience by turning apparent loss into more substantial gain. In the paragraph's closing recognition, Wordsworth then consolidates the newly claimed ground of his authority.

The key to this entire movement is the shift in economic metaphors by which Wordsworth treats his memory and inner resources as a kind of estate instead of as a divine gift. The closing recognition, in which Wordsworth triumphantly displays the "anchor" of his moral authority, reaps the harvest of this transformation. Interrogating his memory, the storehouse of "nature and the language of the sense," ends up doing for Wordsworth the poet what cultivating the rural estate does for Virgil the Roman citizen:

> hanc olim veteres vitam coluere Sabini,
> hanc Remus et frater, sic fortis Etruria crevit
> scilicet et rerum facta est pulcherrima Roma.
> (*Georgics*, 2.532–34)

[Such a life the old Sabines once lived, such Remus and his brother. Thus, surely, Etruria waxed strong, thus Rome became of all things the fairest].

Wordsworth's retrospect affirms the poet's continued access to the radical source of his strength. It also shifts the basis of his authority away from its earlier metaphysical and mythical ground and toward something relatively more social. Thus the relation between his interior drama and the community he hopes to address must change, too. The plot of "Tintern Abbey's" second movement, then, is largely a matter of superseding a version of poetic authority that takes its form from the Christian apocalypse by rewriting the poet's authority as a kind of civic virtue.

Nothing is more typical of "Tintern Abbey" than that Wordsworth only acknowledges the reality of loss after he has already professed his determination to overcome it:

> And now, with gleams of half-extinguish'd thought,
> With many recognitions dim and faint,
> And somewhat of a sad perplexity,
> The picture of the mind revives again:
> While here I stand, not only with the sense
> Of present pleasure, but with pleasing thoughts
> That in this moment there is life and food
> For future years. And so I dare to hope
> Though changed, no doubt, from what I was . . .

Most readers probably share some of Wordsworth's perplexity here, because it is quite difficult to make literal sense of the first four lines. What is his thought, and why is it half-extinguished? Why so many recognitions, dim and faint though they be? And why is it "the picture of the mind" that "revives again?" Does this picture belong to the mind, or does it portray it? If the picture is reviving again, how often has it faded away? These lines seem to require a completion the poet pointedly neglects to furnish, but the suspension of meaning does not suggest so much that more is available as that something has been left out or obscured. The next five lines then proceed to compensate for this vague sense of loss by asserting, first, a "sense / Of present pleasure"; second, confidence "That in this moment there is life and food / For future years"; and third, the poet's declaration that he "dare[s] to hope." Only then does the fact of loss begin to take a definite form. The reader is thereby allowed to understand in retrospect that the poet's perplexity has something to do with sustaining thought, reviving a past sense of pleasure, and coming to a clearer recognition of the poet's debts, losses, and profits. The most telling image is finally the poet's desire for "life and food / For future years." Here the earlier economy of angelic assimilation of the "forms of beauty" to "the life of things" gives way most clearly to an emerging process of laborious cultivation.

The poet then introduces a new version of his former self "when first / [He] came among these hills." What he describes is apparently no more than an earlier touristic excursion,[31] yet Wordsworth now attributes an erotic intensity to the younger man's pleasure in the landscape: it was "like a passion," "an appetite," "A feeling and a love," full of "aching joys" and "dizzy raptures." In one sense this younger Wordsworth represents the antithesis of the "blessed mood," because for the younger tourist the absolute self-sufficiency of the body's pleasures lays the mind to sleep: the "colours" and "forms" of the landscape "had no need of a remoter charm, / By thought supplied." Yet in another sense this tourist seems just as passive as the entranced visionary. The point of comparing him to a hunted deer ("like a roe / I bounded o'er the mountains . . . more like a man / Flying from something that he dreads, than one / Who sought the thing he loved") is to emphasize that his desires drive him precipitously forward without any sense of pursuing a rational goal. The result, however implicit it remains at this point, is to have already claimed that loss is gain, as the overwhelming but superficial intensity of the tour has already faded into the powerful visionary depth of the "blessed mood."

The most complex economic figure for the younger tourist's experience is that it "had no need of . . . any interest / Unborrowed from the eye." The primary signification of "interest" is presumably "human interest," the kind of relationship based on mutual needs and enterprises that is fundamental to the coherence of any community. The younger tourist's pleasure in the landscape (which is appropriately gothic rather than pastoral in this passage) is entirely detached from any "interest" of this sort in the scenes he passes through. His extravagant superficiality is not quite that of the simple and unreflective objects of conventional sympathy; the "glad animal movements" of his childhood are only brought up parenthetically in order to be distinguished from his self-absorbed aesthetic consumption of "nature." Rather, the young tourist's "interest" is *borrowed* "from the eye": meaning that it is evanescent, that it represents no lasting bond with the scene because it results from no rational or laborious investment in the place. This situation will be reversed when the poet returns to the sublime a few lines later. The "still, sad music of humanity" furnishes precisely the human interest that is lacking in the younger tourist's pleasure; sympathy eventually lends interest to vision.

Here a secondary connotation of interest and borrowing may be brought into play. The figure also suggests usury or, better, investment in the public funds. If the voluptuous and suspiciously autoerotic pleasures of the younger tourist suggest some of the meteoric instability associated with public credit in the eighteenth century,[32] the older tourist's interest suggests a steady income— an income likely to be founded on ownership of an estate, but not inevitably so. Wordsworth's ability to supply interest to vision clearly resembles the kind of civic virtue based on "real" property. Yet the mature visionary is still only a tourist, and the entire economic figure suggests his class position. On the one hand, the tourist seems rootless and marginal, neither an owner nor a worker. His appreciation of the landscape is necessarily abstract, so that both the earlier "cataracts" and the later "pastoral farms" end up being idealized into "forms of beauty" and "the language of the sense." The younger tourist's absorption in his experience is balanced by his detachment from the scene, which allows him to move on, free of the demands of labor or subsistence, and yet to continue drawing "interest" on it from afar (see "The Solitary Reaper")— and Wordsworth's sublime detachment in the "blessed mood" seems to be only a hyperbolic extension of the young tourist's self-absorption. In the mature tourist, on the other hand, a firmer sense of his own experiential ground seems at last to galvanize the middle-class spectator's nostalgia for rural simplicity into deep participation in the universal "interest" of humanity. Yet the estate the mature Wordsworth cultivates remains entirely an abstract, idealizing form of individual pleasure.

The second sublime passage goes on to celebrate Wordsworth's "sense sublime / Of something far more deeply interfused." This sense, insofar as it grows out of the "language of the sense,"[33] is the substance of the poet's claim for moral authority. The vagueness of

"something" expresses precisely the pathos that separates Wordsworth's stance from the more secure ground connecting poetry,
metaphysics, ethics, and society for Milton, Denham, Pope, or, for
that matter, Edmund Burke. Yet the perspective the sublime sense
affords Wordsworth is familiar enough. "Tintern Abbey's" second
sublime passage combines the hymns to cosmic harmony in Thomson's *The Seasons* with the ethos of correspondence between sensitivity to natural beauty and the moral sense in Akenside's *The
Pleasures of Imagination.*[34] It also recalls the exultant hilltop moments in Coleridge's recent poetry and points back with them to
such commonplaces as Cowper's elevated prospect in book 1 of
The Task ("Now roves the eye, / And posted on this speculative
height / Exults in its command" [288–90])[35] and Thomson's "eye
excursive" roaming over the prospect at Hagley Park ("Spring"
956).

Nonetheless the claim, "Therefore am I still / A lover," remains
remarkably fragile. The continuing tension between the poet's assertions of growth and of constancy amplifies the already established tone of consolation for unacknowledged loss and indicates
that there is an unresolved problem involving the hierarchical status of undisturbed purity, on the one hand, and of experiential
wisdom, on the other. In this context the movement from declaring
himself a "lover" of nature, which recalls the barely submerged
eroticism of the young tourist's pleasures, to calling nature his
nurse, guide, and guardian indicates that, whatever the scope of
vision or sympathy claimed in the second sublime passage, "something" at the level of passion and kinship remains to be addressed.
The feminization of nature, first implicitly in the young tourist's
appetites and passions, then explicitly in the paragraph's closing
recognition, prepares the way for the poem's final turn to the
poet's sister.

The final verse paragraph of "Tintern Abbey" could be characterized as a series of assertions of invulnerability. Wordsworth begins by turning from the figurative nurse, guide, and guardian he
has just recognized to his real sister, and he declares that her familiar presence would sustain his spirits even if his "abundant recom-
pence" were lacking. He then prays for her, blesses her, and
predicts her future happiness and strength of spirit. Her future
strength depends upon a plot of maturation similar to his own, in
which she trades in her "wild ecstasies" for "sober pleasure." But
in Dorothy Wordsworth's case, instead of the sympathetic capacity
to hear the "music of humanity," he stresses her ability to preserve
and make permanent her present pleasures: ". . . thy mind / Shall

be a mansion for all lovely forms, / Thy memory be as a dwelling-place / For all sweet sounds and harmonies." Dorothy's maturation justifies William's earlier hope for "life and food / For future years" by establishing within her the Horatian self-sufficiency Pope longs for in his "Ode on Solitude:"

> Happy the man, whose wish and care
> A few paternal acres bound,
> Content to breathe his native air,
> In his own ground.
>
> Whose herds with milk, whose fields with bread,
> Whose flocks supply him with attire,
> Whose trees in summer yield him shade,
> In winter fire.[36]

The final verse paragraph of "Tintern Abbey" manages to recapitulate both the economies of sublimation and of exchange in terms of the idealized subsistence economy of the *beatus ille* tradition.

Yet this entire paragraph is also, and increasingly as it goes on, shot through with anxieties. After his first confident acknowledgement of her unequivocal presence, the relation between the poet and his sister becomes more and more tenuously mediated. With each new assertion of invulnerability, the poet also adds new denials of what will be prevented, so that the list of possible ills becomes quite impressive: the poet fears the loss of his powers; he fears being overcome with weariness and despair; he fears solitude, pain, and grief; he fears death. His initial certitude quickly wanders into an ambiguous area between declaration and wish, and his final statements hover between prediction and supplication. Thus, if the turn to Dorothy picks up a recurrent gesture of closure from Coleridge and Thelwall (with clear precedents in Cowper and Thomson as well),[37] then Wordsworth's revision of the Horatian domestic establishment and its idyllic self-sufficiency is also consistently undercut by the denials and fears that hedge it in.

What precipitates the poet's turn to his sister, after the supremely confident phrases that ring out the second sublime passage, is a re-emergence of anxiety about his "decay":

> Nor, perchance,
> If I were not thus taught, should I the more
> Suffer my genial spirits to decay:
> For thou art with me, here, upon the banks

> Of this fair river; thou, my dearest Friend,
> My dear, dear Friend, and in thy voice I catch
> The language of my former heart, and read
> My former pleasures in the shooting lights
> Of thy wild eyes. Oh! yet a little while
> May I behold in thee what I was once,
> My dear, dear Sister!

It has often been remarked that Wordsworth's introduction of a second character into the scene is not just odd, coming as late in the poem as it does, but also somewhat illusory, since Dorothy Wordsworth seems to be little more than a surrogate for the poet.[38] She is first of all a substitute or recompense for the energies he has lost, and, second, a repository or representation of those energies, so that Wordsworth can claim not to have really lost them after all. She is therefore the very embodiment of his defensive posture, both a compensation for loss and a denial of it; and her comforting presence turns out to be riven by that contradiction. The unresolved tension appears in the exclamation, "Yet a little while / May I behold in thee what I was once," which may declare Wordsworth's reassurance of at least limited access to his former self, but equally expresses his fear that those "former pleasures" will quickly disappear again.

Dorothy's status as a representation seems also to overshadow her humanity in the preceding lines, where the poet catches a very personal kind of "language" in her voice and "reads" another reminder of himself in her eyes. The diction here inevitably recalls the two earlier sublime passages, both of which proceed in their different ways through Wordsworth's introspective consideration of an esoteric set of signs. But where earlier he could "see into the life of things" and then later "recognize . . . the anchor of [his] purest thoughts," now he catches at and reads an objectified version of them. The authority he is claiming for himself has been diluted from a metaphysical grasp of essential reality to something merely linguistic and quasi-social. But his third passage to knowledge also quite clearly suggests literary mediation. When Dorothy enters the poem, the actual lineaments of a literary form of authority and a literarily mediated community appear along with her.

This is all the more interesting in that it is presumably the heightened "interest" of family affection that motivates the poet's introduction of his sister into the poem. The community of sympathy the poet declares in the second sublime passage seems to strive against the marginal, spectatorial position dictated by Wordsworth's social class by elevating his metaphorical bond to nature closer and closer to kinship. Once he has moved from his "nurse, guide, and guardian" to his actual human companion, he continues gradually mounting from "thou" to "Friend" to "Sister," so that the phrase "My dear, dear Sister!" climaxes a careful and drawn-out development. Two things follow quickly from this climax. First, Wordsworth immediately includes a deliberate echo of Coleridge's "This Lime-Tree Bower My Prison" ("And this prayer I make, / Knowing that Nature never did betray / The heart that loved her"), and he proceeds from there to the blessing of Dorothy that so elegantly alludes to "Frost at Midnight." Second, the poet also returns within a few lines to the first-person-plural pronoun, as in "Tintern Abbey"'s first sublime passage. However, the status of the first-person plural is quite different when it returns. In the first sublime passage, the first-person plural announces the universality of Wordsworth's experience in its paradoxical emergence from a severe form of solitude. The instabilities of this paradox then help move the poet's claim to universal experience toward a more social form in the second sublime passage, where the sympathetically "interfused" spectator constructs a symptomatically abstract and detached version of civic virtue. Out of the pathos of this detachment, finally, develops the poet's climactic naming of a familial bond with a real person, so that "we" at this point may refer only to two people or to a very small group that, by the force of allusion, would also include the other "Friend," Coleridge. Yet the force of the first-person plural to refer beyond this small group remains strong, particularly since the poet continues to address "Nature" in interpersonal terms. The effect is to leave the pronoun reference suspended between assured fact and lofty wish in perfect keeping with the tone of "Tintern Abbey's" entire final movement.

The problem developed in the passage between the two Coleridge allusions has to do with the practices that constitute communities and hold them together:

> And this prayer I make,
> Knowing that Nature never did betray
> The heart that loved her; 'tis her privilege,
> Through all the years of this our life, to lead
> From joy to joy: for she can so inform
> The mind that is within us, so impress
> With quietness and beauty, and so feed
> With lofty thoughts, that neither evil tongues,
> Rash judgments, nor the sneers of selfish men,
> Nor greetings where no kindness is, nor all

> The dreary intercourse of daily life,
> Shall e'er prevail against us, or disturb
> Our chearful faith that all which we behold
> Is full of blessings.

The contrast between the community of "chearful faith" and its antithesis is based upon the commonplaces concerning country life versus the court and city in the *beatus ille* tradition. But Wordsworth's treatment of that contrast is highly individual. Nature's guidance and sustenance hold together Wordsworth's community; the language simultaneously suggests religion and kinship. It is both passionate and pious, joyful and quiet. The emphasis on quietness and on the act of beholding recalls the importance of the "face" of community in *The Borderers*. Indeed the antithetical world of "daily life" that threatens "chearful faith" recalls Wordsworth's handling of the theme of theatricality in *The Borderers*, and the passage's initial fear of betrayal further solidifies the connection. The lines describing the antithetical world may seem puzzlingly undermotivated and both misanthropic and banal in their final rejection of everyday social interaction. But this judgment would miss the point that Wordsworth lists the world's evils in a pattern of descending magnitude and increasing generality. "Evil tongues" echoes Milton in exile (*Paradise Lost*, 7.26) and suggests a context of political persecution with all the seriousness of fundamental religious issues and prophetic responsibility. Rashness and selfishness descend from the Satanic level of a Rivers to the more ambiguous failings of Mortimer and his band, while the next two lines bring the corrupting influence of falsehood and artifice to bear in the broadest possible context.

The crux of the contrast between faith and betrayal is Nature's benevolent guidance, which, although it seems at times to simply set language against silent vision, actually only opposes one kind of communication within one set of rituals to another. The "language" Wordsworth "reads" in Dorothy's eyes indicates, on the one hand, the kind of spontaneous recognition based on the passionate bonds of the family or authentic community in *The Borderers*, but, on the other, it refers to Wordsworth's literary circle. The two allusions to Coleridge adumbrate the same double reference. In "Frost at Midnight," Coleridge blesses his infant son, but in "This Lime-Tree Bower My Prison" he speaks to Lamb and the Wordsworths. Thus the community of "chearful faith," held together in its familial and religious aspects by Nature, also refers to a literary community held together and indeed constituted by poetry itself. The role of

Wordsworth's turn to his sister in "Tintern Abbey" is to intensify literary ritual by virtually identifying it with the closest natural and sacred ties between people. The sympathetic community's anonymity and detachment are being revised and resolved in the tight-knit web of family and faith.

The power of Wordsworth's solution can hardly be denied. Many a reader, myself among them, has joyfully answered Wordsworth's call to enlist in the quasi-monastic brother-and-sisterhood of "chearful faith," and this is much more true in terms of the literary institution he merely suggests than of the explicit metaphysical and social claims he presses. It is most true, perhaps, insofar as the twists and turns of the meditative, self-interpreting, and self-revising subject who speaks in "Tintern Abbey" have so often been read as the poem's *problem* rather than, in their very tortuousness and their uncanny suspension of tone and reference, the *solution* of a prior historical dilemma. For the poet's true problem is not establishing continuity with his past (he is really breaking off in a new direction) or dealing with a loss of power (he is really gaining poetic power) but rather formulating his role in the grand historical drama. The important question is not, am I still what I was? It is, to whom do I speak, and to what end? Thus the strangely defensive and yet exalted postures he assumes are a way of standing for—and virtually *as*—authentic liberty and genuine social cohesion, but within a wholly vicarious community.

The form of freedom in "Tintern Abbey" is nowhere more beautifully or cogently realized, for instance, than in the blessing the poet pronounces upon his sister:

> Therefore let the moon
> Shine on thee in thy solitary walk;
> And let the misty mountain winds be free
> To blow against thee.

Wordsworth's blessing of his sister enacts a basic human commitment between them as passionate and nurturing, perhaps, as Coleridge's to his son; this commitment is what justifies Wordsworth's use of "therefore." Wordsworth balances family and metaphysics more delicately than Coleridge, however, by first invoking the virginal light of the moon, then wrapping Dorothy in the disembodied but tactile embrace of the wind. Though she be solitary, she walks in the very medium and substance of her communion with William. In fact, the "wind" of Wordsworth's blessing surely recalls the creator's life-giving breath in *Genesis* and thus makes Dorothy

Wordsworth into a kind of Eve repairing the poet's solitude and making whole the bond of "humanity" and nature. Her freedom thus becomes an almost Miltonic accession to the quasi-divine forces playing upon her. Yet is it not troubling that Wordsworth's blessing nonetheless delivers her to solitude, lovely and graceful though it be? For solitude here *represents* community, as it does throughout "Tintern Abbey," and the freedom Wordsworth rediscovers in the poem can be no less paradoxical than that representation.

Here the context of Miltonic solitude and mediation gathers its full force. Wordsworth's turn to his sister alludes in its entirety to the Miltonic source he quotes in its course:

> Standing on Earth, not rapt above the Pole,
> More safe I Sing with mortal voice, unchang'd
> To hoarse or mute, though fall'n on evil days,
> On evil days though fall'n, and evil tongues;
> In darkness, and with dangers compast round,
> And solitude; yet not alone, while thou
> Visit'st my slumbers Nightly, or when Morn
> Purples the East: still govern thou my Song,
> *Urania,* and fit audience find, though few.
>
> (*Paradise Lost,* 7.23–31)

Wordsworth transforms the metaphysical authority that delivers Milton from his solitude and defines Milton's "fit audience" into the paradigmatic experience of isolation and vicarious community "Tintern Abbey" itself constructs and so powerfully reproduces. But since divine inspiration has been traded for sympathetic passion, the poem no longer grants access to a form of freedom beside which political misfortune loses its substance. On the contrary, all it can afford is a kind of safe haven, an enchanted circle of self-determination, that remains as contingent as the corrupt world it fences out. That contingency is what threatens Wordsworth's self-assurance throughout the poem, and it is what dictates the metaphor of the "mansion" and the Horatian economy of subsistence, which become the final bulwarks of freedom in "Tintern Abbey."

The last half of the fifth verse paragraph of "Tintern Abbey" recapitulates the schemes of maturation and sublimation from the poem's first two movements in such a way as to enclose them within a kind of charmed circle. The first nine lines sketch a pattern of alienation and return over the scheme of maturation:

> and in after years,
> When these wild ecstasies shall be matured
> Into a sober pleasure, when thy mind
> Shall be a mansion for all lovely forms,
> Thy memory be as a dwelling-place
> For all sweet sounds and harmonies; Oh! then,
> If solitude, or fear, or pain, or grief,
> Should be thy portion, with what healing thoughts
> Of tender joy wilt thou remember me,
> And these my exhortations!

The economy of exchange that characterizes maturation in "Tintern Abbey" here insures that energies lost can be regained because they circulate within the tight-knit community of family and faith. The "mansion" and "dwelling-place" therefore figure an ideal subsistence economy that seems to relieve the middle-class spectator's sympathy of its marginality and detachment. The cost of doing so, however, is to abstract the poet into a virtual identification with his "exhortations." His alienated return comes not as poet but as poem, and the "interest" that holds together this community becomes literally nothing but words.

The poem's final lines recapitulate the scheme of sublimation:

> Nor, perchance,
> If I should be, where I no more can hear
> Thy voice, nor catch from thy wild eyes these gleams
> Of past existence, wilt thou then forget
> That on the banks of this delightful stream
> We stood together; and that I, so long
> A worshipper of Nature, hither came,
> Unwearied in that service: rather say
> With warmer love, oh! with far deeper zeal
> Of holier love. Nor wilt thou then forget,
> That after many wanderings, many years
> Of absence, these steep woods and lofty cliffs,
> And this green pastoral landscape, were to me
> More dear, both for themselves, and for thy sake!

Alienation and return here become death and resurrection, and the language appropriately turns to the imagery of religious worship. But the institution really being invoked to preserve the poet's love and zeal is poetry, not religion. How tenuous a comfort comes of resurrecting the self as a poem instead of as a person appears in the repeated formula, "Nor wilt thou then forget," which snatches its shred of hope from the jaws of death only by surrendering to the most severely mediated of satisfactions. Both of the times Wordsworth speaks the formula, the clause ends in one of those characteristic half-assertions, the suspended comparison.[39] The effect of the suspended comparison is to force the reader to posit the missing half of the comparison,[40] so that "far deeper zeal" ends up meaning, perhaps, simply a zeal deeper than any you were asked to acknowledge up till now. Ultimately the point of the technique is to form a kind of community in the very act of suspending reference. "We" become more dear, both for ourselves and for the sake of the poem, than we were without it.

"Tintern Abbey's" ritual of worship does not celebrate a communion of tourist with nature or even of brother with sister nearly so powerfully as it celebrates the paradoxical community and isolation of the literary spectator, the reader. The form of freedom it represents the poet as discovering—that is, the form of freedom Wordsworth here invents—corresponds to the reader's detachment and invulnerability in the interlude of poetic representation. That interlude occupies a privileged space that emerges from the deeply political literary tradition of rural retirement, a tradition that is often quite explicit about the class standing necessary to gain access to its detached perspective. In "Tintern Abbey" social class remains integral to the poem, where, besides providing the ground of the poet's vision, it also becomes the source of the pathos that haunts his ambitions of universality. These same ambitions push the poem toward a myth of individual transcendence and toward the illusion that apolitical, virtuous self-sufficiency can here proclaim its triumph over "the world." To label these myths the poem's ideology, however, is to undervalue the desperation— or call it tact—with which the poet hedges in and hollows out his claims of invulnerability. "Tintern Abbey" is not doctrinally surefooted, much as it attempts to appear so, and any attempt to define its ideology will have to take on its ambiguities and doubts along with its mystifications and self-promotion. A better response, perhaps, is to simply try to gauge the protean quality of the poem's salvational and self-interpretive gestures. The community invented in "Tintern Abbey" may prove to be precisely as substantial, as open-ended, and as indeterminate as the practices of reading that preserve and communicate its pleasures.

Conclusion: Originality, Sympathy, and the Critique of Ideology

THE READINGS OFFERED IN THIS STUDY HAVE BEEN SO TIGHTLY focused on a small period of time and a few crucial, canonical texts that the project's limitations are no doubt obvious. Nonetheless, it is worthwhile to meditate on the significance of those limits. Following the hint thrown out in the last sentence of the chapter on "Tintern Abbey," one could ask just what are the practices of reading that preserve and communicate the pleasures of Wordsworth's community of recognition? Or to put it another way, if this entire study can present itself finally as an attempt to lay bare the singularity of Wordsworth's poetic originality, then what exactly does that originality originate?

These questions highlight a problem implied by the thesis that Wordsworth's achievement has to do with inventing a form of community that is realized not in the agrarian settings he idealized, but in the literary space he mapped out. If Wordsworth is in an important way an originator of the set of practices we call today, simply, literature, then literature here has to be understood in a certain way: not as a millenia-old body of writing, but rather as a much more recently assembled apparatus devoted to the production, distribution, reception, and transmission of certain kinds of texts. My attempt to grasp Wordsworth's community of recognition in its historical materiality as a poetic artifact hopes to contribute to an ongoing critical transformation of the concept of literature itself from a transhistorical category immanent in human potential (the capacity for creating imaginative verbal artifacts) to a set of practices with a specific social, political, and economic context (broadly speaking, the development of capitalism and the culture of the European bourgeoisie).[1] This rethinking of the concept of literature not only denaturalizes Wordsworth's achievement, but also, more importantly, it calls into question the object of literary studies. Thus it enables us to elaborate upon the problem of what Wordsworth's originality can be said to originate by asking whether the power of Wordsworth's poetry is grounded in the texts of the poems or whether, on the contrary, the poems have merely become fetishes of an institutional ensemble usually called, by a metonymic transference, literature.

What is involved here is first of all a change of focus. Imagine that you relax your gaze on some pages of Wordsworth's poetry that you have subjected to a long, intense scrutiny, and as a consequence (perhaps even with a "shock of mild surprise") you find yourself staring at a background that was there all along. What you see may be a library, an office, a study; almost surely there are books, lots of books; and your presence there no doubt implies a set of privileges and responsibilities—privileges that have to do with access and time to learn what the books have to communicate and responsibilities for taking part in the transmission and reproduction of that privileged access. And it must be admitted that this is a comfortable scene for most of its inhabitants. For as the import of this background sinks in, its supportive function may begin to bear a striking resemblance to Wordsworthian nature. Are not these book-filled rooms uncannily like Dorothy Wordsworth as the repository of the "Tintern Abbey" poet's lost vitality, as the "mansion" of literary economy and embodiment of a vicarious community—even, perhaps, as amanuensis of your own mimic hootings?

This scene does not, of course, point to nature but rather to the institutional network that supplies the books, grants the privileges, and enforces the responsibilities that support it; and looking more closely at this abiding background presence is not really likely to be comforting. On the contrary, focusing on the way the literary text's importance and value depend upon scholarly, critical, and pedagogic activities changes what seemed like a set of secondary and supplementary adjuncts to a primary object into something less parasitic, more symbiotic, but also more suspicious. Indeed, recent studies of literary education have predominantly agreed that a complex array of somewhat unsavory interests shores up literature's institutional framework, including those of class hegemony, racism, imperialism, governmental schemes for superintendence and social welfare—and, of course, the collective aspirations of a professional class of academic literary scholars.[2]

There can be little doubt that literature's power has been heavily overdetermined (and sometimes downright perverted) by its institutional setting. I have argued that whatever ideological power the poetry has wielded or become an instrument for wielding must itself presuppose the poetry's ability to give pleasure. In response to the barbarities of literary history, therefore, I have proposed that we shift our understanding of the politics of Wordsworth's poetry away from the thematics of exclusion and repression and toward a critique of the pleasures of recognition. The pleasures of recognition Wordsworth offers have to do with the way his poetry constructs community, and they are complicated by the vicissitudes of different notions of virtue, the play of his antitheatricality over the imagery of natural and familial presence, the class pressures that undermine the poems' universalizing gestures, and so on. But the reproach lurking in the problem of the study's limits and in the suspicion that the poetic text may derive its power fetishistically from its institutional setting is that my focus on the close reading of a few canonical texts marginalizes or excludes the material that would make the source of the poetry's power visible. If the sources of the power enacted in and through a poem lie outside it—for instance, in the institutional, political, or economic arrangements that determine its distribution or manage its reception—it may not be possible for an analysis of poetic power to work from the inside of canonical poems without simply reenacting what it proposes to critique. Thus the tight group of familiar texts convened here may merely reproduce in its way the charmed circle of invulnerability Wordsworth attempts to fashion in "Tintern Abbey."

If an unexamined exclusivity and elitism have been allowed to slip into this project through the back door of its very commitment to close reading, then perhaps no more will have been accomplished than a certain stylization or, more accurately, a gentrification of old-fashioned Wordsworthian humanism. It has been my belief, however, that, although a wider scope or a greater variety of texts would enhance this study's ability to make generalizations about, for instance, Wordsworth's historical context or his class standing, his poetic originality could best be grasped through the close reading of specific poems. Let me sketch an argument, then, that any serious meaning we give to poetic originality must be grounded in the poetic text and not in the vagaries of reception history and that a critique of poetic pleasure not only must also be grounded in the text, but is inseparable from, and crucial to, any understanding of poetry's power.[3]

This argument takes the form of a three-part narrative—a scheme, really—concerning the moment of sympathy in a reader's apprehension of a poem. In each of the three cases, the moment of sympathy registers the way a poem's originality communicates or imposes itself upon the reader. The first is Wordsworth's own account. Sympathy comes as the touch of the universal, a true essence always already present in the reader and encountered as a rediscovery of the self in the poem. The second is the account given by the critique of Romantic ideology: sympathy is a mask for domination. It works by imposing a false universality, and this repression of difference and of contingency must be undone in order for power to be revealed in its naked, brutal shape. The moment of sympathy does not disappear with this unmasking, however. Rather, it is displaced from the touch of universality to the realization of contingency. The third moment offers nothing new, in a sense, but rather consists in achieving a certain kind of perspective on the other two. It results from working through the critique of false universality in a way that does not arrive at a different version of the true essence (for instance, by positing History instead of Humanity as the ground of poetic power), but rather insists that the universal is both impossible *and* necessary. Sympathy becomes, at this point, a productive paradox.[4]

Wordsworth's insistence in the "Preface to *Lyrical Ballads*" that poetry's main function is to give pleasure and that poetic pleasure derives from sympathetic apprehension of one's share in universal "humanity" has already been mentioned more than once here. More to the point at present is Wordsworth's analysis of poetic power in his "Essay Supplementary to the Preface of 1815," which is far more thoughtfully devoted to the tangled problems of poetic originality and reception. There, perhaps recalling his praise of the poet's "empire" in the "Preface to *Lyrical Ballads*" or the apostrophe to "Imagination" in book 6 of *The Prelude,* Wordsworth represents poetic originality as a quasi-military triumph: "an advance, or a conquest, made by the soul of the Poet" (PrW3 82). The conquest he has in mind is the original poet's triumph over passively applied conventions of reading, a struggle the poet must win in order to create the active understanding necessary to the poetry's proper appreciation and evaluation. Passive convention appears at the lowest level of understanding as mere appetency, and in this connection poetic originality can be apprehended as the poet's success in clearing out a new space for imaginative exercise: ". . . the introduction of a new element into the intellectual universe . . . the application of powers to objects on which they had not before been exercised" (PrW3 82). The problem reappears, however, in a more dangerous form as allegiance to "system" among the class of readers who apply "the best power of their understandings" to poetry (PrW3 66). No doubt one of Wordsworth's models for this latter class of "Critics too petulant to be passive to a genuine Poet, and too feeble to grapple with him" (PrW3 66) was Francis Jeffrey, who could open his review of Southey's *Thalaba* with the statement that "Poetry has this much, at least, in common with religion, that its standards were fixed long ago, by certain inspired writers, whose authority it is no longer lawful to call into question."[5] In relation to such readers, poetic originality consists in eliciting a power of judgment capable of overturning stale conventions.

It might seem, then, that in the matter of originality Wordsworth places power before pleasure: "Every great Poet with whose writings men are familiar, in the highest exercise of his genius, before he can be thoroughly enjoyed, has to call forth and communicate *power*" (PrW3 82; Wordsworth's emphasis). But the equivocation in the phrase "call forth and communicate" brings the pleasures of sympathy back into the process even before a more thorough enjoyment of poetry becomes possible. What is called forth, rather than communicated, by poetic power surely has to be a recognition on the reader's part of something he or she already possesses. The power of originality has to operate between equals, in kind if not in degree, in order for it to operate at all. In other words, before the original poet can make any conquest over passive covention, his "empire" has to have been posited already in a prelegislative form as the "humanity" that, as I began this book saying, is the transcendental signified of any successful poem in Wordsworth's ideal community of readers.

Against this account of poetic originality as a benign augmentation of the reader's powers of imagination by contact and sympathy with the poet's, we can set out, in an admittedly schematic way, the critique of Romantic ideology, which holds that the poetry's power is not based on sympathy, but rather *produces* sympathy precisely by exercising a power that must not appear to be what it is. Here the real content of Wordsworth's humanity, for instance, will be read as egotism masking its self-absorption, naiveté projecting the fantasy of transcending class barriers, or chauvinism clinging to an evasion of history. Thus the Wordsworthian conquest over passive convention can be seen to rest not on a prior moment of essentialist sympathy, but rather on its precise opposite, the obliteration of differences. The operation of sympathy as a false universal thereby points the alert critic to all that the poetry has excluded or silenced. For instead of remembering or recovering one's humanity, the reader interpellated by this ideology forgets it. Humankind assumes a single form (gendered, racialized, classed, nationalized) that turns all others into its distorted images. Any pleasures of recognition available within this paradigm of poetic power are going to be reserved not for the effects of poetic originality, but rather for the act of critical demystification. If poetry works by hiding the real thing, then only the critic's rediscovery of poetry's repressed content can impart the power over judgment that Wordsworth assigns to poetic originality.

There is more than a coincidental similarity between the Wordsworthian rediscovery of the self and this critical reclamation of the repressed other, since the second procedure is based upon undoing or demystifying the first. It should not, therefore, come as a surprise that when the critique of Romantic ideology sets itself the task of reformulating poetry's historical contingency, situatedness, and interests, the moment of sympathy (even humanity) enjoys an uncanny return. If poetic power operates through false universality, the pleasures of demystification find their objects in its inversion, the true individuation of history's myriad anonymous others. Consider the disarming confession in Alan Liu's epilogue to *Wordsworth: The Sense of History,* when he asks himself:

> *Is it not true that the "facts" you have perused in your researches have often moved you more than any literature—least of all that of your chosen poet—could ever do? We have seen you reading books of "facts" with all your skeptical guard down, alive to the materiality of the past in a way you are not alive to literature in your most imaginative moment.*[6]

The danger implied by embracing the pathos of "facts," as Liu goes on to say, is that History threatens to take over Humanity's status as the transcendental signified of poetry. The problem with the critical rediscovery of historical contingency that deflates Romantic ideology is precisely the temptation to regard contingency as the real thing.

The ironic, self-defeating tendency of an analysis of poetry that stresses its power at the expense of its pleasures is that the analysis seems to end up by rendering poetry impotent. But is not this movement itself a symptom of the institutional status that canonical poets like Wordsworth have attained? Liu finds his intellectual vigor refreshed by "facts" precisely because the canonical poem has been reread so insistently and repeatedly that it has almost disappeared under the weight of its commentary, so as to become a veritable palimpsest of critical controversy. Arguably, it is just this kind of institutional compulsion to repeat certain texts that renders them into the sort of sacralized, lawgiving icons Jeffrey believed in and whose authority Wordsworth felt it was the task of the original poet to challenge. Is it not precisely the ideological effects of power associated with the canonical or institutionalized poem that make the specification of historical contingency so vital to the contemporary analysis of poetic originality, because these effects themselves so vividly depend on and demonstrate the way the poems' intentions or manifest contents have been emptied out into the historical accidents of their reception?

Fortunately this is not the end of the story. The institutional dynamics of sacralization and exhaustion do not simply cancel one another out, nor do they reduce the canonical poem to an arbitrary cipher for critical manipulation. On the contrary, the positive content of ideology critique, the fruit of its labors, prevents it from collapsing back into essentialist ideology. The history reclaimed by ideology critique is not an essence, like Humanity, but rather an archive, endlessly recoverable, factual, articulable, but always conceptually incomplete and never perfectly coherent. Rather than another version of the universal, history is strictly nonuniversal in the sense that ideology critique's relentless shuttle between exposing false universality and recovering true individuation can never resolve history into the sum of its individuals. The crucial point regarding this nonuniversal character of history is that it makes analyzing the relationship between a poem and its historical context a one-way operation. The attempt to specify the real things that radiate in so many eccentric ways from a poetic composition cannot work backward so as to make the poem into the answer that the things pose as a question. Any historical narrative will no doubt have to commit itself to positing some determinate form that gives a shape to the "facts," but insofar as this shape arranges itself around the analysis of a poem the specification of "facts" becomes a way of endlessly refining and repeating the question, "What must the poem have been in order to take such a place in our world?" The ground of the critical and historical analysis of a poem is necessarily the poem itself *as* the question that gives a form to the (incalculable) sum of its effects as an answer.

The nonuniversal character of history thus makes it clear that ideology critique's desire to achieve sympathy with humanism's repressed others in their true individuation is an impossible demand. But perhaps this is a symptomatic reflection of something that was already impossible about the moment of sympathy in the essentialist version of the pleasures of recognition. If poetic originality consists in the poem's ability to "call forth" its readers and "communicate *power*" to them on the basis of some inescapable identification, the effects of power and judgment have to do with the very impossibility of that moment of identification. That is, sympathy imparts power to readers by informing them of their insufficiency—an insufficiency not constituted by the gap between the individual reader and the poet, but rather by the structure of their identification. The act of identification itself posits an ideal subjectivity, the transcendental "humanity" of Wordsworth's formulations, which is always necessarily violated or exceeded when it is appropriated by specific individuals. As soon as a particular person purports to represent humanity, the act of representation itself immediately theatricalizes and subverts this claim. Because the "man speaking to men" is always *someone* saying *something,* his "humanity" recedes, an empty and unattainable form, the moment it comes to view.

Yet the impossible demand for identification cannot simply be foregone. As Kant articulates so clearly in his paradoxical formulations of the character of aesthetic judgments, there is no passage from sympathy to evaluation or from passive convention to critical judgment, except by way of the impossible concept of a subjective universality, that is, by attributing legislative validity to an entirely individual moment of "free play." Perhaps all we can ask of an original poem, then, is that it restores the feeling of emptiness to conventional representation or that it *both* conjures the fantasy of full identification with the understanding person who comprehends others perfectly *and* instructs us of its own nonfulfillment of that ideal. For the limits of representation do not merely bar the way to the perfect moment of sympathy, but actually constitute that moment as the significance of their finitude. The pleasure of recognition is always a fantasy, I am arguing, but a fantasy constituted by a *lack* in the poem.

This is the lack that drives Wordsworth's deepest, most troubling anxiety, the desire to know to whom his poetry is speaking and to what end—and so to overcome the mediations of print, to turn the *Gesellschaft* of the literary audience into the *Gemeinschaft* of his community of recognition. That is why, rather than attempting a comprehensive account of Wordsworth's notions of community, I have chosen to focus on the recurrent moments in Wordsworth's early career when his poetry turns inward in order to make its claim to universality. Unlike Wordsworth's perhaps nostalgic attachment to the rural (with its attendant anxieties about his own uselessness in that setting), Wordsworth's literary community of recognition takes its shape as well as its impetus from the experience of modernity. Wordsworth's counterrevolutionary turn is to assert that poetry itself can lodge a quasi-familial intimacy in the interstices of a class-riven commercial society. The interior of Wordsworth's community of recognition crystallizes civil society into a consolatory image where sympathetic virtue claims to re-store the lost presence of a "natural" immediacy in the very act of reading its traces. Yet the solitude inherent in the act of reading always shadows such a consolation. The claim for Wordsworth's originality should finally be lodged in the poems' articulation of the pathos of reading, that is, in the way the poetry demands its readers attend to the distance between their participation in the poem and their detachment from it. This play of participation and detachment, pleasure and power, affords the reader a place to exer-cise judgment, recast convention, revalue tradition.[7]

Appendix: The Versions of *The Ruined Cottage*

Version	Date	Title	Mss.	Remarks
1	1797	"Tale of Margaret"	STC letter 6/10/97 Ms. A Racedown NB Christabel NB	Robert/Margaret diptych theme of contingecy of virtue inscription as protest poem conjectural: fragmentary and incomplete evidence
2a	1798	*The Ruined Cottage*	Ms. B	diptych → tale/frame, Community Lost/ Community Found short biography of the pedlar sequence of pedlar's visits and progressive decline of Margaret and the cottage abrupt ending; no final consolation
2b	1799	*The Ruined Cottage*	Ms. D	frame/tale achieves formal symmetry no pedlar biography; pedlar → Armytage final consolation sequence added
3a	1798	*The Ruined Cottage*	Ms. B (10 new leaves inserted in 2a)	diptych→ pedlar/Margaret long biography authorizing pedlar's vision long, homiletic consolation passage, later transferred to *The Excursion*, book 4
3b	1803–4	*The Pedlar*	Ms. E	new pedlar biography (the old one having been plundered for *The Prelude*) resets the poem in the Lake District
3c	1806–12	"The Wanderer"	Excursion Ms. P	book 1 of *The Excursion* authorization of the pedlar (now the wanderer) complicated by context of *Excursion* 2–9

Notes

CHAPTER 1. WORDSWORTH'S COMMUNITY OF RECOGNITION

1. The quotations in the preceding paragraph are all from PrW 1: 128–30 (on city life) and PrW1 124 (on the country).

2. Unless otherwise noted, quotations of *The Prelude* throughout the book are from the "AB-Stage Reading Text" of 1805–6, as presented by Mark Reed in his edition of *The 13-Book Prelude*, 2 vols. (Ithaca, NY: Cornell University Press, 1991), 1:107–324.

3. The most sustained and complex instances of Wordsworth's association of the London crowd with commerce and theatricality occur in *The Prelude* book 7. On theatricality and the problem of representation in book 7, see Geraldine Friedman, "History in the Background of Wordsworth's 'Blind Beggar,'" *ELH* 56 (1989): 125–48; and on the more general problem of comprehensibility in relation to the country/city dichotomy, David Simpson's *Wordsworth and the Figurings of the Real* (Atlantic Highlands, NJ: Humanities Press, 1982).

4. To be fair to the poet, any thematic assessment of the significance of Dorothy Wordsworth's role as William's amanuensis ought to also take into consideration William's complaints that the act of writing aggravated certain of his physical ailments. See LEY 406–07, 436, 452–53.

5. On "civic virtue," see J. G. A. Pocock, *The Machiavellian Moment: Florentine Political Thought and the Atlantic Republican Tradition* (Princeton: Princeton University Press, 1975) and *Virtue, Commerce, and History: Essays on Political Thought and History, Chiefly in the Eighteenth Century* (Cambridge: Cambridge University Press, 1985). The gendered terms "man" and "men" in Wordsworth's "Preface" are entirely appropriate to the tradition Pocock describes.

6. Wordsworth's description of the "files of strangers" he watched in France bears a striking contrast to a number of passages about the urban crowd in London, for instance, 7.171 ff. or 7.215 ff. The blind beggar episode, 7.589–623, is discussed in chap. 3.

7. Alan Liu's readings of the crossing of the Alps and the climbing of Mount Snowdon are the best recent accounts of the tension between poetic ambition and political history in *The Prelude;* see "The History in 'Imagination,'" *ELH* 51 (1984): 505–48, later recast as chap. 1 of *Wordsworth: The Sense of History* (Stanford: Stanford University Press, 1989) and *Wordsworth: The Sense of History,* chap. 9. On the parallelism between Wordsworth's crises of maturation and the Revolution, see also Ronald Paulson, *Representations of Revolution,* (New Haven: Yale University Press, 1983) 248–75.

8. Jon Klancher, *The Making of English Reading Audiences,* (Madison: University of Wisconsin Press, 1987), 139, 147.

9. Literature as an institutionalized practice will be taken up most explicitly in the conclusion. Clifford Siskin's essay on "inventing literature" (*The Historicity of Romantic Discourse* [New York: Oxford University Press, 1988] 67–93) argues that Wordsworth's attack upon personification produced a figure of community

that was "the product of communication rather than its prerequisite" (83). My argument here and throughout the rest of the book attempts to give this literarily forged community a different degree of specificity within a quite different compass from Siskin's analysis.

10. No one raises the stakes of the "Julia and Vaudracour" episode higher than Gayatri Spivak, "Sex and History in *The Prelude* (1805): Books Nine to Thirteen," *Texas Studies in Language and Literature* 23 (1981): 324–60; see also the cogent feminist and deconstructionist reading of Mary Jacobus, "The Law of/and Gender: Genre Theory and *The Prelude*," *Diacritics* 14:4 (1984): 47–57. Both should be compared to the full and balanced account of the French Revolution books in Eugene Stelzig's "'The Shield of Human Nature': Wordsworth's Reflections on the Revolution in France," *Nineteenth-Century Literature* 45 (1991): 415–31.

11. Geoffrey Hartman's handling of the relations between experience, memory, composition, and interpretation in *The Prelude*, book 6 is perhaps the classic statement of this problem (*Wordsworth's Poetry 1787–1814* [New Haven: Yale University Press, 1971], 33–69). The best use of the concept of screen memory to read the spots of time is probably Thomas Weiskel, *The Romantic Sublime: Studies in the Structure and Psychology of Transcendence* (Baltimore: Johns Hopkins University Press, 1976), 167–85; while the fullest psychoanalytic reading is that of Richard Onorato, *The Character of the Poet: Wordsworth in The Prelude* (Princeton: Princeton University Press, 1971). See also the original and provocative reading of the process of revision and its thematic importance in *The Prelude* in Charles Altieri's "Wordsworth's Wavering Balance: The Thematic Rhythm of *The Prelude*," *The Wordsworth Circle* 4 (1973): 226–39.

12. *William Wordsworth: A Life* (Oxford: Clarendon Press, 1989), 5–7.

13. Cf. Kenneth Johnston, "Wordsworth and *The Recluse:* The University of Imagination," *PMLA* 97 (1982): 80–81.

14. See Mark Reed's presentation of the evidence in CEY; and compare the pointed arguments of David Erdman, "Wordsworth as Heartsworth, or Was Regicide the Prophetic Ground of Those 'Moral Questions'?" in *The Evidence of the Imagination,* ed. Donald Reiman et. al. (New York: New York University Press, 1978), 12–41, and Kenneth Johnston, "Philanthropy or Treason? Wordsworth as 'Active Partisan,'" *Studies in Romanticism* 25 (1986): 371–409.

15. Nathaniel Teich surveys estimates of Wordsworth's political significance from Jeffrey to Hazlitt in "Evaluating Wordsworth's Revolution: Romantic Reviewers and Changing Tastes," *Papers in Language and Literature* 11 (1975): 206–23. Teich concludes, "Wordsworth did not regard himself, nor did his contemporaries regard him, as an equalitarian reformer" (219). The most balanced and thorough reading of Wordsworth's explicit politics throughout the entire span of his career is Carl Woodring's chapter on Wordsworth in *Politics in English Romantic Poetry* (Cambridge: Harvard University Press, 1970). Extreme but acute assessments of Wordsworth's politics include, on the right, Thomas McFarland, *Romanticism and the Forms of Ruin: Wordsworth, Coleridge, and Modalities of Fragmentation* (Princeton: Princeton University Press, 1981), 137–215; and, on the left, Nicholas Roe, *Wordsworth and Coleridge: The Radical Years* (Oxford: Clarendon Press, 1988). Roe's argument fleshes out the thesis of E. P. Thompson, "Disenchantment or Default: A Lay Sermon," in *Power and Consciousness,* ed. Conor Cruise O'Brien and William Dean Vanech (London: University of London Press, 1969), 149–81. On the question of how early in his career Wordsworth could be called a conservative, James Chandler pushes the date up to sometime

before 1798 in *Wordsworth's Second Nature: A Study of the Poetry and Politics* (Chicago: University of Chicago Press, 1984); but see Alan Grob's critique of Chandler's argument, "Afterword: Wordsworth and the Politics of Consciousness," *Critical Essays on William Wordsworth* ed. by H. Gilpin (Boston: G. K. Hall, 1990), 339–56. The sequence of articles on the topic of the early Wordsworth's politics by George Watson ("The Revolutionary Youth of Wordsworth and Coleridge," *Critical Quarterly* 18 : 3 [1976]: 149–66), John Beer ("The 'Revolutionary Youth' of Wordsworth and Coleridge: Another View," *Critical Quarterly* 19 : 2 [1977]: 79–87), and David Ellis ("Wordsworth's Revolutionary Youth: How We Read *The Prelude*," *Critical Quarterly* 19 : 4 [1977]: 59–67) provides particularly clear examples of the variety of positions and the scope of the issues at stake.

16. *Marxism and the Philosophy of Language,* trans. Ladislav Matejka and I. R. Titunik (New York: Seminar Press, 1973), 23. On the double sense of representation as advocacy and mimesis, compare Gayatri Spivak's discussion of *vertreten* and *darstellen* in Marx ("Can the Subaltern Speak?" *Marxism and the Interpretation of Culture,* ed. Cary Nelson and Lawrence Grossberg [Urbana: University of Illinois Press, 1988], 275–79).

17. On nature as a political concept in Wordsworth's writing see John Beer, "Nature and Liberty: The Linking of Unstable Concepts," *The Wordsworth Circle* 14 (1983): 201–13. Chandler, *Wordsworth's Second Nature,* and Roe, *Wordsworth and Coleridge,* advance strongly opposed but well-informed arguments concerning Wordsworth's attitude to French Revolutionary thought. On Wordsworth and English republicanism see Zera Fink, "Wordsworth and the English Republican Tradition," *Journal of English and Germanic Philology* 47 (1948): 107–26, and John Williams, *Wordsworth: Romantic Poetry and Revolution Politics* (Manchester: Manchester University Press, 1989); and on Wordsworth's use of classical sources, Jane Worthington, *Wordsworth's Reading of Roman Prose, Yale Studies in English* 102 (1946), and Barbara Gates, "Wordsworth's Lessons from the Past," *The Wordsworth Circle* 7 (1976): 133–41; and compare Alan Hill, "Wordsworth and the Two Faces of Machiavelli," *Review of English Studies* n.s. 31 (1980): 285–304.

18. On the politicization of aesthetic categories, see Liu, *Wordsworth: The Sense of History,* chap. 3; Paulson, *Representations of Revolution;* and Theresa Kelley, *Wordsworth's Revisionary Aesthetics* (Cambridge: Cambridge University Press, 1988) chap. 4. On the affiliations of eighteenth-century landscape poetry with English republicanism, see Williams, *Wordsworth and Revolution Politics,* chap. 1, and James Turner, *The Politics of Landscape: Rural Scenery and Society in English Poetry 1630–1660* (Oxford: Basil Blackwell, 1979). On landscape and the politics of imperialism, see Laurence Goldstein, *Ruins and Empire: The Evolution of a Theme in Augustan and Romantic Literature* (Pittsburgh: University of Pittsburgh Press, 1977). On the transformation of the countryside, the classic treatment is Raymond Williams, *The Country and the City* (New York: Oxford University Press, 1973), especially chap. 10; I have also benefited from John Barrell's *The Dark Side of the Landscape: The Rural Poor in English Painting 1730–1840* (Cambridge: Cambridge University Press, 1980) and *The Idea of Landscape and the Sense of Place* (Cambridge: Cambridge University Press, 1972).

19. On the role of domestic affection in Wordsworth's nationalism, see Robert C. Gordon, "Wordsworth and the Domestic Roots of Power," *Bulletin of Research in the Humanities* 81 (1978): 90–102. Simpson's discussions of commercial ideology in *Wordsworth and the Figurings of the Real,* chap. 3, and *Wordsworth's Historical Imagination: The Poetry of Displacement* (London: Methuen, 1987)

chap. 2, are extremely useful. On the agrarian revolution see Kenneth Maclean's *Agrarian Age: A Background for Wordsworth, Yale Studies in English* 115 (1950) and compare E. P. Thompson's treatment of paternalism in "Eighteenth Century English Society: Class Struggle without Class?" *Social History* 3:2 (1978): 133–65. The literature on the problem of sympathy is quite large; see chap. 3 below.

20. See Ohmann, *English in America: A Radical View of the Profession* (New York: Oxford University Press, 1976), esp. chap. 12.

21. Characteristic examples include McGann, *The Romantic Ideology: A Critical Investigation* (Chicago: University of Chicago Press, 1983), 90–91; Levinson, *Wordsworth's Great Period Poems: Four Essays* (New York: Cambridge University Press, 1986), 16–17; Liu, *Wordsworth: The Sense of History,* 20–23, 447–49.

22. "Insight and Oversight: Reading 'Tintern Abbey,'" in *Wordsworth's Great Period Poems,* 14–57.

23. On the contemporaneity of *Lyrical Ballads* see also John Jordan, *Why the Lyrical Ballads? The Background, Writing, and Character of Wordsworth's 1798 Lyrical Ballads* (Berkeley: University of California Press, 1976) and Heather Glen, *Vision and Disenchantment: Blake's Songs and Wordsworth's Lyrical Ballads* (Cambridge: Cambridge University Press, 1983), chap. 2.

24. See particularly Liu, *Wordsworth: The Sense of History,* 212–14. Richard Bourke's *Romantic Discourse and Political Modernity: Wordsworth, the Intellectual and Cultural Critique* (New York: St. Martin's Press, 1993) argues a variant of the repressive hypothesis of McGann and Levinson with a comprehensiveness very far superior to the earlier critics. Yet when he concludes that "Wordsworth enacted the ideological impotence which was to be imposed as a political constriction upon the intellectual from Coleridge to Arnold" (270), he too seems to undervalue the ideological power of literature because he reads literary pleasure as a defensive formation repressing the "political constriction" of the intellectual.

25. Slavoj Zizek, *The Sublime Object of Ideology* (New York: Verso, 1989), 49.

26. This is to say that a poem's political resonance and its historicity may be two quite different things. Noteworthy critiques of New Historicist readings of Wordsworth include Susan Wolfson, "Questioning 'The Romantic Ideology': Wordsworth," *Revue Internationale de Philosophie* 44 (1990): 429–47; Laurence Lerner, "Wordsworth's Refusal of Politics," *SEL* 31 (1991): 673–91; and Alan Liu, review of *Wordsworth's Historical Imagination,* by David Simpson, *The Wordsworth Circle* 19 (1988): 172–81. I find myself most in agreement with Peter Manning's "Placing Poor Susan: Wordsworth and the New Historicism," *Studies in Romanticism* 25 (1986): 351–69, written in response mainly to Glen's treatment of Wordsworth in *Vision and Disenchantment.*

27. Marilyn Butler, *Romantics, Rebels, and Reactionaries* (New York: Oxford University Press, 1981).

28. See *Wordsworth's Historical Imagination.*

29. See *The Making of English Reading Audiences.* David Perkins's argument, in "The Construction of 'The Romantic Movement' as a Literary Clasification," *Nineteenth-Century Literature* 45 (1990): 129–43, that the apparent repression of politics that McGann imputes to Wordsworth's poetry is actually the product of late-nineteenth-century habits of reading is also very pertinent in this context. Perkins implies that the "romantic ideology" has more to do with an institutional history, the history of literary studies in the academy, than with Wordsworth's poetry in its original historical context. See the conclusion to this book, and cf. my comments on Perkins and Klancher in "Wordsworth and Romanticism in the

Academy," in *At the Limits of Romanticism: Essays in Cultural, Feminist, and Materialist Criticism,* ed. Mary Favret and Nicola Watson (Bloomington: Indiana University Press, 1993), 21–39.

30. Siskin, *The Historicity of Romantic Discourse,* chap. 4, and "Wordsworth's Prescriptions: Romanticism and Professional Power," *The Romantics and Us: Essays on Literature and Culture,* ed. Gene W. Ruoff (New Brunswick, NJ: Rutgers University Press, 1990), 303–21; Arac, *Critical Genealogies: Historical Situations for Postmodern Literary Studies* (New York: Columbia University Press, 1989), 34–49; and Liu, *Wordsworth: The Sense of History,* chap. 6.

31. *Wordsworth, Dialogics, and the Practice of Criticism* (Cambridge: Cambridge University Press, 1992), chap. 1.

32. See Michel Foucault, *The History of Sexuality: Volume One: An Introduction,* trans. Robert Hurley (New York: Random House, 1978), esp. 122–27.

33. Some of the more recent contributions to this line of interpretation include Don Bialostosky, *Making Tales: The Poetics of Wordsworth's Narrative Experiments* (Chicago: University of Chicago Press, 1984), Michael Friedman, *The Making of a Tory Humanist: William Wordsworth and the Idea of Community* (New York: Columbia University Press, 1979), and studies already cited by Chandler, Goldstein, McFarland, and Simpson.

34. On Wordsworth's notion of virtue, see Fink, Worthington, John Williams, Hill, Gordon, and Kurt Heinzelmann, "The Cult of Domesticity: Dorothy and William Wordsworth at Grasmere," in *Romanticism and Feminism,* ed. Anne K. Mellor (Bloomington: Indiana University Press, 1988), 52–78.

35. Wordsworth's anxiety-ridden sense of vocation has been a central concern in the work of Geoffrey Hartman throughout his career; an excellent recent example is "'Was It For This . . . ?': Wordsworth and the Birth of the Gods," in *Romantic Revolutions: Criticism and Theory,* ed. Kenneth Johnston, Gilbert Chaitin, Karen Hanson, and Herbert Marks (Bloomington: Indiana University Press, 1990), 8–25. On Wordsworth's economic anxieties see also Kurt Heinzelmann, *The Economics of Imagination* (Amherst: University of Massachusetts Press, 1980); Liu, *Wordsworth: The Sense of History,* chap. 7; and Stuart Peterfreund, "The Evolving Notion of Work in English Romantic Poetry," *Works and Days* 2.1 (1984): 19–44.

36. On the relation between the theme of community and Wordsworthian solitude, see Richard Eldridge, "Self-Understanding and Community in Wordsworth's Poetry," *Philosophy and Literature* 10 (1986): 273–94.

CHAPTER 2. WORDSWORTH'S ETHOS: VIOLENCE, ALIENATION, AND MIDDLE-CLASS VIRTUE

1. PrW1 20–21.

2. On the widespread currency of the term "the friends of liberty," see Albert Goodwin, *The Friends of Liberty: The English Democratic Movement in the Age of the French Revolution* (Cambridge: Harvard University Press, 1979).

3. *Miscellaneous Works* (New York: D. Appleton & Co., 1870), 420.

4. For Wordsworth's use of Sidney's *Discourses concerning Government* in the *Letter to Llandaff,* see Fink, 115; on the topicality of the relation between virtue and institutions and Wordsworth's exposure to this debate, see Worthington, 3–4 and 19–42; and Roe, 38–83.

5. *Virtue, Commerce, and History,* 197.

6. Quotations of Burke are followed by parenthetical citations to volume and page number of his *Works*.

7. On Burke's analysis of the class situation in France in terms of protean energy versus inertial stability, see Pocock's "The Political Economy of Burke's Analysis of the French Revolution," in *Virtue, Commerce, and History,* 193–212. Burke's rhetoric in the *Reflections* is one of the clearest examples in the late eighteenth century of the kind of hysterical anxieties about paper money, stocks, credit, and public debt that Pocock analyzes in the wake of the financial revolution of the 1690s in "The Mobility of Property and the Rise of Eighteenth-Century Sociology," in *Virtue, Commerce, and History,* 103–23, esp. 110–14, and in *The Machiavellian Moment,* 451–75.

8. Quotations of Paine are from his *Complete Writings,* and are followed by volume and page in parentheses.

9. *Miscellaneous Works,* 406. For the argument that the "swinish multitude" became a virtual rallying cry for the embryonic class consciousness of Burke's opponents, see E. P. Thompson, *The Making of the English Working Class* (New York: Pantheon, 1963), 90 and ff.

10. Adam Smith, *The Theory of Moral Sentiments,* ed. D. D. Raphael and A. L. Macfie (Oxford: Clarendon Press, 1976), 56.

11. Paine continues, a few paragraphs later: "It appears to general observation, that revolutions create genius and talents; but those events do no more than bring them forward. There is existing in man, a mass of sense lying in a dormant state, and which, unless something excites it to action, will descend with him, in that condition, to the grave. As it is to the advantage of society that the whole of its faculties should be employed, the construction of government ought to be such as to bring forward, by a quiet and regular operation, all that extent of capacity which never fails to appear in revolutions" (1.368).

12. Paine's faith in commerce is conventional rather than idiosyncratic. Compare, for instance, this panegyric on "that middle rank among whom almost all the sense and virtue of society reside," penned by Mackintosh in the section of *Vindiciae Gallicae* titled "Of the Composition and Character of the National Assembly": "The commercial or monied interest has in all nations of Europe (taken as a body) been less prejudiced, more liberal, and more intelligent than the landed gentry. Their views are enlarged by a wider intercourse with mankind; and hence the important influence of commerce in liberalizing the modern world. We cannot wonder then that this enlightened class ever prove the most ardent in the cause of freedom, and the most zealous for political reform" (426).

13. Roe, 129–30.

14. Richard Watson, Bishop of Llandaff, *Miscellaneous Tracts on Religious, Political, and Agricultural Subjects,* 2 vols. (London: T. Cadell and W. Davies, 1815), 1.487. Further citations to Watson are followed by volume and page number in parentheses.

15. The theory paraphrased in the text could be that of Hobbes or Locke, but also pertains to Wordsworth's pamphlet. In the *Letter to Llandaff,* property constitutes a natural hierarchy prior to and independent of government, but also the ground that leads out of the state of nature into the social contract: "Another distinction will arise amongst mankind, which, though it may be easily modified by government, exists independent of it; I mean the distinction of wealth which always will attend superior talents and industry. . . . It cannot be denied that the security of individual property is one of the strongest and most natural motives to induce men to bow their necks to the yoke of government." The way Words-

worth's rhetoric proclaims that the rule of law simultaneously transforms men into beasts of burden under its yoke is somewhat more distinctive. Nonetheless Wordsworth looks to law not only as a mode of securing property, but also as a way of correcting economic inequality: "A legislator . . . should not suppose that, when he has ensured to their proprietors the possession of lands and moveables against the depredation of the necessitous, nothing remains to be done. The history of all ages has demonstrated that wealth not only can secure itself but includes even an oppressive principle" (all quotes PrW1 42).

16. Wordsworth writes that "[Aristocracy] has a natural tendency to dishonour labour . . . it binds down whole ranks of men to idleness while it gives the enjoyment of a reward which exceeds the hopes of the most active exertions of human industry." The terms "industry" and "idleness" are moral, not economic. The aristocrats are "bound down" by their idleness because of the moral decay they suffer as a result of it; and the bad effects of aristocratic indolence are not registered in terms of an unfair distribution of wealth and labor, but as the spread of vice: "Reflecting on the corruption of public manners, does your lordship shudder at the prostitution which miserably deluges our streets? You may find the cause in our aristocratical prejudices. . . . Do you lament that such large portions of mankind should stoop to occupations unworthy the dignity of their nature? You may find in the pride and luxury thought necessary to nobility how such servile arts are encouraged" (all quotes PrW1 45).

17. From Jeffrey's review of Southey's *Thalaba the Destroyer, Edinburgh Review* 1 (October 1802): 63–83; quoted in Lionel Madden, ed., *Robert Southey: The Critical Heritage* (London: Routledge & Kegan Paul, 1972), 77.

18. I take the terms "effective" and "affective" in this context from Friedman, *The Making of a Tory Humanist.*

19. Chandler, *Wordsworth's Second Nature,* 75. Chandler's description of the movement in Wordsworth's thematics away from reason and toward manners, habit, and custom is extremely helpful, in my view, as long as one resists his exaggerated identification of ideas about "second nature" with Burkean conservatism.

20. Thomas Hobbes, *Leviathan,* ed. C. B. Macpherson (New York: Viking Penguin, 1968), 223.

21. Adam Smith makes this point in the section on Hobbes in the *Theory of Moral Sentiments:* "In order to confute so odious a doctrine [i.e., that the state of nature is a condition of warfare], it was necessary to prove that, antecedent to all law or positive institution, the mind was naturally endowed with a faculty, by which it distinguished, in certain actions and affections, the qualities of right, laudable, and virtuous, and in others those of wrong, blameable, and vicious" (318).

22. A. A. Cooper, 3d Earl of Shaftesbury, *Characteristicks of Men, Manners, Opinions, Times,* 3d ed., 3 vols. (London: J. Darby, 1723), 2.134.

23. Bernard Mandeville, *The Fable of the Bees: Or, Private Vices, Publick Benefits,* ed. F. B. Kaye, 2 vols. (Oxford: Clarendon Press, 1924), 1.4.

24. On the various attempts of eighteenth-century writers to adequately represent the economically constituted social order, see John Barrell, *English Literature 1730–1780: An Equal, Wide Survey* (New York: St. Martin's Press, 1983).

25. *The Progress of Civil Society* (London: G. Nicol, 1796), 4, 73.

26. 4, 125–36. On the intersection between the figure of *concordia discors* and procommercial ideology in the early eighteenth century, particularly in Pope's *Windsor Forest,* see Earl Wasserman, *The Subtler Language: Critical Readings*

of Neoclassical and Romantic Poems (Baltimore: Johns Hopkins University Press, 1959), 162–68.

27. Joseph Fawcett uses the metaphor of "complicated Traffic's trembling web" to this effect in *The Art of War,* 2d ed. (London: J. Johnson, 1795), 34; the passage is quoted at greater length below in chap. 4. Wordsworth himself developed the figure of the web at some length in *The Convention of Cintra;* see PrW 1: 340, lines 4851–56.

28. Cf. Pocock, *The Machiavellian Moment,* 497–505.

29. The quotation is Richard Teichgraber's formulation of the so-called Adam Smith Problem, in *"Free Trade" and Moral Philosophy: Rethinking the Sources of Adam Smith's Wealth of Nations* (Durham: Duke University Press, 1986), 10; see also Laurence L. Dickey, "Historicizing the 'Adam Smith Problem': Conceptual, Historiographical, and Textual Issues," *Journal of Modern History* 58 (1986): 579–609. I. Hont and M. Ignatieff argue that Smith's concept of economic totality is derived from the natural jurisprudential tradition of Grotius and Pufendorf in "Needs and Justice in *The Wealth of Nations:* An Introductory Essay," in *Wealth and Virtue: Political Economy in the Scottish Enlightenment,* ed. I. Hont and M. Ignatieff (Cambridge: Cambridge University Press, 1983), 1–44. Their argument is directed against Pocock's construction of Smith's work as emerging primarily from the debate between virtue and commerce in the civic humanist tradition. It is also still well worth consulting C. B. Macpherson's attempt to place Smith in an emerging procapitalist tradition traced from Hobbes through Locke in *The Political Theory of Possessive Individualism: Hobbes to Locke* (Oxford: Clarendon Press, 1962).

30. Lukacs's concept of reification and his attendant critique of bourgeois philosophy may be found in "Reification and the Class Consciousness of the Proletariat," *History and Class Consciousness,* trans. Rodney Livingstone (Cambridge: MIT Press, 1971): 83–222, esp. 83–149.

31. *Theory of Moral Sentiments,* 86.

32. Thompson questions the reliability of the letter as a statement of Coleridge's real political views in "Disenchantment or Default," 153.

33. Cf. also the diary entry of Wordworth's friend James Losh on 31 December 1798: "Tho' I retain my opinion of the value of Liberty in general, and of the corruptions of our own government in particular, I am resolved to withdraw for ever from Politics, never to interfere farther than by calm discussion, and when that cannot be had I am determined to be silent—nothing I trust shall ever induce me to take any active part with any *party* whatever" (quoted in Roe, 241).

34. The basic reference on country ideology is Caroline Robbins, *The Eighteenth-Century Commonwealthman: Studies in the Transmission, Development and Circumstances of English Liberal Thought from the Restoration of Charles II until the War with the Thirteen Colonies* (Cambridge: Harvard University Press, 1959) and on civic humanism, Pocock's *The Machiavellian Moment.* Lawrence Stone provides the following concise paraphrase of the political tenets of the country ideology: "'The business of Parliament is to preserve the independence of property, on which is founded all human liberty and human excellence. The business of government is to govern, and that is a legitimate authority; but to govern is to wield power, and power has a natural tendency to encroach. It is more important to supervise government than to support it, because the preservation of independence is the ultimate political good'" (*The Family, Sex, and Marriage in England 1500–1800* [New York: Harper & Row, 1977], 231).

35. Gordon argues for a strong Harringtonian influence in Wordsworth's letter to Fox, in "Domestic Roots of Power," 96–98.

36. The most provocative and original recent treatment of Wordsworth's political sonnets of 1802 is Liu's in *Wordsworth: The Sense of History,* 427–36 and 459–85. The relation between political and domestic virtue in these sonnets receives excellent commentary in Heinzelman, "The Cult of Domesticity," 62–65. On the tension between public and private themes see also Judith W. Page, "'The weight of too much liberty': Genre and Gender in Wordsworth's Calais Sonnets," *Criticism* 30 (1988): 189–203.

37. Gill, *Wordsworth: A Life,* 108–9.

38. Thomas Erskine, *A View of the Causes and Consequences of the Present War with France* (London: J. Debrett, 1797), 128–30.

39. *Wordsworth: The Sense of History,* 475–85.

40. *Wordsworth, Dialogics, and the Practice of Criticism,* 87. For a thorough review of the extensive prior commentary on this sonnet, see Bialostosky's "symposium" on it, *Wordsworth, Dialogics, and the Practice of Criticism,* 79–133.

41. *Wordsworth's Poetry,* 1–30.

42. Although the poem's title dates it 3 September 1803 in the 1807 volume, and in later editions 3 September 1802, there is evidence that it was actually composed on 31 July 1802, on the way to Calais rather than on Wordsworth's return from France. See Liu's discussion of the various dates Wordsworth assigned the poem, *Wordsworth: The Sense of History,* 476–77, 486, 492.

CHAPTER 3. THE ECONOMY OF VISION

1. Unsigned article "On the Importance of the Middle Ranks of Society," *The Oeconomist* 1 (1798): 7.

2. On the relation of the *Letter* to *The Rights of Man,* see E. N. Hooker, "Wordsworth's *Letter to the Bishop of Llandaff,*" *Studies in Philology* 28 (1931): 522–31.

3. Beatrice and Sidney Webb's history of the poor laws in *English Local Government,* parts 1 and 2 (London: Longmans, Green, & Co., 1927–29) argues the importance of the New Poor Law to the growth of a centralized national government in England. The best detailed account of the debates of the years of scarcity is J. R. Poynter's in *Society and Pauperism: English Ideas on Poor Relief, 1795–1834* (London: Routledge & Kegan Paul, 1969), 45–185.

4. Karl Polanyi, *The Great Transformation* (1944; rpt. Boston: Beacon Press, 1957), 83–84.

5. Because of its explicit social theme, "The Old Cumberland Beggar" has received a great deal of attention from historically focused critics in the last decade. The recent readings of "The Old Cumberland Beggar" I have found most useful are those of Chandler, 84–89; Simpson, *Wordsworth's Historical Imagination,* 162–74; Gary Harrison, "Wordsworth's 'The Old Cumberland Beggar': The Economy of Charity in Eighteenth-Century Britain," *Criticism* 30 (1988): 23–42; and Mark Koch, "Utilitarian and Reactionary Arguments for Almsgiving in Wordsworth's 'The Old Cumberland Beggar,'" *Eighteenth-Century Life* 13 (1989): 18–33.

6. Quotations of "The Old Cumberland Beggar" are from LB 228–34, and are followed by line numbers in parentheses.

7. Cleanth Brooks, "Wordsworth and Human Suffering: Notes on Two Early

Poems," in *From Sensibility to Romanticism: Essays Presented to Frederick A. Pottle,* ed. Frederick W. Hilles and Harold Bloom (New York: Oxford University Press, 1965), 376. Harrison makes a similar judgment: "The poem appeals to an economy of charity . . . which only perpetuates the division of the community into beggars and their benefactors. Of course, this process implies that the beggar is a kind of communal property exchanged within a marketplace of virtue from which he is excluded" (27).

8. Chandler first made the argument that "The Old Cumberland Beggar" is Burkean (84–89); see also Harrison, 28. Simpson (172–74) disagrees, and Koch (21–22) qualifies the claim in a way more similar to the position taken here.

9. Harrison describes the "prevalent view . . . that almsgiving should produce a self-congratulatory return" (31). For a literary representation of this convention, take for example the incident early in Ann Radcliffe's *The Mysteries of Udolpho* when the hero, Valancourt, is presented with a choice between "raising a family from ruin to happiness" by giving them most of the money he has and facing "the difficulties of pursuing his journey with so small a sum as would be left." After performing the charitable act, "Valancourt had seldom felt his heart so light as at this moment; his gay spirits danced with pleasure; every object around him appeared more interesting, or beautiful, than before" (*The Mysteries of Udolpho,* ed. Bonamy Dobree [New York: Oxford University Press, 1966], 52–53).

10. King's table is reproduced, among other places, in Frederick Morton Eden, *The State of the Poor: An History of the Labouring Classes in England, from the Conquest to the Present Period,* 3 vols. (London: J. Davis, 1797), 1.228.

11. All quotations from Eden 1.1–3.

12. Joseph Townsend's *Dissertation on the Poor Laws* provides a clear instance of the attitude that poverty stems from vice and is natural and inevitable: "It is notorious, that with the common people the appetite for drink is their prevailing appetite. When therefore, by the advance in wages, they obtain more than is sufficient for their bare subsistence, they spend the surplus at the alehouse, and neglect their business. . . . If a new and equal division of property were made in England, we cannot doubt that the same inequality which we now observe would soon take place again: the improvident, the lazy, and the vicious, would dissipate their substance; the prudent, the active, and the virtuous, would again increase their wealth" (*A Dissertation on the Poor Laws, by a Well-Wisher to Mankind* [London: C. Dilly, 1786], 25, 44).

The opposite assumption can be found in *The Philanthropist,* possibly the very journal Wordsworth and William Matthews projected in 1794, in an essay that Kenneth Johnston has supposed might even bear marks of Wordsworth's own hand: "The general happiness of a country depends much more on the comfortable state of the lower orders than is commonly imagined. Not only the character and morals of the lower orders, but the general national character, are affected by it. The wretchedness resulting from extreme poverty has a direct tendency to debase the human character" (No. 37 [14 December 1795]: 6).

In 1797 one can find both views being aired in the pages of the *Monthly Magazine.* An anonymous correspondent in January argues that, if the "lower orders" are "seditiously inclined," the solution is to grant tenant cottagers freehold interest in their property: "Being now possessed of a property, [the cottager] is of consequence in his own estimation—he has a stake in the country—he has something to lose by tumult and internal commotion; and therefore, he will not only be unwilling to promote riot, but readily lend his aid to suppress popular outrage. He naturally becomes a better man, and a better citizen" (3 [January–June, 1797]:

3). But another anonymous correspondent in December is more apt to see property relations as the result of morality than as its effects: "That some place ought to be appointed, to which persons may be carried and taken care of when sick, who have no home of their own, I allow; but I would ask, *why has not every person a home of their own?* If poor people were honestly employed in getting their living, they would have some place of residence" (4 [July–December, 1797]: 432).

13. *Natural Theology, or, Evidences of the Existence and Attributes of the Deity, Collected from the Appearances of Nature* (Philadelphia: John Morgan, 1802), 363.

14. *Observations Preliminary to a Proposed Amendment of the Poor Laws* (London: John Nichols, 1788), 48. Harrison (31) draws a very similar quotation from Eden 3.300.

15. See S. and B. Webb, part 1, 151.

16. *An Examination of Mr. Pitt's Speech, in the House of Commons, on Friday, February 12, 1796, Relative to the Condition of the Poor* (London: W. Richardson, 1796), 28–29.

17. *The Idea of Poverty: England in the Early Industrial Age* (New York: Alfred A. Knopf, 1984), 76.

18. Eden 1.467.

19. *Works,* ed. John Bowring, 11 vols. (Edinburgh: William Tait, 1838–42), 8.366.

20. *Works* 8: 384. Bentham's use of the term "luxury" in this passage opens onto another complex and important discursive history. The best exposition of the concept's history is part 1 of John Sekora's *Luxury: The Concept in Western Thought, Eden to Smollett* (Baltimore, Johns Hopkins University Press, 1977), 23–131. In its archaic sense "luxury" refers not to surplus expenditure but to any excess over what has been naturally ordained. The concept of luxury is closely allied to the rigid and static version of class hierarchy that it was one of the original functions of the Elizabethan Poor Law to protect. Sekora says the concept was almost defunct by the end of the eighteenth century, having by that time been nearly erased by the newer concepts of political economy (112); I would suggest, however, that the older form of the concept still exercised a strong residual influence, even within the discourse of political economy, during the period from 1795 to 1834.

21. In *Wordsworth's Historical Imagination* Simpson calls Wordsworth's position "anti-Benthamite." This is not a distortion of Wordsworth's ideology, but it is a misleading way to characterize it. One of Simpson's cogent reasons for rejecting Chandler's identification of the poem as Burkean—"To argue that the poem is *dominantly* expressive of support for Burke would entail the assumption that Burke's case was *the* primary object of attention at the time of writing, so that any reference, however implicit, would have instantly signalled the poem's allegiance" (174)—seems to me to apply even more strongly to his own term.

22. The most important single event in this contest over the form and social significance of "reason" was Malthus's crushing critique of Godwinism in his *Essay on the Principle of Population*. Gertrude Himmelfarb argues that the real object of Malthus's polemic is not Godwin but Adam Smith's far more moderate hopes for social amelioration (*Idea of Poverty,* 108). Given Paine's procommercial tendencies, this would render Malthus's essay all the more devastating to the party of reason.

23. A few years before dictating the Fenwick note, Wordsworth included a

lengthy critique of the New Poor law in his "Postscript of 1835"; see PrW3. 240–48.

24. Bialostosky, *Making Tales,* 76–77.

25. *Making Tales,* 81.

26. John F. Danby, *The Simple Wordsworth: Studies in the Poems 1797–1807* (London: Routledge & Kegan Paul, 1960), 39.

27. Thomas Percy, *Reliques of Ancient English Poetry,* 3 vols. (London: L. A. Lewis, 1839), 1.xxix.

28. *Economics of Imagination,* 221.

29. The 1850 version of these lines is somewhat clearer: ". . . things that are, are not, / As the mind answers to them, or the heart / Is prompt, or slow, to feel" (7.669–71).

30. See Eve Walsh Stoddard, "'All Freaks of Nature': The Human Grotesque in Wordsworth's City," *Philological Quarterly* 67 (1988): 37–61. Stoddard comments specifically on the anticapitalist critical function of the Bartholomew Fair description, 44–50.

31. *The Borders of Vision* (Oxford: Clarendon Press, 1982), 304.

32. Quotations of *The Castle of Indolence* are from the text in James Thomson, *The Seasons and The Castle of Indolence,* ed. James Sambrook (Oxford: Clarendon Press, 1972), and are followed by canto and stanza number in parentheses. "False luxury" is from the epigraph of book 1, canto 1.

33. The earliest draft of the poem was composed before Coleridge's marriage to Sara Hutchinson; the lines on the "coy maid" belong to this stage of composition. The full poem, however, including the noontime scene on the hill, was composed after the wedding. See H. J. W. Milley, "Some Notes on Coleridge's 'Eolian Harp,'" *Modern Philology* 36 (1938–39), 365–68.

CHAPTER 4. CIVIC VIRTUE AND SOCIAL CLASS AT THE SCENE OF EXECUTION: THE SALISBURY PLAIN POEMS

1. On *The Philanthropist,* see Johnston, "Philanthropy or Treason?" Despite the fact that Wordsworth worked on the Juvenal imitation in 1796 and perhaps even 1797, the Juvenal project and its idiom belong to London and 1795. Wordsworth includes some satiric couplets in a letter to Wrangham in November 1795, e.g.: "Heavens! who sees majesty in George's face? / Or looks at Norfolk and can dream of grace?" (LEY 157). Mark Reed dates the rest of Wordsworth's extant work on the imitation as all or mainly in March 1796 (CEY 340–41). But all of this work seems to have been undertaken out of a sense of obligation to his friend Wrangham. His comments to Matthews in March 1796 do not indicate a very intense interest in the project: "As to writing it is out of the question. Not however entirely to forget the world, I season my recollection of some of its objects with a little ill-nature, I attempt to write satires" (LEY 169). The "writing" that is out of the question at this point may be any more serious poetic composition than the imitation of Juvenal, as Reed supposes (CEY 341); but Wordsworth may also be declaring to Matthews his complete unwillingness to engage in any more journalistic work, to which he links the satire as a similar but lesser evil. In either case, the imitation of Juvenal seems quite foreign to Wordsworth's most serious work at this period. It lacks any of the dramatic and psychological interest that distinguishes his recent work on *Adventures on Salisbury Plain* and that will occupy him soon in *The Borderers.* Whatever interest Wordsworth once had in

the poem had entirely disappeared by the time he sent Wrangham a set of verses for it in February 1797; his letter merely says the verses "will do" even though most of them are "sad stuff" (LEY 178).

2. From the preface to *The Minstrel,* in James Beattie, *The Minstrel; Or, The Progress of Genius: in Two Books, with Some Other Poems* (London: C. Dilly, 1797). Further quotations are followed by book and stanza number in parentheses.

3. Dorothy Wordsworth wrote in 1793 that "the whole character of Edwin [the main charcter of *The Minstrel*] resembles much what William was when I first knew him after my leaving Halifax" (LEY 101); and in 1802 Wordsworth drew upon the same lines alluded to by Dorothy in the 1793 letter for his description of himself in the "Stanzas Written in My Pocket-Copy of Thomson's *Castle of Indolence.*"

4. J. Williams associates Beattie and some other eighteenth-century locodescriptive poets who influenced Wordsworth, especially Mark Akenside and William Crowe, with the political tradition of the Commonwealthmen; see chap. 1 of *Wordsworth: Romantic Poetry and Revolution Politics.*

5. Stephen Gill assigns the bulk of the revisionary work on ASP to September through November of 1795 (SPP 7–12).

6. Cf. Paul Sheats, *The Making of Wordsworth's Poetry, 1785–1798* (Cambridge: Harvard University Press, 1973), 83–105; Stephen Gill, "Wordsworth's Breeches Pocket: Attitudes to the Didactic Poet," *Essays in Criticism* 19 (1969): 385–401; and Mary Jacobus, *Tradition and Experiment in Wordsworth's Lyrical Ballads 1798* (Oxford: Clarendon Press, 1976), 148–58.

7. All quotations of SP and ASP are from the reading texts in SPP and are followed by stanza numbers in prentheses.

8. Roe, 124–35.

9. Joseph Fawcett, *The Art of War,* 2d ed. (London: J. Johnson, 1795), 34–35. Further quotations of *The Art of War* are followed by page numbers in parentheses.

10. See Arthur W. Beatty, "Joseph Fawcett: *The Art of War,*" *University of Wisconsin Studies in Language and Literature* 2 (1918): 224–26; and Stephen Gill, "'Adventures on Salisbury Plain' and Wordsworth's Poetry of Protest, 1795–97," *Studies in Romanticism* 11 (1972): 48–65.

11. *Wordsworth's Poetry,* 117.

12. *Tradition and Experiment,* 159.

13. Quotations of the additions to Ms. 1 are from the transcriptions in SPP 109–17, cited by ms. page. Gill dates these additions between April-May 1794 and November 1795, that is, between the copying of the manuscript of *Salisbury Plain* and the beginning of Wordsworth's full-scale revision of the poem into *Adventures on Salisbury Plain.* I have edited these passages so far as to choose a readable version from the additions and deletions faithfully reproduced in Gill's transcriptions.

14. See chap. 2, note 14.

15. The apologetic structure of Watson's sermon can also be noted in his contradictory portrayal of acquisitiveness. Watson more or less equates the pursuit of wealth with rational virtue by identifying poverty with folly and vice: "Men are sometimes classed into different orders, according to the diversity of the professions or trades which they pursue; but the end aimed at, by men of every profession and every trade, is to advance themselves from a state of poverty to a state of riches, or from the possession of a smaller portion of wealth to a larger. Men, on the other hand, are addicted to various vices, and pursue a strange

multiplicity of follies; but the usual end of vice and folly is to reduce men from riches to poverty. It may be truly said, that all the pursuits of mankind, whether they be laudable or disreputable, have a natural tendency to introduce a disparity of property; to establish the great distinction of the human species into rich and poor" (1: 451–52). The pursuit of riches appears to be ultimately irrational, however, when Watson later in the sermon enumerates the miseries entailed upon wealth and luxury: "The body, by indolence, becomes enervated, unequal to fatigue, and prone to disease. . . . An idle mind . . . preys upon itself, becomes peevish and discontented" (1: 458). Perhaps the only consistently rational behavior (although Watson does not make this suggestion) would be to work for very low wages, so as never to be tempted to stop.

16. William Paley, *Reasons for Contentment: Addressed to the Labouring Part of the British Public* (London: R. Faulder, 1793). Quotations of Paley will be followed by page number in parentheses.

17. Gill, for reasons explained in SPP 9–10 and 121, prints the *Lyrical Ballads* text of "The Female Vagrant" as stanzas 30–44 and 48–62 of ASP. The stylistic advances evident in the female vagrant's narrative may well be less decisive if the 1795 text were available.

18. The most relevant argument in this connection is Gill's in "Wordsworth's Breeches Pocket."

Chapter 5. The Politics of Theatricality and the Crime of Abandonment in *The Borderers*

1. SPP 12.

2. The text of *The Borderers* cited by act, scene, and line in this essay is the reading text of the Early Version in *The Borderers*, ed. Robert Osborn (Ithaca, NY: Cornell University Press, 1982), hereafter cited as B. Other material in B is cited by page number or, in the case of the reading text of the Later Version, by line number.

3. Osborn notes: "These lines, a garbled reference to events after the battle of Evesham, are the only ones in the play that could be thought to refer to the year 1265 in particular, though Wordsworth seems to prefer to remain vague" (B 172).

4. I use the Early Version (EV) of *The Borderers* rather than the text Wordsworth published in 1842 (LV) primarily because of its obvious superiority as evidence in a developmental study of political themes in Wordsworth's writing. Aside from the renaming of characters, Wordsworth's revisions of the earlier text in the 1842 version are mostly of three kinds. First, there are numerous helpful clarifications of specific lines and of minor incidents in the plot. Some needlessly obscure lines are simply eliminated (e.g., EV 2.1.48–51). Second, there is a marked economizing of speeches, especially in the last scene, where 275 lines are pared down to 234, but, far more strikingly, 135 speeches are reduced to 59. The LV is altogether an easier text to read. Third, the LV often tones down the play's philosophical and topical vocabulary, as in its elimination of the naked/clothed opposition in EV 2.1.88–100, or in the closely related change of "ground as free as the first earth / Which nature gave to man" (EV 2.1.112–13) to simply "open ground" (LV 655). The general effect of these changes is to associate Oswald somewhat more straightforwardly and polemically with Jacobin Error. That this was Wordsworth's intention receives additional support from his decision to re-

name the tempter Oswald, an allusion to the English Jacobin John Oswald that David Erdman has explored at length in "Wordsworth as Heartsworth."

5. "Wordsworth as Heartsworth," 19.

6. See Hartman's influential discussion of *The Borderers* in *Wordsworth's Poetry,* esp. 126–27, 129, and 369, n. 26; and Robert Osborn, "Meaningful Obscurity: The Antecedents and Character of Rivers," in *Bicentenary Wordsworth Studies,* ed. Jonathan Wordsworth (Ithaca: Cornell University Press, 1964): 393–424.

7. See Peter Thorslev, "Wordsworth's *Borderers* and the Romantic Villain-Hero," *Studies in Romanticism* 5 (1964): 84–103; Roger Sharrock, *"The Borderers:* Wordsworth on the Moral Frontier," *Durham University Journal* 56 (1964): 170–83; Eve Stoddard, *"The Borderers:* A Critique of both Reason and Feeling as Moral Agents," *The Wordsworth Circle* 11 (1980): 93–97; and the discussions in Woodring and Roe.

8. Osborn, "Meaningful Obscurity," 409, and W. J. B. Owen, *"The Borderers* and the Aesthetics of Drama," *The Wordsworth Circle* 6 (1975): 227 argue against the relevance of the later commentary to the 1797 play. On the status of sublimity in the two versions, see Paul Magnuson, *Coleridge and Wordsworth: A Lyrical Dialogue* (Princeton: Princeton University Press, 1988), 54–55; and Theresa Kelley, *Wordsworth's Revisionary Aesthetics,* (Cambridge: Cambridge University Press, 1988), 72–90.

9. "Wordsworth's *The Borderers:* The Poet as Anthropologist," *ELH* 36 (1969): 343.

10. Reeve Parker, "Reading Wordsworth's Power: Narrative and Usurpation in *The Borderers,"* *ELH* 54 (1987): 299–331; Liu, "The Tragedy of the Family," chap. 6 of *Wordsworth: The Sense of History.*

11. The specific political context is, however, central to Liu's entire project in *Wordsworth: The Sense of History.* In particular, chap. 4, "The Poetics of Violence," establishes the terms for an original reading of *The Borderers* as a dialogic intervention in contemporary political discourse.

12. I offer *The Monk* for comparison despite the fact that Wordsworth's more direct indebtedness to Radcliffe's *The Romance of the Forest* has long been established (B 29), because what is at stake here is not the character type of the Gothic villain (Radcliffe's Marquis Montalt as precursor of Rivers) but the deployment of Gothic convention as expositor of the passions. Whatever Wordsworth's opinion or acquaintance with *The Monk* may have been—there is no evidence of his having read it—one can measure the seriousness of Wordsworth's approach to Gothic horror by the disdain he professed, in April 1798, for Lewis's own softening of the Gothic into low comedy and theatrical extravaganza in *The Castle Spectre* (LEY 210–11).

13. The trope of the unholy contract also appears in full Gothic trappings in 5.2.56–57, and the Rough Notebook's "Edge of a Heath" scene (Ms. 1, 57v [B, 430–31]).

14. Mayo, 491.

15. See Charles J. Smith, "The Effect of Shakespeare's Influence on Wordsworth's 'The Borderers,'" *Studies in Philology* 50 (1953): 625–39.

16. Owen, *"The Borderers* and the Aesthetics of Drama," *The Wordsworth Circle* 6 (1975): 230.

17. Owen, 232, quoting William Richardson's *Essays on Some of Shakespeare's Dramatic Characters.*

18. Reeve Parker offers some intriguing suggestions about the relevance of two French adaptations of Schiller's play during Wordsworth's stay in France in "'In

Some Sort Seeing with My Own Proper Eyes': Wordsworth and the Spectacles of Paris," *Studies in Romanticism* 27 (1988): 369–90.

19. Friederich Schiller, *The Robbers* (London, 1792; rpt. Oxford: Woodstock, 1989), 176.

20. *King Lear,* ed. Russell Fraser (New York: New American Library, 1963), 3.2.20. The allusion to *Lear* appears already in the strongly Gothic "Edge of a Heath" scene in the Rough Notebook (Ms. 1, 56r [B, 424–25]).

21. *King Lear* 3.4.108–11.

22. For different considerations of Wordsworth's handling of his Shakespearean sources, see Alan Richardson, *A Mental Theater: Poetic Drama and Consciousness in the Romantic Age* (University Park: Penn State University Press, 1988), 20–42; and Reeve Parker's comments on the influence of *The Tempest* and of contemporary French productions of *Macbeth* in "Narrative and Usurpation," 300–304, 317–22.

23. *The Political Theory of Possessive Individualism,* 20. Wordsworth uses the terminological opposition of passions and manners in the Fenwick note. If he had written the play later in his career, he says, "The manners also wd have been more attended to—my care was almost exclusively given to the passions & the characters, & the position in which the persons in the Drama stood relatively to each other, that the reader (for I had then no thought of the Stage) might be moved & to a degree instructed by lights penetrating somewhat into the depths of our Nature" (B 814).

24. See Bewell's treatment in *Wordsworth and the Enlightenment: Nature, Man, and Society in the Experimental Poetry* (New Haven: Yale University Press, 1989) of the relation of the paradigm of moral philosophy to the *Recluse* project (3–17), of the use of a "contemporary state of nature" in *Tintern Abbey* (36–38), and of Wordsworth's belief "that in France he had walked in a world that, in the sphere of culture, had returned to the world's postdiluvian origins" (252).

25. Cf. also Sharrock's exposition of the setting of Wordsworth's play as a "symbolic border" based upon the real experience of the French Reign of Terror ("Moral Frontier," 172–74).

26. On Adam Smith's view of theatricality and on the antitheatrical tradition in England, see Jonas Barish, *The Anti-Theatrical Prejudice* (Berkeley: University of California Press, 1981) and David Marshall, *The Figure of Theater: Shaftesbury, Defoe, Adam Smith, and George Eliot* (New York: Columbia University Press, 1986).

27. *Enquiry concerning Political Justice and Its Influence on Morals and Happiness,* 3d ed., ed. F. E. L. Priestley, 3 vols. (Toronto: University of Toronto Press, 1946), 2: 49. All quotations of *Political Justice* are from this edition.

28. Smith is in qualified agreement with Godwin on this point; but his qualification is itself a good example of the political error Godwin condemns: "This disposition to admire, and almost to worship, the rich and the powerful, and to despise, or, at least, to neglect persons of poor and mean condition, though necessary both to establish and to maintain the distinction of ranks and the order of society, is, at the same time, the great and most universal cause of the corruption of our moral sentiments" (61).

29. Gill, *Wordsworth: A Life,* 108–9.

30. Although I have stressed the English context of Wordsworth's antitheatricality, there is also a complex and powerful debate in France, including, in addition to the whole problem of the use of public spectacle in revolutionary France, the arguments in Rousseau's *Lettre à d'Alembert* and Diderot's antitheatrical stric-

tures on contemporary painting. Michael Fried comments on Diderot, for instance: "In Diderot's writings on painting and drama the object-beholder relationship as such, the very condition of spectatordom, stands indicted as theatrical, a medium of dislocation and estrangement rather than of absorption, sympathy, and self-transcendence; and the success of both arts, in fact their continued functioning as expressions of the human spirit, are held to depend on whether or not the painter and dramatist are able to undo that state of affairs" (*Absorption and Theatricality: Painting and Beholder in the Age of Diderot,* [Berkeley: University of California Press, 1980], 104).

31. As the execution scene at the conclusion of *Adventures on Salisbury Plain* might imply, even theater is probably too much like real life, and the spectatorship Wordsworth privileges is actually literary rather than dramatic. On Wordsworth's antitheatrical prejudice, see Mary Jacobus, "'That Great Stage Where Senators Perform': *Macbeth* and the Politics of Romantic Theater," *Studies in Romanticism* 22 (1983): 353–87; and David Marshall's suggestive reading in "The Eye-Witnesses of *The Borderers*," *Studies in Romanticism* 27 (1988): 392–98.

32. See also 3.5.18–21; Osborn notes the echo of Genesis 2:24.

33. The Later Version clarifies the plot by revising 1.3.20 to "She paces round and round an Infant's grave."

34. Miguel Abensour, "Saint-Just and the Problem of Heroism in the French Revolution," *Social Research* 56 (Spring 1989), 192. Saint-Just's philosophy, as expounded by Abensour, is remarkably similar in some of its basic assumptions to that of Wordsworth as I find it articulated in *The Borderers.* The important similarities would include the common presumption of a harmonious, prepolitical sociality; the importance of the locale in granting a quasi-chthonic "identity of origin"; and the role of heterogeneity in destroying this state of affairs and instituting civil order in its stead: "For Saint-Just the state of nature meant, in the usage of the political theory of the time, 'the state of man before civil governments were instituted.' He describes this state as social, for society, a natural given and a fundamental and historically earliest phenomenon, precedes the individual and not vice versa. . . . Saint-Just's first proposition concerns the societal state as a harmonious alliance between independence and life in society. . . . Identity of origin, the precondition for this state, and its corollary, equality, make it possible to rid social life of every instance of domination caused by some difference in power. . . . Inequality of any kind destroys the original identity and introduces into the species or society a heterogeneity which is necessarily a catalyst of dissolution . . . As a result, otherness is the source of an antisocial state, namely, the 'savage' or 'political' state" (189–91). There is no question of direct influence, since Saint-Just's *De la nature* remained unpublished until 1951.

35. William Godwin, *The Enquirer: Reflections on Education, Manners, and Literature, in a Series of Essays* (London, 1797; rpt. New York: Augusus Kelley, 1965), 191.

36. *Works* 8:401.

37. Townsend, *Dissertation on the Poor Laws,* 6.

38. *Monthly Magazine,* 2 (December 1796), 859.

39. Parker's interpretation of this first scene and of its relation to the Female Beggar's testimony ("Narrative and Usurpation," 304–12) has been very helpful to me in formulating the interpretation offered in this essay. Of Herbert's story about saving Matilda from the flames, Parker comments: "The tale of the loss of the mother, the embrace of the daughter with its covert plea for self-pity, is a screen to mask and displace the censored truth of self-usurpation. The birth of

narrative is in an illegitimate appeal to pity disguising the self-usurpation of the tale-teller and coinciding with the illegitimate repression of the mother" (309).

40. The opposition between the sniping mothers in the Female Beggar's speech and the compassionate fathers called upon by Mortimer hints at a problem I have not integrated into my argument, the play's representation of misogyny. Rivers, like Iago in *Othello,* is its most explicit spokesman (e.g., 2.3.388–91); but Mortimer's wildly vacillating trust and suspicion of Matilda clearly partake of it as well (e.g., 3.3.51–57, 3.5.156–60). It seems to me that, rather than receiving the kind of critical representation afforded to Wordsworth's antiaristocratic political ideology in the character of Clifford, gender ideology pervades the text in a generalized and less deliberate way. It would seem to call for interpretation as part of the historical underpinning of Wordsworth's play rather than as an aspect of its political intention; see note 45.

41. In Alan Liu's provocative and often dazzling reading of *The Borderers,* it is not Herbert's pandering but the suspicion that he has *bought* Matilda that represents the most profound violation of Mortimer's sense of legitimacy. Liu reads the final twenty-three lines of 1.3, during which the Female Beggar recounts a business meeting between Herbert and Clifford, as a "supernumerary deception" (231); Mortimer's cry of "Enough!" at 1.3.143 signals that, at the mere discovery of Matilda's illegitimacy, "he really feels pity and fear only for himself— for a tragedy of illegitimacy in which he must now act" (*Wordsworth: The Sense of History,* 231). Liu builds much of his argument on the inadequate motivation of Mortimer's reaction, and therefore he puts strong emphasis on the difference between Mortimer's reaction in 1.3 and the band's relative complacency, during the trial scene, until Mortimer levels the accusation of pandering against Herbert. I am arguing, on the contrary, that it is pandering that so deeply disturbs Mortimer and that the supposed discrepancy between his reaction and the band's does not exist. Mortimer's cry of "Enough" is motivated largely by the hints about Herbert and Clifford that Rivers has fed him in 1.1; the revelation of Matilda's illegitimacy begins to make Rivers's uncertain accusations much too credible. At the same time, Mortimer's outburst is at least as much a cry of impatience with the Female Beggar's irrelevant details about her marriage to Gilfrid as it is an announcement of conclusive evidence. When Mortimer dismisses the Female Beggar from the stage and then calls her back, this is not a "supernumerary" movement, but rather it dramatizes the conflict between his desire to avoid having his worst fears confirmed and his desire of gaining a full revelation of Herbert's perfidy.

42. My sense of the power of Herbert's face is indebted to Paul DeMan's brief analysis of "the speaking face of earth and heaven" (*Prelude* 5. 12) and the "Blest the infant Babe" passage in book 2 ("Wordsworth and the Victorians," in *The Rhetoric of Romanticism* [New York: Columbia University Press, 1984], 89–91). DeMan's analysis leads him to a question that, I would argue, is fully thematized in *The Borderers:* "How are we to reconcile the *meaning* of face, with its promise of sense and of filial preservation, with its *function* as the relentless undoer of its own claims" (92)?

43. Rivers also ascribes a special power to Herbert's appearance, but, like his suborned witness, he considers it deceptive:

> 'Tis his own fault if he hath got a face
> Which doth play tricks with them that look upon it:
> 'Twas he that put it in my thought—his countenance—
> His step, his figure.
>
> (2.3.227–30)

44. On Rivers's irrationality, see Osborn, "Meaningful Obscurity," 407–13, and Stoddard.

45. Alan Liu employs a similar strategy to that adopted here when he situates the psychological and philosophical (esp. Hegelian, i.e., Hartmanian) interpretations of *The Borderers* within the context of the social history of the family and of the way class relationships are expressed in fantasies about the family unit; see *Wordsworth: The Sense of History,* 300–306. My own approach is perhaps less ambitious. The major difference, as I see it, is that I am here trying to render the play as Wordsworth's highly conscious and deliberate intention, rather than trying to delineate the way that history expresses itself in the text despite Wordsworth's intentions, and indeed, by means of the deformations that signal his repression of it.

46. Cf. also 2.1.5–8, and Osborn's note.

CHAPTER 6. FRAMING *THE RUINED COTTAGE*

1. The two most famous instances are Francis Jeffrey's review in *The Edinburgh Review* 24 (1814): 1–30, and Coleridge's letter to Wordsworth of 30 May 1815.

2. Percy Bysshe Shelley, *Shelley's Poetry and Prose,* ed. Donald H. Reiman and Sharon B. Powers (New York: Norton, 1977), 70. Shelley misquotes slightly.

3. On the relation between "Alastor" and *The Excursion,* see John Rieder, "Description of a Struggle: Shelley's Radicalism on Wordsworth's Terrain," *boundary 2* 13 (1985): 267–87; Earl Wasserman, *Shelley: A Critical Reading* (Baltimore: Johns Hopkins University Press, 1971), 3–42, esp. 19–21 and 41–42; and Yvonne Carothers, "*Alastor:* Shelley Corrects Wordsworth," *Modern Language Quarterly* 42 (1981): 21–47.

4. *The Music of Humanity: A Critical Study of Wordsworth's RUINED COTTAGE Incorporating Texts from a Manuscript of 1799–1800* (London: Thomas Nelson and Sons, 1969), xiii.

5. *Romantic Ideology,* 82–85.

6. *Wordsworth's Second Nature,* 135, 140.

7. Levinson, *The Romantic Fragment Poem,* (Chapel Hill: University of North Carolina Press, 1986), 229.

8. Liu, *Wordsworth: The Sense of History,* 319.

9. See Thomas De Quincey, "On Wordsworth's Poetry," in *Collected Writings,* ed. David Masson, 14 vols. (London: A. & C. Black, 1896–97), 11: 294–325; and Cleanth Brooks, "Wordsworth and Human Suffering: Notes on Two Early Poems," in *From Sensibility to Romanticism: Essays Presented to Frederick A. Pottle,* ed. Frederick W. Hilles and Harold Bloom (New York: Oxford University Press, 1965), 373–88.

10. *Wordsworth: The Sense of History,* 325.

11. Quotations of Wordsworth's poetry in this chapter are from RC&P unless otherwise indicated. Reading texts are cited by page number; other citations indicate the manuscript page followed by the page number of the transcription in RC&P.

12. See "Wordsworth and *The Recluse:* The University of Imagination," *PMLA* 97 (1982): 60–82, and *Wordsworth and The Recluse* (New Haven: Yale University Press, 1984).

13. One problem with these two criticisms is that they apparently constitute a

demand that art refer to historical events and take a clearly committed stance toward them. Despite the considerable descriptive accuracy of McGann's, Chandler's, and Levinson's strictures upon this poem, their tendency toward prescription is a symptom that the ideological critique is somehow misconceived. Johnston argues that the critique itself is (as McGann says of the "Romantic ideology") already in the text and is based upon feelings of guilt about the privileged position poets and academics enjoy with respect to those who suffer the evils they only write about ("Self-Consciousness, Social Guilt, and Romantic Poetry: Coleridge's Ancient Mariner and the Old Pedlar," in *Beyond Representation: Philosophy and Poetic Imagination,* ed. Richard Eldridge (Cambridge: Cambridge University Press, 1966), 216–48.

14. My account of textual and compositional matters is heavily indebted throughout to Butler's thorough Cornell edition (RC&P).

15. LEY 199.

16. *Music of Humanity,* 9–16.

17. "*The Ruined Cottage* Restored: Three Stages of Composition," in *Bicentenary Wordsworth Studies in Memory of John Alban Finch,* ed. Jonathan Wordsworth (Ithaca: Cornell University Press, 1970), 29–49. J. Wordsworth actually posits a shorter text as well, speculating that a poem of about one hundred twenty lines was read to Coleridge in June, then expanded into the 370-line version and read to Lamb in July (*Music of Humanity,* 14–15).

18. Finch's mistake involved Dorothy Wordsworth's misnumbering of the lines of part 2 in Ms. B. Dorothy wrote "140" and "160" next to lines 240 and 260 (RC&P 251–53), and Finch guessed, plausibly but erroneously, that the final pages of this version were transferred from an earlier, lost manuscript numbering 174 lines.

19. RC&P 12.

20. A coherent, hypothetical reading text can be assembled from the materials in RC&P as follows: 1) Christabel NB, 3r–3v (99–101); 2) fifty-six and one-half lines from MS. A, arranged as follows: p. 81, lines numbered 165–70; p. 85, 170–71; p. 83, 172–89; p. 87, 190–214; p. 83, 215–43; 3) a reworked version of Racedown NB, 5v and 8r (91); the Ms. B reading text of lines 318–33 (60) and 467–70 (68) can be substituted to produce a readable version; 4) Christabel NB, 4v (103) and the lines implied by the stub of 5r (96); 5) the lines in Coleridge's letter to Estlin (95).

21. On the female vagrant in contemporary literature, see *Music of Humanity,* 50–67.

22. Cf. Liu's understanding of "textualization" in the poem, in *Wordsworth: The Sense of History,* 325–41, and Karen Swann's reading of this passage as an example of Derridean "reelism," in "Suffering and Sensation in *The Ruined Cottage,*" *PMLA* 106 (1991): 85–87.

23. The "Lines Left upon a Seat in a Yew-tree" were included in the "Poems Proceeding from Sentiment and Reflection" rather than the "Inscriptions" in the 1815 *Poems,* perhaps because this poem, like the Estlin fragment, is somewhat uncertainly poised between conversation and pure inscription.

24. See Butler's introduction to the two poems, RC&P 461–62.

25. I am indebted to Peter Sacks's psychoanalytic account of the relation between elegiac conventions and the work of mourning, in *The English Elegy: Studies in the Genre from Spenser to Yeats,* (Baltimore: Johns Hopkins University Press, 1985), 1–37.

26. "Wordsworth, Inscriptions, and Romantic Nature Poetry," *Beyond Formal-*

ism: Literary Essays 1958–1970 (New Haven: Yale University Press, 1970), 222–23.

27. *Wordsworth: The Sense of History,* 341–57; *The Romantic Fragment Poem,* 221–22.

28. *Wordsworth and The Recluse,* 36.

29. Johnston, "Self-Consciousness, Social Guilt, and Romantic Poetry." I draw the phrase "substituting catharsis for responsibility" from the manuscript version of this essay, which Ken Johnston generously shared with me before its publication.

30. See J. Wordsworth, *Music of Humanity,* 184–241.

31. Liu compares Wordsworth's crisis of debt, associated with the Calvert legacy and the suit against Lowther, to the crisis in the weaving industry, where the different form of capitalization becoming dominant in southern England threatened to destroy the virtuous "independence" of Northern weavers (*Wordsworth: The Sense of History,* 325–47). Thus Wordsworth's invocation of Burns is overdetermined by his advocacy of Northern independence and of a pre-capitalistic, or at least differently capitalized, cottage industry.

32. Robert Burns, *Poems and Songs,* ed. James Kinsley (Oxford: Oxford University Press, 1971), 69–72.

33. Johnston, "Self-Consciousness, Social Guilt, and Romantic Poetry"; Liu, *Wordsworth: The Sense of History,* 327–32.

34. "Wordsworth, Margaret, and the Pedlar," *Studies in Romanticism* 15 [1976]: 197, 205–6.

35. I have not included the addition of lines 361–75 of Butler's reading text of Ms. D in this discussion, since Butler could well have included this passage in the reading text of Ms. B. The lines, written on Ms. B, 36v, are marked for insertion in Ms. B, 36r and are included in Dorothy Wordsworth's count of the lines at the end of 2a (see Butler's note, RC&P 241).

36. Peter Manning argues that "the Pedlar is a partial self-portrait; the poem which became Book I of *The Excursion* is a multi-faceted one, and we need to have it whole to understand Wordsworth" ("Wordsworth, Margaret, and the Pedlar," 215). Thus the tale of Margaret turns into a facet of Wordsworth's complex self-portrait. An antithetical defense of *The Excursion* is made by William Galperin in *Revision and Authority in Wordsworth: The Interpretation of a Career* (Philadelphia: University of Pennsylvania Press, 1989), 29–63, esp. 32–44. Where Manning privileges the autobiographical self of *The Prelude* and values "The Wanderer" as a species of self-portrait, Galperin prefers *The Excursion* because it ironizes Wordsworthian selfhood. Nonetheless, Galperin's argument similarly dissolves the tale of Margaret into a test case for a version of Wordsworthian subjectivity.

A second argument in favor of "The Wanderer" observes, very reasonably, that the elaborate metaphysical grounding given to the wanderer's authority as "chosen son" ought to make his consolation speech more convincing than Armytage's similar efforts in Ms. D (Phillip Cohen, "Narrative and Persuasion in *The Ruined Cottage*," *Journal of Narrative Technique* 8 [1978]: 185–99, and Peter F. McInerney, "Natural Wisdom in Wordsworth's *The Excursion*," *The Wordsworth Circle* 9 [1978]: 188–99). Those who prefer Ms. D will no doubt agree that the pedlar/wanderer is a more authoritative teacher than Armytage, but that is one of the reasons the later poems are duller. For instance, Cohen writes that "whether or not the universe is indifferent or benevolent is not left open to question in Book I as it is in *The Ruined Cottage*" (193); this is true because it was *not* the question in the earlier poem, especially not in Ms. D, where the problem is how to cope with the social implications of Margaret's suffering and of the act of recounting it.

A more interesting case can be made in terms of "The Wanderer"'s inability to be fully persuasive: "Both Margaret and the wanderer are forced to cope with what seems for Wordsworth an inevitable falling away from possession and communion. Their responses are profoundly different, so different as to seem antithetical, and the power of the poem comes partly from our recognition that Wordsworth's sympathies for each cannot be reconciled" (Reeve Parker, "'Finer Distance': The Narrative Art of Wordsworth's 'The Wanderer,'" *ELH* 39 [1972]: 103). Parker argues that "The Wanderer" is superior precisely because it fully realizes the antithetical tension between Margaret and the wanderer. The difficulty with Parker's argument, however, is that the wanderer's losses concern things that no one but Wordsworth could take seriously as causes for grief: his adolescent experiences of communion with nature. How can this sort of loss be put in the balance with Margaret's? In fact, Parker ends up very close to the hagiography/ *exemplum* interpretation: the wanderer's is an "ideal human response" (103) to loss, while "Margaret's fixity of hope is a paralysis of life" (108).

37. Rieder, "Description of a Struggle."

38. On the importance of the implicit protocol, see V. N. Volosinov, "Discourse in Life and Discourse in Art (Concerning Sociological Poetics)," in *Freudianism,* trans. I. R. Titunik (New York: Academic Press, 1976), 93–116, where the fact that a value judgment is unstated is a sign of its unquestioned rule; cf. the status of hegemonic values as "obvious" in Louis Althusser, "Ideology and Ideological State Apparatuses (Notes toward an Investigation)," in *Lenin and Philosophy,* trans. Ben Brewster (New York: Monthly Review Press, 1971), 173, or as "common sense" in Williams, *Marxism and Literature,* 110.

39. *Marxism and Literature,* 45–54; see also Stone, 226–29, on the importance of new literary genres and habits of reading to the development of what he calls "affective individualism."

40. John B. Radner, "The Art of Sympathy in Eighteenth-Century British Moral Thought," *Studies in Eighteenth-Century Culture* 9 (1979): 189–210.

41. Cf. the "emotion recollected in tranquility" passage's emphasis on pleasure as well as on the *technique* of reviving remembered emotional responses to something like their original intensity through a kind of internalized theatricality. Paul Magnuson's argument, in "Wordsworth and Spontaneity," in *The Evidence of Imagination,* ed. Donald H. Reiman, et. al. (New York: New York University Press, 1978), 101–18, that Wordsworth uses "spontaneous" in the "Preface to *Lyrical Ballads*" to mean voluntary, without constraint, and self-generated, but *not* unpremeditated strips the idea of a technique of spontaneity of its apparently oxymoronic quality.

42. The change of "bosom" to "breast" may be motivated by a desire to repair the weak caesura in the Ms. B version of the line.

43. See Sacks, 19–26.

44. The pedlar's lament also carries apocalyptic political and religious overtones in its allusion to Isaiah 34:13: "And thorns shall come up in her palaces, nettles and brambles in the fortresses thereof: and it shall be a habitation of dragons, and a court for owls." Isaiah 34–35 comprises a strong scriptural source for the sequence of devastation and regeneration worked out in the pedlar's lament and consolation. See note 60.

45. Compare Johnston on the eroticism of this passage, which he connects to the rejected possibilities of sensationalism and pornography in the rest of the

narrative (*Wordsworth and the Recluse,* 43–51); on Wordsworth's treatment of sensationalism, see Swann.

46. "Il Penseroso," 131–54; "Summer," 522–63; see Neil Hertz, "Wordsworth and the Tears of Adam," *Studies in Romanticism* 7 (1967): 15–33, and Parker, "Finer Distance," 90–96.

47. Thomson, *The Castle of Indolence,* 1.7; Barrell, *The Dark Side of the Landscape,* 46–47.

48. A. O. Aldridge, "The Pleasures of Pity," *ELH* 16 (1949): 78.

49. See Aldridge, "The Pleasures of Pity," and Radner, "The Art of Sympathy in Eighteenth-Century British Moral Thought."

50. A particularly good example is Dugald Stewart's analysis of compassion in his *Elements of the Philosophy of the Human Mind* (1792): "What we commonly call sensibility depends, in a great measure, on the power of imagination, . . . [and] the apparent coldness and selfishness of mankind may be traced, in a great measure, to a want of attention and a want of imagination" (quoted by Radner, "The Art of Sympathy," 193). Stewart's concerns are consonant with Wordsworth's own choice of subject matter in the 1790s: "[Stewart] contrasts two ways of responding to the sight of a man who has suddenly been reduced to poverty. One person 'feels merely in proportion to what he perceives by his sense.' But another 'follows, in imagination, the unfortunate man to his dwelling and partakes with him and his family in their domestic distress.' He fleshes out the whole scene, listens to conversations filled with disappointment, and pictures 'all the various resources delicacy and pride can suggest, to conceal poverty from the world'; and 'as he proceeds in the painting, his sensibility increases, and he weeps, not for what he sees, but for what he imagines'" (193–94).

51. Norman S. Fiering, "Irresistible Compassion: An Aspect of Eighteenth-Century Sympathy and Humanitarianism," *Journal of the History of Ideas* 37 (1976): 212–13.

52. "On Wordsworth's Poetry," 305.

53. Edmund Spenser, *The Faerie Queene* (New York: Dutton, 1910), 1.9.44. Despair's speech in *The Faerie Queene* also proceeds from two earlier scenes of morally dangerous repose in shady spots: at 1.2.28–32, where the spot itself generates a narrative, the story of Fradubio, and 1.7.2–7, where Duessa seduces the Redcrosse knight.

54. The words in brackets were erased in Ms. D, and no substitutes inserted; Butler's reading text leaves them blank and supplies the erased text in a footnote.

55. Jacques Derrida, "White Mythology: Metaphor in the Text of Philosophy," in *Margins of Philosophy,* trans. Alan Bass (Chicago: University of Chicago Press, 1982): 207–71, esp. 242–45 and 250–51; cf. Liu, *Wordsworth: The Sense of History,* 317.

56. "White Mythology," 213.

57. *Music of Humanity,* 125.

58. The connection of the visionary moments in Wordworth's poetry to radical Protestantism, so important to the best twentieth century criticsm of his poetry, e.g., by Abrams and Hartman, was obvious to discerning contemporaries as well, for instance to Charles Lamb in his review of *The Excursion:* ". . . an internal principle of lofty consciousness . . . stamps upon [Wordsworth's] opinions and sentiments (we were almost going to say) the character of an expanded and generous Quakerism" (*Lamb as Critic,* ed. Roy Park, [Lincoln: University of Nebraska Press, 1980], 196). For a scholarly account of Wordsworth's relation to the Evangelical movement, see Richard E. Brantley, *Wordsworth's "Natural Methodism"*

(New Haven: Yale University Press, 1975), which takes its title from Lamb's review of *The Excursion*.

59. RC&P 11–14 and 105–7.

60. J. Wordsworth, *Music of Humanity,* 127 compares various descriptions of ruin in the poem to Isaiah 13 : 20–22; the more extended vision of destruction and regeneration in Isaiah 34–35, cited by Blake in *The Marriage of Heaven and Hell,* is also appropriate.

CHAPTER 7. "THEREFORE AM I STILL": THE POET'S AUTHORITY IN "TINTERN ABBEY"

1. The text of "Tintern Abbey" used in this discussion will be the 1798 *Lyrical Ballads* text, LB 116–20.

2. Jacobus, *Tradition and Experiment,* 113–18; cf. the importance granted to Bowles in two now-classic essays on the Romantic lyric, William K. Wimsatt, "The Structure of Romantic Nature Imagery," in *The Verbal Icon: Studies in The Meaning of Poetry* (Lexington: University of Kentucky Press, 1954), 103–16, and M. H. Abrams, "Structure and Style in the Greater Romantic Lyric," in *From Sensibility to Romanticism: Essays Presented to Frederick A. Pottle,* ed. Frederick W. Hilles and Harold Bloom (New York: Oxford University Press, 1965), 527–60.

3. This disparity is Geoffrey Hartman's starting point in both *The Unmediated Vision: An Interpretation of Wordsworth, Hopkins, Rilke, and Valery* (New York: Harcourt, Brace, & World, 1954), 3 and *Wordsworth's Poetry,* 3–4. Levinson's "Insight and Oversight" provocatively explores a different approach to the disparity between occasion and emotion.

4. For the dating of the fragment, see CEY 27 and 346.

5. See Mark Foster, "'Tintern Abbey' and Wordsworth's Scene of Writing," *Studies in Romanticism* 25 (1986): 75–95, for a description of the performative or "projective" dimension of "Tintern Abbey."

6. For a full psychoanalytic rendering of this conflict, see Onorato, 29–87.

7. On the details of William and Dorothy's July 10–13 tour of the Wye see CEY 243 and Levinson, *Period Poems,* 53–55. On the political resonance of the date, see J. R. Watson, "A Note on the Title of 'Tintern Abbey,'" *Wordsworth Circle* 10 (1979): 379–80, and on the possible association of the locale with the radical John Thelwall's farm at Llyswen (cf. "Anecdote for Fathers"), see Geoffrey Little, "'Tintern Abbey' and LLyswen Farm," *Wordsworth Circle* 8 (1977): 80–82.

8. See Johnston on "the use Wordsworth did *not* make of Gilpin," "The Politics of 'Tintern Abbey,'" *The Wordsworth Circle* 14 (1985): 8; Gill, *Wordsworth,* 152–53; and Levinson, *Period Poems,* 14–37. My argument with Levinson in chap. 1 has to do with the significance of Wordsworth's omissions, not the fact that they were made.

9. "Politics of 'Tintern Abbey,'" 13.

10. See Johnston, *Wordsworth and The Recluse,* chapters 3, 6, and 7; and also M. H. Abrams, *Natural Supernaturalism: Tradition and Revolution in Romantic Literature* (New York: W.W. Norton & Co., 1971), 17–70.

11. Unless otherwise noted, translations of Virgil and Horace are cited by page number from Abraham Cowley, *The Essays and Other Prose Writings,* ed. Alfred B. Gough (Oxford: Clarendon Press, 1915).

12. Maren-Sofie Røstvig, in her thorough survey of the *beatus ille* tradition

in English poetry, uses Cowley's essays as her starting point because of their comprehensive selection of classical sources and because they comprise a sustained exposition of the tradition (*The Happy Man: Studies in the Metamorphoses of a Classical Ideal,* 2 vols., 2d ed. [New York: Humanities Press, 1971], 1: 15–41). The most important essay, according to Røstvig, is "Of Agriculture," which includes Cowley's translations of both the "*O fortunatos nimium*" and the "*beatus ille procul negotiis*" passages (Cowley, 154–60). My quotations of Cowley's prose are all from the essay "Of Agriculture." My discussion of all of these texts is deeply indebted to Røstvig's scholarship.

13. Røstvig 2: 10.

14. Cowper's *The Task* also belongs in the series that runs from Thomson to Wordsworth. The relevance of all three poems to "Tintern Abbey" might well be gauged by their appearance in John Hayden's amusing *cento* of eighteenth-century locodescriptive and meditative verse, "The Road to Tintern Abbey," *The Wordsworth Circle* 12 (1981): 211–16. Hayden's 187-line collocation bears a rather striking similarity to "Tintern Abbey," leading Hayden to conclude that it is "difficult to say whether Thomson and Akenside are more 'Pre-Romantic' or Wordsworth more 'Post-Augustan'" (216). Hayden's *cento* includes thirty-two lines from *The Seasons,* thirty-four from *The Pleasures of Imagination,* and fifty-five from *The Task.*

15. On the "good man" in "Tintern Abbey," see Robert A. Brinkley, "Vagrant and Hermit: Milton and the Politics of 'Tintern Abbey,'" *The Wordsworth Circle* 16 (1985): 127, and Roe, 213.

16. Røstvig 2: 245.

17. See Røstvig 2: 231.

18. James Turner, *The Politics of Landscape: Rural Scenery and Society in English Poetry 1630–1660* (Oxford: Basil Blackwell, 1979), 85–112.

19. "Structure and Style in the Greater Romantic Lyric."

20. John Thelwall, *Political Lectures* (London: J. Thelwall, 1795), 8–9.

21. John Thelwall, *The Rights of Nature, Against the Usurpation of Establishments* (London: H. D. Symonds, 1796), 21.

22. Magnuson's *Wordsworth and Coleridge* seems unlikely to be surpassed any time soon in the care and detail of its readings. I have also benefitted from Lucy Newlyn, "'In City Pent': Echo and Allusion in Wordsworth, Coleridge, and Lamb, 1797–1801," *The Review of English Studies* n.s. 32 (1981): 408–28; Richard Matlak, "Classical Argument and Romantic Persuasion in 'Tintern Abbey,'" *Studies in Romanticism* 25 (1986): 97–129, and the comparison of "Tintern Abbey" and "Fears in Solitude" in Roe, 263–75.

23. STCL 1: 397–98; "Fears in Solitude" is dated 20 April 1798.

24. Cf. Johnston's reading of the Ms. B passage in *Wordsworth and The Recluse,* 25.

25. See especially Harold Bloom, *Poetry and Repression: Revisionism from Blake to Stevens* (New Haven: Yale University Press, 1976), 52–82, and Brinkley.

26. *Georgics* 2. 490, in *Eclogues, Georgics, Aeneid I–VI,* with translation by H. Rushton Fairclough, Loeb Classical Library, rev. ed. (Cambridge: Harvard University Press, 1978); the Loeb edition translates: "Blessed is he who has been able to win knowledge of the causes of things." Further Latin quotations and the accompanying prose translations of Virgil are from this edition.

27. *Paradise Lost* 3. 54–55, in *Complete Poems and Major Prose,* ed. Merritt Y. Hughes (New York: Bobbs-Merrill, 1957). Further quotations of *Paradise Lost* are from this edition.

28. Robert Brinkley reaches a similar conclusion in "Vagrant and Hermit: Milton and the Politics of 'Tintern Abbey'": "In 'Tintern Abbey,' the anchor of Wordsworth's moral being is not a law but an experience of the sublime . . . . If, as Gilles Deleuze suggests, it is only in the *Critique of Judgment* that Kant provides a 'foundation for Romanticism,' it is because freedom no longer *governs* in this aesthetic. . . . Similarly, in the Wordsworthian sublime it is *a freedom that does not govern* which is taken to be the truth" (131).

29. Jonathan Wordsworth devotes an entire chapter of *The Borders of Vision* to the ways in which Wordsworth uses the pattern of the Fall in *The Prelude* without ever quite acknowledging that a fall has taken place: "There is no doubt that Wordsworth intended to impose on his poem the paradise-lost-and-regained pattern. . . . But alongside his preoccupation with loss, and with the possible sublimity of primal vision restored, there is an extraordinary refusal to believe that his imagination has ever truly been impaired" (234–35).

30. The concluding lines of Thomson's "Autumn" are a likely intermediate text between Virgil's and Wordsworth's turns from the sublime to the rural scene. Thomson puts this passage at the end of his translation and adaptation of the "*O fortunatos nimium*" passage, "Autumn," 1235–1373 (quoted from *The Seasons and The Castle of Indolence*, ed. James Sambrook [Oxford: Clarendon Press, 1972]). In the first line, "that" refers to Thomson's ambition to gain comprehensive knowledge of nature's works:

> But, if to that unequal—if the blood
> In sluggish streams about my heart forbid
> That best ambition—under closing shades
> Inglorious lay me by the lowly brook,
> And whisper to my dreams. From thee begin,
> Dwell all on thee, with thee conclude my song;
> And let me never, never stray from thee!

The way the "lowly brook" whispers to Thomson's dreams further suggests a connection between this passage, the opening of "Tintern Abbey," and the origins of Ms. JJ, particularly if the famous "Was it for this" passage in that manuscript represents a kind of detour from the rigorous and comprehensive philosophic plan of *The Recluse* (cf. Johnston, *Wordsworth and The Recluse*, 61–65).

31. On the factual inaccuracy of Wordsworth's representation of his earlier self, see Gill, *Wordsworth*, 153–54.

32. See Pocock, *Virtue, Commerce, and History*, 110–14.

33. Cf. William Empson, "Sense in *The Prelude*," in *The Structure of Complex Words* (London: Chatto & Windus, 1951), 289–305.

34. Hayden uses Thomson's "Spring," [1738] 859–77 as the parallel passage in "The Road to Tintern Abbey." *The Pleasures of Imagination* (1744), 3, 593–633 (in Akenside's *Poetical Works*, ed. Alexander Dyce [1845; rpt. New York: AMS Press, 1969]) is also strikingly similar, especially if Akenside's closing lines are set alongside Wordsworth's recognition of "the language of the sense":

> Thus the men
> Whom Nature's works can charm, with God himself
> Hold converse; grow familiar, day by day,
> With his conceptions, act upon his plan;
> And form to his, the relish of their souls.

(629–33)

35. *Poetical Works,* ed. H. S. Milford, 4th ed. (Oxford: Oxford University Press, 1934).

36. Alexander Pope, *The Poems,* ed. John Butt (New Haven: Yale University Press, 1963), 265.

37. See "Spring" 904–1176, especially the last verse paragraph; and Cowper's repeated praise of domestic peace in "The Garden," book 3 of *The Task,* as well as the long paragraph beginning "He is the happy man," which concludes the entire poem.

38. Lawrence Kramer writes of Dorothy Wordsworth's role in "Tintern Abbey" as that of "a self-object, a representation of the other in which the self is fully fused" ("Victorian Sexuality and 'Tintern Abbey,'" *Victorian Poetry* 24 [1986]: 402), and Onorato discerns "a subtle and persistent confusion of Dorothy with [William Wordsworth] himself" (82). On Dorothy Wordsworth's tendency toward self-effacement, see Susan Levin, *Dorothy Wordsworth and Romanticism* (New Brunswick: Rutgers University Press, 1987), 1–10. Richard Fadem, "Dorothy Wordsworth: A View from 'Tintern Abbey,'" *The Wordsworth Circle* 9 (1978): 17–32, and James Holt McGavran, Jr. "Xanadu, Somersetshire, and the Banks of the Wye: A Study of Romantic Androgyny," *Papers on Language and Literature* 26 (1990): 334–45, both concentrate more closely on the role Dorothy Wordsworth plays in "Tintern Abbey," but I have found neither of these essays very useful. It is my general impression that interpretations of "Tintern Abbey" devote a disproportionately small amount of attention to the poem's final verse paragraph and that the turn to Dorothy is usually read only as a gloss on the earlier sublime passages, where the poem's theme is (they imply) really delivered.

39. See Isobel Armstrong's analysis of Wordsworth's use of the "hovering comparison" in "'Tintern Abbey': From Augustan to Romantic," in *Augustan Worlds,* ed. J. C. Hilson, M. M. B. Jones, and J. R. Watson (New York: Barnes & Noble, 1978), 266.

40. For an exemplary instance, see Hartman, *Unmediated Vision:* "The phrase 'of more deep seclusion' has a referent of which we are hardly conscious because a transcendent one immediately suggests itself. It is the cliffs that cause the scene to appear more secluded, it is the thoughts that are by nature more secluded even than the scene, but the suggestion persists that the cliffs and the scene have, by the very fact of entering the mind, caused a deepening there" (22).

CONCLUSION: ORIGINALITY, SYMPATHY, AND THE CRITIQUE OF IDEOLOGY

1. Raymond Williams's chapter on the concept of literature in *Marxism and Literature* and Pierre Macherey and Etienne Balibar's "Literature as an Ideological Form: Some Marxist Propositions," trans. James Kavanaugh, *Praxis* 5 (1981): 43–58 are now classic examples of this argument; Clifford Siskin argues for the specificity and historical limitation of the category of literature in the context of ideas about Romanticism in *The Historicity of Romantic Discourse,* chap. 4; John Guillory's discussion of the changing forms of the canon in *Cultural Capital: The Problem of Literary Canon Formation* (Chicago: University of Chicago Press, 1993), 55–82, is a very useful consolidation of the entire theme.

2. For example: Terry Eagleton, "The Rise of English," chap. 2 of *Literary Theory: An Introduction* (Minneapolis: University of Minnesota Press, 1983) and Guillory emphasize class hegemony; Franklin Court's *Institutionalizing English*

Literature: The Culture and Politics of Literary Study, 1750–1900 (Stanford: Stanford University Press, 1992) stresses the role played by racism in nineteenth century literary theory; the argument linking literary education to imperialism is advanced in Gauri Viswanathan's *Masks of Conquest: Literary Study and British Rule in India* (New York: Columbia University Press, 1989); Ian Hunter's *Culture and Government: The Emergence of Literary Education* (London, Macmillan, 1988) grants a central role in the development of literary education to social welfare schemes; professional aspiration is a main theme for Ohmann and for Gerald Graff, *Professing Literature: An Institutional History* (Chicago: University of Chicago Press, 1987).

3. This is not to say, however, that a poem's power in a "field of cultural production" can be adequately understood solely on the basis of the poem's intrinsic characteristics. Clearly the two endeavors—close reading of poetry and sociohistorical analysis of the field of production—supplement one another. Cf. Pierre Bourdieu's argument concerning the limitations of the intrinsic analysis of works of art in "The Field of Cultural Production," *Poetics* 12 (1983): 311–55.

4. The inspiration for the three-part scheme proposed here is Slavoj Zizek's analysis of Hegelian logic in *Tarrying with the Negative: Kant, Hegel, and the Critique of Ideology* (Durham, NC: Duke University Press, 1993), chap. 4.

5. Madden, ed., *Robert Southey: The Critical Heritage,* 68.

6. 501; Liu's italics.

7. The most pervasive trope of literary scholarship bears witness to the same fantastic structure as the one at work in original poetry. I am referring to the trope of citation, which is so inescapable because it is based on the implacable demand for originality. But this demand, which rules that whatever an individual stakes out to be done must be presented as having been left unfinished or incomplete elsewhere, has as its corollary the fantasy of comprehensiveness, in which every scholarly project becomes a fragment of some collective one that will ultimately complete it.

Works Cited

Abensour, Miguel. "Saint-Just and the Problem of Heroism in the French Revolution." *Social Research* 56 (Spring 1989): 188–211.

Abrams, M. H. *Natural Supernaturalism: Tradition and Revolution in Romantic Literature.* New York: W. W. Norton & Co., 1971.

———. "Structure and Style in the Greater Romantic Lyric." In *From Sensibility to Romanticism: Essays Presented to Frederick A. Pottle,* edited by Frederick W. Hilles and Harold Bloom, 527–60. New York: Oxford University Press, 1965.

Akenside, Mark. *Poetical Works.* Edited by Alexander Dyce. 1845; rpt. New York: AMS Press, 1969.

Aldridge, A. O. "The Pleasures of Pity." *ELH* 16 (1949): 76–87.

Althusser, Louis. "Ideology and Ideological State Apparatuses (Notes toward an Investigation)." In *Lenin and Philosophy,* translated by Ben Brewster, 127–86. New York: Monthly Review Press, 1971.

Altieri, Charles. "Wordsworth's Wavering Balance: The Thematic Rhythm of *The Prelude*." *The Wordsworth Circle* 4 (1973): 226–39.

Arac, Jonathan. *Critical Genealogies: Historical Situations for Postmodern Literary Studies.* New York: Columbia University Press, 1989.

Armstrong, Isobel. "'Tintern Abbey': From Augustan to Romantic." In *Augustan Worlds,* edited by J. C. Hilson, M. M. B. Jones, and J. R. Watson, 261–79. New York: Barnes & Noble, 1978.

Barish, Jonas. *The Anti-Theatrical Prejudice.* Berkeley: University of California Press, 1981.

Barrell, John. *The Dark Side of the Landscape: The Rural Poor in English Painting 1730–1840.* Cambridge: Cambridge University Press, 1980.

———. *English Literature 1730–1780: An Equal, Wide Survey.* New York: St. Martin's Press, 1983.

———. *The Idea of Landscape and the Sense of Place.* Cambridge: Cambridge University Press, 1972.

Beattie, James. *The Minstrel; Or, The Progress of Genius: in Two Books, with Some Other Poems.* London: C. Dilly, 1797.

Beatty, Arthur. "Joseph Fawcett: *The Art of War*." *University of Wisconsin Studies in Language and Literature* 2 (1918): 224–69.

Beer, John. "Nature and Liberty: The Linking of Unstable Concepts." *The Wordsworth Circle* 14 (1983): 201–13.

———. "The 'Revolutionary Youth' of Wordsworth and Coleridge: Another View." *Critical Quarterly* 19:2 (1977): 79–87.

Bentham, Jeremy. *Works.* Edited by John Bowring. 11 vols. Edinburgh: William Tait, 1838–42.

Bewell, Alan. *Wordsworth and the Enlightenment: Nature, Man, and Society in the Experimental Poetry.* New Haven: Yale University Press, 1989.

Bialostosky, Don H. *Making Tales: The Poetics of Wordsworth's Narrative Experiments*. Chicago: University of Chicago Press, 1984.

———. *Wordsworth, Dialogics, and the Practice of Criticism*. Cambridge: Cambridge University Press, 1992.

Bloom, Harold. *Poetry and Repression: Revisionism from Blake to Stevens*. New Haven: Yale University Press, 1976.

Bourdieu, Pierre. "The Field of Cultural Production." *Poetics* 12 (1983): 311–55.

Bourke, Richard. *Romantic Discourse and Political Modernity: Wordsworth, the Intellectuals, and Cultural Critique*. New York: St. Martin's Press, 1993.

Brantley, Richard E. *Wordsworth's "Natural Methodism"*. New Haven: Yale University Press, 1975.

Brinkley, Robert A. "Vagrant and Hermit: Milton and the Politics of 'Tintern Abbey.'" *The Wordsworth Circle* 16 (1985): 126–33.

Brooks, Cleanth. "Wordsworth and Human Suffering: Notes on Two Early Poems." In *From Sensibility to Romanticism: Essays Presented to Frederick A. Pottle*, edited by Frederick W. Hilles and Harold Bloom, 373–88. New York: Oxford University Press, 1965.

Burns, Robert. *Poems and Songs*. Edited by James Kinsley. Oxford: Oxford University Press, 1971.

Butler, Marilyn. *Romantics, Rebels, and Reactionaries*. New York: Oxford University Press, 1981.

Carothers, Yvonne. "*Alastor*: Shelley Corrects Wordsworth." *Modern Language Quarterly* 42 (1981): 21–47.

Chandler, James K. *Wordsworth's Second Nature: A Study of the Poetry and Politics*. Chicago: University of Chicago Press, 1984.

Cohen, Phillip. "Narrative and Persuasion in *The Ruined Cottage*." *Journal of Narrative Technique* 8 (1978): 185–99.

Court, Franklin. *Institutionalizing English Literature: The Culture and Politics of Literary Study, 1750–1900*. Stanford University Press, 1992.

Cowper, William. *Poetical Works*. Edited by H. S. Milford. 4th ed. Oxford: Oxford University Press, 1934.

Danby, John F. *The Simple Wordsworth: Studies in the Poems 1797–1807*. London: Routledge & Kegan Paul, 1960.

De Man, Paul. "Wordsworth and the Victorians." In *The Rhetoric of Romanticism*, 83–92. New York: Columbia University Press, 1984.

De Quincey, Thomas. "On Wordsworth's Poetry." In *Collected Writings*, edited by David Masson, 11: 294–325. 14 vols. London: A. & C. Black, 1896–97.

Derrida, Jacques. "White Mythology: Metaphor in the Text of Philosophy." In *Margins of Philosophy*, translated by Alan Bass, 207–71. Chicago: University of Chicago Press, 1982.

Dickey, Laurence. "Historicizing the 'Adam Smith Problem': Conceptual, Historiographical, and Textual Issues." *Journal of Modern History* 58 (1986): 579–609.

Eagleton, Terry. *Literary Theory: An Introduction*. Minneapolis: University of Minnesota Press, 1983.

Eden, Frederick Morton. *The State of the Poor: An History of the Labouring Classes in England, from the Conquest to the Present Period*. 3 vols. London: J. Davis, 1797.

Eldridge, Richard. "Self-Understanding and Community in Wordsworth's Poetry." *Philosophy and Literature* 10 (1986): 273–94.

Ellis, David. "Wordsworth's Revolutionary Youth: How We Read *The Prelude*." *Critical Quarterly* 19:4 (1977): 59–67.

Empson, William. "Sense in *The Prelude*." In *The Structure of Complex Words*, 289–305. London: Chatto & Windus, 1951.

Erdman, David. "Wordsworth as Heartsworth, or Was Regicide the Prophetic Ground of Those 'Moral Questions'?" In *The Evidence of the Imagination*, edited by Donald Reiman et. al., 12–41. New York: New York University Press, 1978.

Erskine, Thomas. *A View of the Causes and Consequences of the Present War with France*. London: J. Debrett, 1797.

Fadem, Richard. "Dorothy Wordsworth: A View from 'Tintern Abbey.'" *The Wordsworth Circle* 9 (1978): 17–32.

Fawcett, Joseph. *The Art of War*. 2d ed. London: J. Johnson, 1795.

Fiering, Norman S. "Irresistible Compassion: An Aspect of Eighteenth-Century Sympathy and Humanitarianism." *Journal of the History of Ideas* 37 (1976): 195–218.

Finch, John Alban. "*The Ruined Cottage* Restored: Three Stages of Composition." In *Bicentenary Wordsworth Studies in Memory of John Alban Finch*, edited by Jonathan Wordsworth, 29–49. Ithaca: Cornell University Press, 1970.

Fink, Zera. "Wordsworth and the English Republican Tradition." *Journal of English and Germanic Philology* 47 (1948): 107–26.·

Foster, Mark. "'Tintern Abbey' and Wordsworth's Scene of Writing." *Studies in Romanticism* 25 (1986): 75–95.

Foucault, Michel. *The History of Sexuality: Volume One: An Introduction*. Translated by Robert Hurley. New York: Random House, 1978.

Fried, Michael. *Absorption and Theatricality: Painting and Beholder in the Age of Diderot*. Berkeley: University of California Press, 1980.

Friedman, Geraldine. "History in the Background of Wordsworth's Blind Beggar." *ELH* 56 (1989): 125–48.

Friedman, Michael H. *The Making of a Tory Humanist: William Wordsworth and the Idea of Community*. New York: Columbia University Press, 1979.

Galperin, William. *Revision and Authority in Wordsworth: The Interpretation of a Career*. Philadelphia: University of Pennsylvania Press, 1989.

Gates, Barbara T. "Wordsworth's Lessons from the Past." *The Wordsworth Circle* 7 (1976): 133–41.

Gill, Stephen C. "'Adventures on Salisbury Plain' and Wordsworth's Poetry of Protest, 1795–97." *Studies in Romanticism* 11 (1972): 48–65.

———. *William Wordsworth: A Life*. Oxford: Clarendon Press, 1989.

———. "Wordsworth's Breeches Pocket: Attitudes to the Didactic Poet." *Essays in Criticism* 19 (1969): 385–401.

Glen, Heather. *Vision and Disenchantment: Blake's Songs and Wordsworth's Lyrical Ballads*. Cambridge: Cambridge University Press, 1983.

Godwin, William. *The Enquirer: Reflections on Education, Manners, and Literature, in a Series of Essays*. London, 1797; rpt. New York: Augustus Kelley, 1965.

————. *Enquiry concerning Political Justice and Its Influence on Morals and Happiness*. 3d ed. Edited by F. E. L. Priestley. 3 vols. Toronto: University of Toronto Press, 1946.

Goldstein, Laurence. *Ruins and Empire: The Evolution of a Theme in Augustan and Romantic Literature*. Pittsburgh: University of Pittsburgh Press, 1977.

Goodwin, Albert. *The Friends of Liberty: The English Democratic Movement in the Age of the French Revolution*. Cambridge: Harvard University Press, 1979.

Gordon, Robert C. "Wordsworth and the Domestic Roots of Power." *Bulletin of Research in the Humanities* 81 (1978): 90–102.

Graff, Gerald. *Professing Literature: An Institutional History*. Chicago: University of Chicago Press, 1987.

Grob, Alan. "Afterword: Wordsworth and the Politics of Consciousness." In *Critical Essays on William Wordsworth*, 339–56. Boston: G. K. Hall, 1990.

Guillory, John. *Cultural Capital: The Problem of Literary Canon Formation*. Chicago: University of Chicago Press, 1993.

Harrison, Gary. "Wordsworth's 'The Old Cumberland Beggar': The Economy of Charity in Late Eighteenth-Century Britain." *Criticism* 30 (1988): 23–42.

Hartman, Geoffrey. *The Unmediated Vision: An Interpretation of Wordsworth, Hopkins, Rilke, and Valery*. New York: Harcourt, Brace, & World, 1954.

————. "'Was It for This. . .?': Wordsworth and the Birth of the Gods." In *Romantic Revolutions: Criticism and Theory,* edited by Kenneth Johnston, Gilbert Chaitin, Karen Hanson, and Herbert Marks, 8–25. Bloomington: Indiana University Press, 1990.

————. "Wordsworth, Inscriptions, and Romantic Nature Poetry." In *Beyond Formalism: Literary Essays 1958–1970,* 206–30. New Haven: Yale University Press, 1970.

————. *Wordsworth's Poetry 1787–1814*. New Haven: Yale University Press, 1971.

Hayden, John O. "The Road to Tintern Abbey." *The Wordsworth Circle* 12 (1981): 211–16.

Heinzelman, Kurt. "The Cult of Domesticity: Dorothy and William Wordsworth at Grasmere." In *Romanticism and Feminism,* edited by Anne K. Mellor, 52–78. Bloomington: Indiana University Press, 1988.

————. *The Economics of Imagination*. Amherst: University of Massachusetts Press, 1980.

Hertz, Neil. "Wordsworth and the Tears of Adam." *Studies in Romanticism* 7 (1967): 15–33.

Hill, Alan G. "Wordsworth and the Two Faces of Machiavelli." *Review of English Studies* n.s. 31 (1980): 285–304.

Himmelfarb, Gertrude. *The Idea of Poverty: England in the Early Industrial Age*. New York: Alfred A. Knopf, 1984.

Hobbes, Thomas. *Leviathan*. Edited by C. B. Macpherson. New York: Viking Penguin, 1968.

Hont, I. and Ignatieff, M. "Needs and Justice in *The Wealth of Nations:* An Introductory Essay." In *Wealth and Virtue: Political Economy in the Scottish Enlightenment,* edited by I. Hont and M. Ignatieff, 1–44. Cambridge: Cambridge University Press, 1983.

Hooker, Edward Niles. "Wordsworth's *Letter to the Bishop of Llandaff.*" *Studies in Philology* 28 (1931): 522–31.

Horace. *The Odes and Epodes.* With translation by C. E. Bennett. Loeb Classical Library. Rev. ed. Cambridge: Harvard University Press, 1978.

Howlett, Rev. J. *An Examination of Mr. Pitt's Speech, in the House of Commons, on Friday, February 12, 1796, Relative to the Condition of the Poor.* London: W. Richardson, 1796.

Hunter, Ian. *Culture and Government: The Emergence of Literary Education.* London, Macmillan, 1988.

Jacobus, Mary. "The Law of/and Gender: Genre Theory and *The Prelude.*" *Diacritics* 14:4 (1984): 47–57.

———. "'That Great Stage Where Senators Perform': *Macbeth* and the Politics of Romantic Theater." *Studies in Romanticism* 22 (1983): 353–87.

———. *Tradition and Experiment in Wordsworth's Lyrical Ballads 1798.* Oxford: Clarendon Press, 1976.

Jeffrey, Francis. Review of Robert Southey, *Thalaba the Destroyer. Edinburgh Review* 1 (October 1802): 63–83.

———. Review of William Wordsworth, *The Excursion. The Edinburgh Review* 24 (1814): 1–30.

Johnston, Kenneth R. "Philanthropy or Treason? Wordsworth as 'Active Partisan'." *Studies in Romanticism* 25 (1986): 371–409.

———. "The Politics of 'Tintern Abbey.'" *The Wordsworth Circle* 14 (1985): 6–14.

———. "Self-Consciousness, Social Guilt, and Romantic Poetry: The Ancient Mariner and the Old Pedlar." in *Beyond Representation: Philosophy and Poetic Imagination,* edited by Richard Eldridge, 216–48. Cambridge: Cambridge University Press, 1996.

———. *Wordsworth and The Recluse.* New Haven: Yale University Press, 1984.

———. "Wordsworth and *The Recluse:* The University of Imagination." *PMLA* 97 (1982): 60–82.

Jordan, John. *Why the Lyrical Ballads? The Background, Writing, and Character of Wordsworth's 1798 Lyrical Ballads.* Berkeley: University of California Press, 1976.

Kelley, Theresa. *Wordsworth's Revisionary Aesthetics.* Cambridge: Cambridge University Press, 1988.

Klancher, Jon. *The Making of English Reading Audiences, 1790–1832.* Madison: University of Wisconsin Press, 1987.

Koch, Mark. "Utilitarian and Reactionary Arguments for Almsgiving in Wordsworth's 'The Old Cumberland Beggar.'" *Eighteenth-Century Life* 13 (1989): 18–33.

Knight, Richard Payne. *The Progress of Civil Society.* London: G. Nicol, 1796.

Kramer, Lawrence. "Victorian Sexuality and 'Tintern Abbey.'" *Victorian Poetry* 24 (1986): 399–410.

Lamb, Charles. *Lamb as Critic.* Edited by Roy Park. Lincoln: University of Nebraska Press, 1980.

Lerner, Laurence. "Wordsworth's Refusal of Politics." *SEL* 31 (1991): 673–91.

Levin, Susan M. *Dorothy Wordsworth and Romanticism.* New Brunswick: Rutgers University Press, 1987.

Levinson, Marjorie. *The Romantic Fragment Poem*. Chapel Hill: University of North Carolina Press, 1986.

———. *Wordsworth's Great Period Poems: Four Essays*. New York: Cambridge University Press, 1986.

Little, Geoffrey. "'Tintern Abbey' and LLyswen Farm." *Wordsworth Circle* 8 (1977): 80–82.

Liu, Alan. "The History in 'Imagination.'" *ELH* 51 (1984): 505–48.

———. *Wordsworth: The Sense of History*. Stanford: Stanford University Press, 1989.

———. Review of *Wordsworth's Historical Imagination,* by David Simpson. *The Wordsworth Circle* 19 (1988): 172–81.

Lukacs, Georg. "Reification and the Consciousness of the Proletariat." In *History and Class Consciousness,* translated by Rodney Livingstone, 83–222. Cambridge: MIT Press, 1971.

Macherey, Pierre, and Etienne Balibar. "Literature as an Ideological Form: Some Marxist Propositions." Translated by James Kavanaugh. *Praxis* 5 (1981): 43–58.

Mackintosh, James. *Miscellaneous Works*. New York: D. Appleton & Co., 1870.

Maclean, Kenneth. *Agrarian Age: A Background for Wordsworth*. Yale Studies in English 115 (1950).

Macpherson, C. B. *The Political Theory of Possessive Individualism: Hobbes to Locke*. Oxford: Clarendon Press, 1962.

Madden, Lionel, ed. *Robert Southey: The Critical Heritage*. London: Routledge & Kegan Paul, 1972.

Magnuson, Paul. *Coleridge and Wordsworth: A Lyrical Dialogue*. Princeton: Princeton University Press, 1988.

———. "Wordsworth and Spontaneity." In *The Evidence of Imagination,* edited by Donald H. Reiman, et. al., 101–18. New York: New York University Press, 1978.

Mandeville, Bernard. *The Fable of the Bees: Or, Private Vices, Publick Benefits*. Edited by F. B. Kaye. 2 vols. Oxford: Clarendon Press, 1924.

Manning, Peter J. "Placing Poor Susan: Wordsworth and the New Historicism." *Studies in Romanticism* 25 (1986): 351–69.

———. "Wordsworth, Margaret, and the Pedlar." *Studies in Romanticism* 15 (1976): 195–220.

Marshall, David. "The Eye-Witnesses of *The Borderers*." *Studies in Romanticism* 27 (1988): 392–98.

———. *The Figure of Theater: Shaftesbury, Defoe, Adam Smith, and George Eliot*. New York: Columbia University Press, 1986.

Matlak, Richard E. "Classical Argument and Romantic Persuasion in 'Tintern Abbey.'" *Studies in Romanticism* 25 (1986): 97–129.

Mayo, Robert. "The Contemporaneity of the *Lyrical Ballads*." *PMLA* 69 (1954): 486–522.

McFarland, Thomas. *Romanticism and the Forms of Ruin: Wordsworth, Coleridge, and Modalities of Fragmentation*. Princeton: Princeton University Press, 1981.

McGann, Jerome. *The Romantic Ideology: A Critical Investigation*. Chicago: University of Chicago Press, 1983.

McGavran, James Holt, Jr. "Xanadu, Somersetshire, and the Banks of the Wye: A Study of Romantic Androgyny." *Papers on Language and Literature* 26 (1990): 334–45.

McInerney, Peter F. "Natural Wisdom in Wordsworth's *The Excursion.*" *The Wordsworth Circle* 9 (1978): 188–99.

Milley, H. J. W. "Some Notes on Coleridge's 'Eolian Harp.'" *Modern Philology* 36 (1938–39): 359–75.

Milton, John. *Complete Poems and Major Prose.* Edited by Merritt Y. Hughes. New York: Bobbs-Merrill, 1957.

Newlyn, Lucy. "'In City Pent': Echo and Allusion in Wordsworth, Coleridge, and Lamb, 1797–1801." *Review of English Studies* n.s. 32 (1981): 408–28.

Ohmann, Richard. *English in America: A Radical View of the Profession.* New York: Oxford University Press, 1976.

Onorato, Richard J. *The Character of the Poet: Wordsworth in "The Prelude."* Princeton: Princeton University Press, 1971.

"On the Importance of the Middle Ranks in Society." *The Oeconomist* 1 (1798): 5–8.

Osborn, Robert. "Meaningful Obscurity: The Antecedents and Character of Rivers." In *Bicentenary Wordsworth Studies,* edited by Jonathan Wordsworth, 393–424. Ithaca: Cornell University Press, 1964.

Owen, W. J. B. "*The Borderers* and the Aesthetics of Drama." *The Wordsworth Circle* 6 (1975): 227–39.

Page, Judith W. "'The Weight of Too Much Liberty': Genre and Gender in Wordsworth's Calais Sonnets." *Criticism* 30 (1988): 189–203.

Paley, William. *Natural Theology, or, Evidences of the Existence and Attributes of the Deity, Collected from the Appearances of Nature.* Philadelphia: John Morgan, 1802.

———. *Reasons for Contentment; Addressed to the Labouring Part of the British Public.* London: R. Faulder, 1793.

Parker, Reeve. "'Finer Distance': The Narrative Art of Wordsworth's 'The Wanderer.'" *ELH* 39 (1972): 87–111.

———. "'In Some Sort Seeing with My Own Proper Eyes': Wordsworth and the Spectacles of Paris." *Studies in Romanticism* 27 (1988): 369–90.

———. "Reading Wordsworth's Power: Narrative and Usurpation in *The Borderers.*" *ELH* 54 (1987): 299–331.

Paulson, Ronald. *Representations of Revolutions (1789–1820).* New Haven: Yale University Press, 1983.

Percy, Thomas. *Reliques of Ancient English Poetry.* 3 vols. London: L. A. Lewis, 1839.

Perkins, David. "The Construction of 'The Romantic Movement' as a Literary Classification." *Nineteenth-Century Literature* 45 (1990): 129–43.

Peterfreund, Stuart. "The Evolving Notion of Work in English Romantic Poetry." *Works and Days* 2:1 (1984): 19–44.

The Philanthropist. London: Daniel Isaac Eaton, 1795. In *Early British Periodicals.* Ann Arbor: Xerox University Microfilms, 1972.

Pocock, J. G. A. *The Machiavellian Moment: Florentine Political Thought and the Atlantic Republican Tradition.* Princeton: Princeton University Press, 1975.

————. *Virtue, Commerce, and History: Essays on Political Thought and History, Chiefly in the Eighteenth Century.* Cambridge, Cambridge University Press, 1985.

Polanyi, Karl. *The Great Transformation.* 1944; rpt. Boston: Beacon Press, 1957.

Pope, Alexander. *The Poems.* Edited by John Butt. New Haven: Yale University Press, 1963.

Poynter, J. R. *Society and Pauperism: English Ideas on Poor Relief, 1795–1834.* London: Routledge & Kegan Paul, 1969.

Radcliffe, Ann. *The Mysteries of Udolpho.* Edited by Bonamy Dobree. New York: Oxford University Press, 1966.

Radner, John B. "The Art of Sympathy in Eighteenth-Century British Moral Thought." *Studies in Eighteenth-Century Culture* 9 (1979): 189–210.

Richardson, Alan. *A Mental Theater: Poetic Drama and Consciousness in the Romantic Age.* University Park: Penn State University Press, 1988.

Rieder, John. "Description of a Struggle: Shelley's Radicalism on Wordsworth's Terrain." *boundary 2* 13 (1985): 267–87.

————. "Wordsworth and Romanticism in the Academy." In *At the Limits of Romanticism: Essays in Cultural, Feminist, and Materialist Criticism,* edited by Mary Favret and Nicola Watson, 21–39. Bloomington: Indiana University Press, 1993.

Robbins, Caroline. *The Eighteenth-Century Commonwealthman: Studies in the Transmission, Development and Circumstances of English Liberal Thought from the Restoration of Charles II until the War with the Thirteen Colonies.* Cambridge: Harvard University Press, 1959.

Roe, Nicholas. *Wordsworth and Coleridge: The Radical Years.* Oxford: Clarendon Press, 1988.

Røstvig, Maren-Sofie. *The Happy Man: Studies in the Metamorphoses of a Classical Ideal.* 2 vols. 2d ed. New York: Humanities Press, 1971.

Sacks, Peter. *The English Elegy: Studies in the Genre from Spenser to Yeats.* Baltimore: Johns Hopkins University Press, 1985.

Schiller, Friederich. *The Robbers.* London, 1792; rpt. Oxford: Woodstock, 1989.

Sekora, John. *Luxury: The Concept in Western Thought, Eden to Smollett.* Baltimore, Johns Hopkins University Press, 1977.

Shaftesbury, A. A. Cooper, 3d Earl of. *Characteristicks of Men, Manners, Opinions, Times.* 3 vols. 3d ed. London: J. Darby, 1723.

Shakespeare, William. *King Lear.* Edited by Russell Fraser. New York: New American Library, 1963.

Sharrock, Roger. "*The Borderers:* Wordsworth on the Moral Frontier." *Durham University Journal* 56 (1964): 170–83.

Sheats, Paul. *The Making of Wordsworth's Poetry, 1785–1798.* Cambridge: Harvard University Press, 1973.

Shelley, Percy Bysshe. *Shelley's Poetry and Prose.* Edited by Donald H. Reiman and Sharon B. Powers. New York: Norton, 1977.

Simpson, David R. *Wordsworth and the Figurings of the Real.* Atlantic Highlands NJ: Humanities Press, 1982.

————. *Wordsworth's Historical Imagination: The Poetry of Displacement.* London: Methuen, 1987.

Siskin, Clifford. *The Historicity of Romantic Discourse.* New York: Oxford University Press, 1988.

———. "Wordsworth's Prescriptions: Romanticism and Professional Power." In *The Romantics and Us: Essays on Literature and Culture,* edited by Gene W. Ruoff, 303–21. New Brunswick, NJ: Rutgers University Press, 1990.

Smith, Adam. *The Theory of Moral Sentiments.* Edited by D. D. Raphael and A. L. Macfie. Oxford: Clarendon Press, 1976.

Smith, Charles J. "The Effect of Shakespeare's Influence on Wordsworth's 'The Borderers.'" *Studies in Philology* 50 (1953): 625–39.

Spenser, Edmund. *The Faerie Queene.* 2 vols. New York: Dutton, 1910.

Spivak, Gayatri. "Can the Subaltern Speak?" In *Marxism and the Interpretation of Culture,* edited by Cary Nelson and Lawrence Grossberg, 271–313. Urbana: University of Illinois Press, 1988.

———. "Sex and History in *The Prelude* (1805): Books Nine to Thirteen." *Texas Studies in Language and Literature* 23 (1981): 324–60.

Stelzig, Eugene. "'The Shield of Human Nature': Wordsworth's Reflections on the Revolution in France." *Nineteenth-Century Literature* 45 (1991): 415–31.

Stoddard, Eve Walsh. "'All Freaks of Nature': The Human Grotesque in Wordsworth's City." *Philological Quarterly* 67 (1988): 37–61.

———. "*The Borderers:* A Critique of both Reason and Feeling as Moral Agents." *The Wordsworth Circle* 11 (1980): 93–97.

Stone, Lawrence. *The Family, Sex, and Marriage in England 1500–1800.* New York: Harper & Row, 1977.

Storch, R. F. "Wordsworth's *The Borderers:* The Poet as Anthropologist." *ELH* 36 (1969): 340–60.

Swann, Karen. "Suffering and Sensation in *The Ruined Cottage.*" *PMLA* 106 (1991): 83–95.

Teich, Nathaniel. "Evaluating Wordsworth's Revolution: Romantic Reviewers and Changing Tastes." *Papers in Language and Literature* 11 (1975): 206–23.

Teichgraber, Richard F., III. *"Free Trade" and Moral Philosophy: Rethinking the Sources of Adam Smith's Wealth of Nations.* Durham: Duke University Press, 1986.

Thelwall, John. *Political Lectures.* London: J. Thelwall, 1795.

———. *The Rights of Nature, against the Usurpation of Establishments.* London: H. D. Symonds, 1796.

Thompson, E. P. "Disenchantment or Default? A Lay Sermon." In *Power and Consciousness,* edited by Conor Cruise O'Brien and William Dean Vanech, 149–81. London: University of London Press, 1969.

———. "Eighteenth-Century English Society: Class Struggle without Class?" *Social History* 3:2 (1978): 133–65.

———. *The Making of the English Working Class.* New York: Pantheon, 1963.

Thomson, James. *The Seasons and The Castle of Indolence.* Edited by James Sambrook. Oxford: Clarendon Press, 1972.

Thorslev, Peter L. "Wordsworth's *Borderers* and the Romantic Villain-Hero." *Studies in Romanticism* 5 (1964): 84–103.

[Townsend, Joseph.] *A Dissertation on the Poor Laws, by a Well-Wisher to Mankind.* London: C. Dilly, 1786.

Turner, James. *The Politics of Landscape: Rural Scenery and Society in English Poetry 1630–1660.* Oxford: Basil Blackwell, 1979.

Virgil. *Ecloques, Georgics, Aenid I–VI.* With translation by H. Rushton Fairclough. Loeb Classical Library. Rev. ed. Cambridge: Harvard University Press, 1978.

Viswanathan, Gauri. *Masks of Conquest: Literary Study and British Rule in India.* New York: Columbia University Press, 1989.

Volosinov, V. N. "Discourse in Life and Discourse in Art (concerning Sociological Poetics)." In *Freudianism,* translated by I. R. Titunik, 93–116. New York: Academic Press, 1976.

———. *Marxism and the Philosophy of Language.* Translated by Ladislav Matejka and I. R. Titunik. New York: Seminar Press, 1973.

Wasserman, Earl. *Shelley: A Critical Reading.* Baltimore: Johns Hopkins University Press, 1971.

———. *The Subtler Language: Critical Readings of Neoclassical and Romantic Poems.* Baltimore: Johns Hopkins University Press, 1959.

Watson, George. "The Revolutionary Youth of Wordsworth and Coleridge." *Critical Quarterly* 18:3 (1976): 149–66.

Watson, J. R. "A Note on the Title of 'Tintern Abbey.'" *Wordsworth Circle* 10 (1979): 379–80.

Webb, Sidney, and Beatrice Webb. *English Local Government: English Poor Law History: Part I: The Old Poor Law.* London: Longmans, Green, & Co., 1927.

———. *English Local Government: English Poor Law history: Part II: The Last Hundred Years.* 2 vols. London: Longmans, Green & Co., 1929.

Weiskel, Thomas. *The Romantic Sublime: Studies in the Structure and Psychology of Transcendence.* Baltimore: Johns Hopkins University Press, 1976.

Williams, John. *Wordsworth: Romantic Poetry and Revolution Politics.* Manchester: Manchester University Press, 1989.

Wiliams, Raymond. *The Country and the City.* New York: Oxford University Press, 1973.

———. *Marxism and Literature.* New York: Oxford University Press, 1977.

Wimsatt, William K., Jr. "The Structure of Romantic Nature Imagery." In *The Verbal Icon: Studies in The Meaning of Poetry,* 103–16. Lexington: University of Kentucky Press, 1954.

Wolfson, Susan J. "Questioning 'The Romantic Ideology': Wordsworth." *Revue Internationale de Philosophie* 44 (1990): 429–47.

Woodring, Carl. *Politics in English Romantic Poetry.* Cambridge: Harvard University Press, 1970.

Wordsworth, Jonathan. *The Borders of Vision.* Oxford: Clarendon Press, 1982.

———. *The Music of Humanity: A Critical Study of Wordsworth's RUINED COTTAGE Incorporating Texts from a Manuscript of 1799–1800.* London: Thomas Nelson and Sons, 1969.

Worthington, Jane. *Wordsworth's Reading of Roman Prose. Yale Studies in English* 102 (1946).

Young, William. *Observations Preliminary to a Proposed Amendment of the Poor Laws.* London: John Nichols, 1788.

Zizek, Slavoj. *The Sublime Object of Ideology.* New York: Verso, 1989.

———. *Tarrying with the Negative: Kant, Hegel, and the Critique of Ideology.* Durham NC: Duke University Press, 1993.

Index

Works and critics cited in the endnotes do not appear in the index. William Wordsworth's works appear only under the author heading with the exceptions of *The Borderers, The Prelude, The Ruined Cottage,* and "Tintern Abbey."